The Bookseller's Tale

MARTIN LATHAM

PARTICULAR BOOKS
an imprint of
PENGUIN BOOKS

PARTICULAR BOOKS

UK | USA | Canada | Ireland | Australia
India | New Zealand | South Africa

Particular Books is part of the Penguin Random House group of companies
whose addresses can be found at global.penguinrandomhouse.com.

Penguin
Random House
UK

First published in Great Britain by Particular Books 2020
001

Text copyright © Martin Latham, 2020

The moral right of the author has been asserted

Set in 12/14.75 pt Dante MT Std
Typeset by Jouve (UK), Milton Keynes
Printed and bound in Great Britain by Clays Ltd, Elcograf S.p.A.

A CIP catalogue record for this book is available from the British Library

ISBN: 978–0–241–40881–0

Front endpaper: An illustration by Ernest Flammarion shows *bouquinistes* along the *quais* in Paris,
1931. *The Print Collector/Print Collector/Getty Images.*

Back endpaper: Ernest Hemingway with Sylvia Beach and friends, in front of Beach's Paris bookshop,
Shakespeare and Company. *Photo Researchers / Alamy Stock Photo.*

www.greenpenguin.co.uk

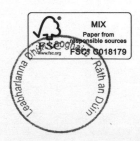

MIX
Paper from
responsible sources
www.fsc.org   FSC® C018179

Penguin Random House is committed to a
sustainable future for our business, our readers
and our planet. This book is made from Forest
Stewardship Council® certified paper.

Contents

List of Illustrations

Introduction

There is a book which has not moved a centimetre in 800 years. It is on the tomb of Eleanor of Aquitaine in Fontevraud Abbey, near Poitiers. Her turbulent life is all behind her as she lies in deep repose, holding up an open Bible. She rests as we all do in bed when, finished with talking or tea, we become one with a book, lost in a private world. The story of humanity's love affair with books is, to a visitor from another galaxy, one of our strangest tales.

This history of the book explores our relationship with the physical book, showing how it has deepened our sense of self. The printed book helped to inaugurate an Earth-wide springtime of consciousness. Curled up with a book, we continue to find new selves.

Such private reading only became widespread in the age of print. In most languages the word 'read' originally meant 'read aloud'. Alexander the Great's men stared in puzzlement when he read silently, and, until the age of print, being read to was commoner than reading privately. With this new privacy came a deepening of emotional involvement, of affect. The pioneer Victorian sociologist Harriet Martineau felt she often *became* the author she was reading, and novels such as *Clarissa* generated extraordinary convulsive weeping and exaltation. Post-Gutenberg, our imagination was mainlining stories, high on new realms.

Private reading gave us new inner dimensions. We feel the truth of this in the stacks of a great library, or in corners of a bookshop, places which give us a sense of immanence, of being on the verge of infinite inner space. The ancient library of Alexandria may not even have existed, but, as the classicist Edith Hall says, the idea of such a library is almost as important to our collective psyche as its reality. We know instinctively that we are both infinite and serendipitous, so we love getting lost in bookshops and libraries, and accidentally finding books which unlock our various hidden selves.

Our passionate relationship with actual books (not 'the text' of literary theorists) has been enacted in many little-documented physical ways. It can be, Virginia Woolf observed, an almost sexual interplay. I have seen this in thirty years of bookselling: customers stroking a book's cover, peeking under the jacket, surreptitiously closing their eyes to smell the valley of pages – this sometimes accompanied by a quiet moan of pleasure – hugging it after purchase, and even giving it a little kiss.

Book users cannot explain why they love holding books, and, after hearing them – a few hundred times over the years – say at length that they cannot explain it, I am beginning to think that they do not want to analyse a feeling so inner.

The book, of paper from trees, is halfway to the forest, that great source of myth. Tech devices are not only made of colder, denatured materials, they are relentlessly demanding. In 1913 Kafka, with astonishing prescience, described the future in a letter to his would-be girlfriend Felice, who sold dictation machines. He detested such machines, and celebrated the way he might stare out of the office window mid-dictation, then hear the soughing of his secretary's nail file as she joined in the secret dawdle. He told Felice that 'faced with such machines' we become 'degraded factory workers'. Today, we all sometimes feel like grunts serving our machines; we do not feel that with the book. Kafka predicted that such machines would end up talking to us, making suggestions as to restaurants, correcting pronunciation even. Such a technology was preposterous even when I started this book a decade ago, but is now commonplace. Poor old Felice did not reply to Franz's bonkers-seeming letter.

The 'cold tech' of digital devices offers 'interactivity', but it is an interactivity with formatting rules, from 'liking' something to blogging, very far from how many interact with books – 'warm tech' – by writing in them. Montaigne's marginalia on his copy of Lucretius represent a whole strand of his thought, as do Blake's heated scribblings on Joshua Reynolds' *Discourses*. Coleridge's marginalia fill an entire volume of his collected works. But marginalia have been literally marginalized by academic librarians, especially in Victorian times, when they were sliced off and binned in rebinding operations and even – this happened to Milton's marginalia – bleached out. The legacy of this Benthamite hygiene is our excessive opposition to writing in books today. One recent historian of marginalia laments that, unless we relax, we won't have a record of our fresh, unmediated reactions to books.

With a similarly irreverent biblio-sensuality, from about 1600 until about 1870, book users cut out favourite passages and pasted them into commonplace books, which were interspersed with their own manuscript thoughts. This craze went largely unrecorded because of the attitude of librarians such as M. R. James, who described commonplace books as 'a sort of residue or sediment'. To add vexation to the librarian's empiricist mind, these books were unclassifiable – were they books or manuscripts? They were thrown out in skiploads until as late as the 1980s.

Racy short books, known in Britain as chapbooks, are another lost part of book history. These narratives of crime, mythology, paranormal activity, romance, philosophy and religion were printed in unrecorded millions worldwide, but looked down upon by librarians and ignored until recently by academics. This is odd because so many titans of literature were fed on these viral tales. Pepys hoarded them, Blake wrote great poems in the format, Dickens was weaned on them, Stevenson loved them so much he wrote one (*Moral Emblems*) and Shakespeare's love for the nomadic bullshitting chapbook seller Autolycus is palpable. But, often with no covers, they only had a street life, and are largely lost.

Jacques Derrida has lamented the baleful influence of a largely male cadre of librarians in editing our culture, coining the term 'patriarchive'. Not for them the interest of this writer in the archaeology of books, the odysseys of nomadic tomes, the secrets hidden in ink and paper, in watermarks and in fore-edge paintings, the stories of pressed flowers and of handwritten dedications. Lovers resent rival stimulation and dictators just want to be loved. East German leader Erich Honecker presided over much persecution but lamented in old age: 'Didn't they see how I loved them?' This jealousy accounts for the great number of books burned by dictators. The survival of underground books is a history yet to be fully told, from the secret photocopying of Solzhenitsyn in Kremlin offices, to East Berlin's hidden cache of *Animal Farm*.

This is the uncensored tale of our love affair with books, an affair which saw the emergence of a more private and reflective self. It is an affair with the physical book which thrives even – perhaps especially – in the digital era.

> I don't know how I learned to read. I only remember my first readings and their effect on me. It is from that time that I date my consciousness of self. (Rousseau's *Confessions*)

1.   Comfort Books

Childhood memories recur, like a door suddenly slammed by the wind in the distant wing of an old house.

Richard Church, in an obscure essay I cannot now trace.

Each one of us should make a surveyor's map of his lost fields and meadows.

Gaston Bachelard, *The Poetics of Space*

It is only recently that I have overcome my education and gone back to that early intuitional spontaneity.

Robert Graves, *Goodbye to All That*

The Low Door in the Wall

An Egyptian in about 2500 BC equated finding the right read with embarking on a small boat. Certain comfort books have this ability to take us away to a better place. These totemic novels are a strange mish-mash of 'trash' and 'classics'.

Editor and biographer Jenny Uglow was once on a panel at the New York Public Library, discussing which classics are still widely read. She came into my shop beforehand to check and got some surprising indications from the computer. Excluding set books and screen adaptations, it was clear that Mrs Gaskell still sells, and Hemingway of course, but only a few of his works. *Middlemarch* is still a bestseller but not Fielding. Although Anthony Powell's *Dance to the Music of Time* has great cultural influence, it sells only occasionally. By contrast the lengthy *Balkan Trilogy* and *Alexandria Quartet* from the early 1960s still 'wash their face' (mysterious business jargon for something which delivers a profit). One might think it was only newish novels which drive stock-turn and 'wash their face', but *Robinson Crusoe* (1719) and *Candide* (1759) are both regularly purchased for pleasure, rather than as set books. Smollett, however, like Boswell's *Life of Johnson*, is stocked out of fond respect rather than commercial necessity, selling in tiny quantities each year. In thirty years I have never been asked for *The Pilgrim's Progress*. Chesterton's *The Man Who Was Thursday*, however, is one of several perennials which are word-of-mouth phenomena. The list of loved shot-in-the-arm books known to most booksellers – which includes much sci-fi and children's books – bears only a partial relation to 'the canon' of classics as perceived by academe, and, I suppose, why should it? To name a few: *Cloud Atlas*, *Against Nature*, *Watchman*, *I Capture the Castle*, *The Catcher in the Rye*, *Tristram Shandy*, *Wide Sargasso Sea*, *To Kill a Mockingbird*, *The Earthsea Trilogy*, *Eragon*, *Lord of the Rings*, Pratchett's Discworld books, *Do Androids Dream of Electric Sheep?*, *Anne of Green Gables*, The Harry Potter books, *The Phantom Tollbooth*, *The Little Prince*, *The Alchemist*, the Jeeves books, *Cold Comfort Farm*.

Lovers of all these books have on occasion felt that they should be reading something more monumental instead. The literary novelist A. S. Byatt was an early fan of Terry Pratchett, in the days when sci-fi and fantasy rarely intruded into broadsheet book reviews. In 1990 when she excitedly bought the new Discworld book in my Canterbury bookshop she said jokingly, 'I love Discworld but I can't be seen buying it in London.'

This state of affairs is a by-product of the modern educational establishment: Chaucer, Shakespeare and Dickens enjoyed a shame-free eclecticism. The Victorian establishment loved the story of heroic Dr Brydon, sole survivor of the 1842 retreat from Kabul, who rode to safety after a bible in his hat stopped an Afghan sword blow. As an old man back home in the Highlands, Brydon debunked the myth (which he had not created). It was not a bible which saved his life, but a volume of *Blackwood's Magazine*, a popular repository of romanticism and horror stories.

Comfort is such an important part of reading, but we need to preserve it, or end up like some of Professor Deirdre Lynch's students at Harvard. She has lamented:

> the frequent undertone of nostalgia in the complaints of . . .
> students in English . . . about how the training in criticism
> and theory to which they must conform smothers the love of
> authors and reading that had brought them to their graduate
> programs in the first place.

The discovery of a comfort book is, like the occasion of falling in love, often an unforgettable experience. For some years, in my early twenties, I used to cycle to Tite Street in Chelsea and lock my gearless student bicycle to the railings of an Edwardian block of flats. The street hummed with a bookish atmosphere: Radclyffe Hall and Oscar Wilde had lived a few doors away. I took the ancient lift to the top floor and, as I slowly reached it, through the grille of the lift gates two feet would come into view on the landing, in worn handmade leather shoes from Tricker's of Jermyn Street. My visits to the writer and traveller Wilfred Thesiger were extended conversations, often into the small hours, as the lights of Albert Bridge twinkled on the Thames outside.

He used to be called the last of the Victorian explorers, but his hatred of the internal combustion engine and respect for indigenous world-views have caused younger writers such as Levison Wood and Rory Stewart to give him a new tag: the first hippy. Although Thesiger is forever associated with befriending the Bedouin and crossing Arabia's Empty Quarter, he was a keen bibliophile, so we spoke a lot about books – here was someone who possessed a subscribers' edition of *The Seven Pillars of Wisdom* with covers made from slices of the wooden propellers of a 1915 Turkish aeroplane downed in the Hejaz, a rarity which no dealer I have spoken to seems to have heard of.

On an index card Thesiger wrote me a list in his tiny, even handwriting of his six all-time comfort books. *Brideshead Revisited* was on there, the first time I had heard of it, but he had to add a rider: Evelyn Waugh, whom he had known well in Abyssinia, was 'an absolutely bloody man', whom he could never identify with such a great book. Thesiger, who was awarded a DSO for bravery fighting Mussolini's forces in Abyssinia and later served in the early SAS, was particularly unimpressed that Waugh, reporting on the Italian invasion, sported a big floppy hat. 'That damned *het*,' Thesiger would say, shaking his head at the memory, but with a shadow of a smile.

Nowadays, as a bookseller – I was not one then, just an earnest history PhD student – I know that *Brideshead* is a comfort book for people of all ages and genders. Waugh's tale of aristocratic life keeps on selling every week because of its heady prose and, for me anyway, the way it conjures something unget-at-able about beauty, and leaves it unget-at-able.

One young woman recently came into my shop and said, 'I've just read *Brideshead Revisited*. It was just so . . . different, it blew my head off and I need something to follow that – y'know, something that *really gets to you*.'

A tough one, which goes to the heart of reading pleasure: there are books with an element of duty in the reading, and books you get up earlier in the morning for, and slow down near the end to delay parting from. For this customer, neither Dostoevsky nor Dickens would have served. She would have understood Nabokov's strange aim in writing. Speaking in a grainy fifties TV interview, he said – so quickly I had to replay it several times to get the words – he wrote not to move hearts or change minds but 'to produce that little sob in the spine of the artist reader'. A shorter, unmediated shot in the vein was required. I thought of some of my own totem-books, *Crash* for instance, by J. G. Ballard? No good – my advocacy of it once started a pub fight in Fulham (I was not a participant). We lined up copies of *I Capture the Castle*, *To Kill a Mockingbird*, *The Shooting Party* and *Frankenstein* for her. I heard later that, as so often, the first book, by Dodie Smith, pleased her greatly, and she wondered why it was not better known.

Another book on Thesiger's list was *Upon That Mountain* (1943) by Eric Shipton. For years, Thesiger would refer to that book as one he had lost long ago and could not get hold of. It dawns upon me in retrospect that he somehow wanted *not* to get hold of the book. It was that obscure object of desire for him, something which – to quote the master-work of his inappropriately hatted friend – represented:

> that low door in the wall, which others, I knew, had found before me, which opened on an enclosed and enchanted garden, which was somewhere, not overlooked by any window.

'Not overlooked' is central to the power of a comfort book. It is utterly personal, rarely a prizewinner or current bestseller, a private discovery, epiphanic, something which created a slow-motion explosion in some previously unvisited desert of the soul.

For some, the comfort book represents the beauty of loss: *Upon That Mountain* is all about fulfilment deliciously denied. Thesiger talked a lot about Nanda Devi, the 'widow-maker' Himalayan peak which repelled all attempts to get near it; Shipton's book was about a failed attempt to climb it. This could explain the book's rarity, it was no 'peak-bagging' chronicle.

This year, seventeen years after Thesiger died, I found a 1956 Pan paperback *Upon That Mountain* in a charity shop; I keep it next to my signed *Arabian Sands*.

Everyone I have asked to explain the appeal of their comfort books becomes evasive, so I don't ask directly any more. Often, like a captured spy in wartime giving name, rank and number, they give title, author and maybe format, paperback or hardback. Then they change the subject, unwilling to give anything away about their magical hinterland. They are protecting their mountain sanctuary, for surely the comfort book is one which always remains a private happening. To put it into prose would be as wrong as a helicopter trip to the top of Nanda Devi.

As we grow up some of our imaginative power slips underneath our administrative self, to resurface, say, in times of love and death, or when out in nature, or curled up with a book. Shipton opens his book with this:

> Every child, I suppose, spends a large proportion of its time in a day-dream about trees, or engines, or the sea . . . Sometimes these longings are submerged, but sometimes sufficient remains to have a decisive effect upon our way of life.

'A decisive effect upon our way of life': the comfort book is a way to keep the effect going. No wonder people clam up about comfort books: in asking about them I am interfering with the surviving mind-stream of their childhood, a tender matter. As kids we are innocent of the administrative matters which will one day muddy that mind-stream. We grow up taking for granted an imaginative world as rich as *The Arabian Nights*.

I am one of eight children and my youngest sibling, Sarah, had a childhood comfort book which she had never talked about until I asked her. In *Children of the Old House*, a large family make do and mend in a run-down home. They thrive, amid many challenges. Sarah grew up in just such a house, and her career in children's nursing started at Great Ormond Street Hospital. I have found time and again that people's childhood comfort book prefigures, to an almost comical degree which they cannot always see, their adult mission in life.

This morning, while I was writing this section in a Canterbury café, a young couple came in with rucksacks and wooden staffs. We got talking and I asked about their childhood comfort books. Both twenty-one, they were walking from Bordeaux to Ireland, wild-camping, with no itinerary. Zakaria Fassi had overcome his domineering father by reading *Un homme ça ne pleure pas* (*Men Don't Cry*) by fellow French Algerian Faïza Guène. His girlfriend, a shaven-headed trucker's daughter called Lelia Galin, made sense of the 'madness' in her childhood home by reading an obscure fairy tale involving an ogre being tamed by love. They talked about the two books quietly, religiously, and said they had never told anyone about them before. The books mapped their sensibility and explained their great escape better than any chit-chat.

On the London to Canterbury train recently I was talking

to Sam, a barrister on the way back from an Old Bailey murder trial.

Self: 'What was your childhood comfort book?'

Sam: 'Oh, I loved the Peter and Jane reading scheme books, and Dickens, *A Tale of Two Cities*, *Les Misérables* and –'

Self [interrupting because I sensed this was a recital of precocity]: 'Stop right there – I mean what book was personal to you as a child?'

Sam: 'Oh, what I really loved was a little hardback *Cinderella*.'

Cinderella, I thought, oppressed by two step-sisters and an evil stepmother, three ugly forces, a spot-on fable for the life of Sam, who somehow stormed the legal establishment despite being Trinidadian, working-class and a woman. She agreed that, despite Cinders' whiteness and the role of the airhead Prince Charming, it was a liberation tale for her.

The same mechanism was at work in the copy of *The Little Red Engine That Could* which came up for sale in New York a few years ago, with childish pencil markings and signs of much wear: it was Marilyn Monroe's.

My comfort book aged about eleven was *The Time Garden*, and it means so much to me that I have never told anybody about it, or thought about why it is so close to me. As with *Upon That Mountain* for Thesiger, I have never for a moment wanted a copy to reread, nor have I thought before this moment about why on earth it means so much to me. It concerns a boy who encounters a natterjack toad on the sunlit brick path of his back garden, and the toad somehow enables him to time travel. That's all my youthful aspirations in a nutshell: mystery, nature, secret gardens, animals who know more than they are giving away, and trips through history.

A few years on, in the storm of adolescence, a new protective amulet emerged for me in the form of *The Silver Sword* – still widely read, this one – a Second World War story about a teacher whose house in the Warsaw ghetto is destroyed by bombing. He meets a homeless boy who keeps a few atmospheric personal treasures in a shoebox, including for some reason a tiny silver sword. When I tried to look this book up I thought it was called *The Sword in the Stone*. It is clear to me now that the horrors of secondary school were destroying the symbolic house of my magic world, but that I could secretly hang on to it all via a few totemic objects in a metaphorical shoebox. The potential of the mini-sword has remained Arthurian, although in the book it was merely the paper knife of the teacher's wife, who died in the bombing. The book's power lives on among my grown-up children ('Loved that sword book,' said Oliver; 'I so wanted that sword!' said India) and among customers.

I read somewhere about a young English girl whose mental uniqueness was unnameable in any of the current 'disorders' like ADHD. Intelligent but somehow continually distracted by something, some need. No doctors could crack the problem until she went to one specialist in London. He arrived late for work and noticed her in the waiting room, tapping her feet continually. When she came into the appointment he said 'she's a dancer, that's all' – she became a principal ballet dancer at Covent Garden. I wonder what her childhood reading was.

Childhood daydreams surface in reading, and outlive childhood. We don't need French thinker Gaston Bachelard to tell us 'what special depth there is in a child's daydream, and how happy the child who really possesses his moments of solitude, and boredom', but we can sympathize when he cries out, 'How often I have wished for the attic of my boredom when life's complications made me lose the very germ of freedom', and commend his optimistic insistence that 'In the realm of absolute imagination, we remain young late in life.'

Comfort books help us to get through what Nietzsche called 'the horror of living'. Montaigne, in his tower library, called his favourite books 'the best munition I have in this humane peregrination'. Sometimes we carry them around like amulets: Alexander the Great carried his Homer on his wanderings – a book full of nostalgia, a word meaning literally longing for home.

Many a fighter used their favourite book to combat the horrors of war. Napoleon carried Goethe's *Sorrows of Young Werther* on his campaigns, an interesting choice because it was famously about an existential crisis leading to thoughts of suicide. Perhaps Napoleon needed fall-back suicidal thoughts to balance Imperial hubris, after the manner of the Roman emperors who had a boy standing behind them on their victory parade chariot whispering 'all glory is fleeting'. (It is hard to imagine that boy not being incredibly annoying.)

The meaning for General Wolfe, fighting the French in Canada, of his battered copy of Gray's *Elegy Written in a Country Churchyard*, apart from reminding him of England, was hinted at by the bit he double-underlined: 'The paths of glory lead but to the grave.' He was killed in Quebec, aged thirty-two. In the First World War, Lawrence of Arabia read Aristophanes' plays in ancient Greek on long camel marches, to remind him of life's absurdity. There was a similar war-neutralizing function for Glasgow carpenter James Murray, who fought in the trenches of Flanders with his favourite Goethe in his pocket – in German. Sharing a loved book in battle is hard to imagine, but Captain Ferguson insisted to Walter Scott that, in the bitterest days of the war against Napoleon in

Spain, he read Scott's epic poem *The Lady of the Lake* to the lads waiting in the battle line: 'the stag-hunt was the favourite among the rough sons of the Fighting Third Division.'

A more convincing frontline reaction is recorded by the novelist Stendhal, who soldiered in Napoleon's terrible retreat from Moscow: his consolation was a red leather copy of Voltaire's satirical sallies, rescued from a burning house in Moscow. Although he tried to read it discreetly by the campfire, he was derided by his comrades who thought it too dilettantish for the setting: he left it behind in the snow.

A pleasingly pacifist reader was William Harvey, discoverer of the vascular system, who spent the Battle of Edgehill in a hedge reading to two boys until, as John Aubrey tells us in his Brief Lives (*c*. 1680), 'a Bullet of a Great Gun grazed on the ground neare them, which made him remove his station.'

Where does the comfort book come from? Often an unexpected source, the very oddness of its arrival lending it *mana*, to use an untranslatable Polynesian word for the vibe an object can possess. (Patrick Leigh Fermor used the word about his green-backed travel journal.) We are not all lucky enough to have, as Alexander did, a tutor like Aristotle to recommend Homer; more likely we stumbled on our favourite childhood book in a library or bookshop. As children's magazine editor Anne Mozley argued in 1870, the book which is 'an event in [the child's] inner history can never be supplied by teachers: a book this influential comes by a sort of chance', like the old *Paradise Lost* found in a meal chest by a boy called David Grieve in Mary Ward's 1891 eponymous novel: 'he devoured it all morning lying in a hidden corner of a sheepfold, the rolling verse imprinting itself by a sort of enchantment.'

Recommendation can be good, but we yearn for the adventitious discovery, for the finding of a book to be in itself fabulous. 'Somehow,' the author of Moby Dick mused, 'the books that prove most companionable are those we pick up by chance.' Dorothy Wordsworth would have agreed, on the day she came down to the firelit snug of a Lakeland inn, wild weather outside. Her brother William

> soon made his way to a library piled up in a corner of the window. He brought out a volume of Enfield's Speaker, & an odd volume of Congreve. We had warm rum & water – we enjoyed ourselves.

If there are hostile observers, the book can become even more electric. The popular Royalist poet Abraham Cowley, as a boy, happened on a copy of *The Faerie Queen* in his mother's room and became 'irrecoverably' a poet. The childhood of the Victorian Augustus Hare centred for a while around retrieving the serial parts of his grandmother's *Pickwick Papers* from her wastepaper basket, whilst another Victorian lad, Edmund Gosse, developed a fetishistic curiosity about a hatbox in the uncarpeted lumber-room. Illicitly opening the box one day, it was: empty! – except for the lining, made from pages of a sensational novel. This he read 'kneeling on the bare floor with indescribable rapture and with delicious fears that my Mother [might return] in the midst of one of its most thrilling sentences'.

Why is reading by torchlight under the covers after bedtime so enjoyable for kids? I recently discovered that all of my five children handed down the technique to each other like a survival skill. In past eras, before torches, it was romantic too: Conan Doyle read Scott's historical novels 'by candle-end . . . into the dead of night' and recalled concisely that 'the sense of crime added zest to the story'.

The Subtle Art of Recommendation

Comfort books can be shared in certain intimate friendships, but it's as subtle as tickling trout or grafting orchids. If you want to get someone to enjoy your heartfelt recommendation, a sort of take-it-or-leave-it insouciance is required. An over-enthusiastic recommendation gives your friend a burden: he or she must also find the book life-changing or profoundly affecting, or they are somehow not deep enough, or insufficiently caring about the friendship itself. And so the borrowed comfort book – we've all experienced this – sits somewhere emitting silent guilt-waves.

Henry Miller, novelist of sex and Bohemia, wrote about this business. He remembers a close friend who had just the right subtlety in luring him to Herman Hesse's *Siddhartha* :

> The man who put the book in my hands employed artful strategy: he said almost nothing about the book except that it was a book for me. Coming from him, this was incentive enough. It came exactly at the right moment.

This book has transformed so many lives. In the seventies it helped a lot of young people decide to avoid the rat race and have a bit more of a journeying existence. It had that effect on me: I got a job in a bookshop and did a lot of shoestring travelling. I remember being sat next to a very upright Berliner in a Sudan Airways Comet over the upper Nile in 1975, the sort of man who felt no need to make conversation. I have the sort of weak personality which leads me to vainly try and fill the silence with these types, like a bird futilely bashing itself against a window. In my mind I cast around for a specious

Germany link – I only knew the country aerially from seeing *The Dambusters*, hardly a happy opening gambit. Then I remembered *Siddhartha*, and I was off: 'Yeah, loads of young people in Britain are reading it now – it's really changing our outlook,' I gushed. Raising his gaze slowly from the vomit bag instructions to the seatbelt alert lights, he just said, 'I can imagine,' before reaching for his month-old *Die Welt*.

If, forty years later, he had been sitting next to Paulo Coelho – third bestselling novelist on earth and author of *The Alchemist* – Coelho would have explained the whole *Siddhartha* thing better than me: in his introduction to one recent edition he says that 'Hesse sensed – decades before my generation – the necessity we all have to claim what is truly and rightfully ours: our own life.' *The Alchemist* is a successor comfort book to *Siddhartha*; I met a customer recently who had read it six times. She knew she would read it more times too, whenever her life went pear-shaped.

Customers who buy *Siddhartha* in my shop usually have a quiet, purposeful air: they have heard it spoken about in a certain way, as you might describe early Bob Dylan songs to an alien, or sometimes they are buying it with a gleam of hope, for a lover.

Miller failed to emulate the strategy that drew him to read *Siddhartha* when he handed friends his own comfort book, the obscure *Seraphita* by Balzac. None of them took the bait, even though he told them the story of the student who accosted Balzac in the street and begged permission to kiss the hand that created this pioneering celebration of androgyny. Miller was just too enthusiastic to achieve the comfort book transfer. In his conversational autobiography, he does stop short of recommending *Siddhartha* to his readers, knowing that 'the less said the better'.

When it comes to 'inner history' books, recommendation is indeed a fine art. Miller points out that it is not the actual words used in a recommendation, but 'the aura that accompanies the words' which might alert the listener to a real comfort book recommendation. Be alive, he suggests, to these 'smouldering vibrations'. I think he gives off such vibrations when he ends a chapter by referring to *The Round* by Eduardo Santiago – not the surfer of insta-fame, nor even the notorious murderer who went to the chair, but an unknown Cuban occultist about whom even the internet yields no information. Miller's phrase, 'I doubt if a hundred people in the world would be interested in this book' is a sure-fire come-on. If a comfort book is outré and hard-to-get, the idea of it is all the more alluring.

I had a highly introverted bookseller in my independent bookshop whom I secretly admired for his literary tastes, although they made me feel inferior. Once, looking up from the catalogue of an obscure American university publisher – he spent hours poring over these catalogues, much to my fury and envy – he quietly enthused in his thick Cumbrian accent, mainly to himself – 'Aaaahh, *The Pit* – reprinted at last.'

I had to ask, 'What's that when it's at 'ome, George?'

'Well, Martin, I'll tell you if you turn this bloody crap off' – I did play a lot of world music in the shop in the eighties – 'What CD is it anyway? Don't tell me: another Mozart of the nose-flute?'

Huffily I defended the Burundian gourd-and-zither combo as a sub-Saharan sensation, but he wasn't listening. I turned it off.

'Onetti?' he said with a raised right eyebrow, Spock-like.

I had never heard of Onetti and so, in disgust, George returned to marking up his catalogues, muttering, 'Next you'll be saying you've never heard of the Premio Cervantes.'

I hadn't, of course, and this ignorance went to the core of my insufficiency as a manager and human being. I enquired, 'OK, what the fuck is it?'

George: 'Oh, it's only the premier literary prize for the second most widely spoken language in the world, but why should you have heard of it when you spend your time reading a tosser like Kipling? Onetti got it in 1980.'

Self: 'Look, just because I once confessed to reading *The Man Who Would Be King* – which your revered Eliot admired – you keep trying to brand me as the person who actually fired the shots at the Amritsar Massacre.'

Pause.

Self, now in conciliatory management tone: 'OK, who is Onetti anyway? I'm sorry I've never heard of him. Pardon me for living. I just have to spend my time finding a decent cleaner so we don't get endless complaint letters about the toilets, which you don't have to reply to – that's why I get the big money and my hair's falling out.'

George, shaking his head, and turning the page of the Arizona State University Press catalogue: 'Juan Carlos Onetti, you benighted southern imperialist, is . . . [looking from our shopfloor desks across the Fiction section] . . . is the Uruguayan Tolstoy.'

Since that memorable literary conversation I have regarded Onetti with the sort of awed reverence which Miller induced for Eduardo Santiago.

Both serendipity and inaccessibility can enchant a book and make it a comfort book, but buying it in a particular bookshop can lend enchantment too, in a completely illogical way. For instance, we buy a local book as a consoling souvenir of our exploration.

I am sure this is a general phenomenon. When I go on

holiday to somewhere very different from homely Kent, for instance, I find myself buying books in a new way, trying to take home some essence of my odyssey. Scanning my shelves I see such purchases, the middle-class version of a stick of rock or sombrero, and perhaps less useful: *The Geology of Mull, Wild Plants of Northern Cyprus* and *Ghosts of North Wales*. As well as looking distinctively local, these arcana feel different, run off clanking printing presses in Oban, Kyrenia and Pwllheli. The physicality of a book is often crucial to its comforting nature. In the fragile rainforest of private emotion, the senses are so alive that a book can become a talisman.

Getting Physical

The comfort book thing is very physical. This would be hard to explain to an alien: the fact that a book, a vehicle of mere words, is loved for its smell or feel. In thirty years working at tills in bookshops I have heard so much talk of changing times – books are dead, dumbed down, too many published, blah-di-blah – but customers' physical reaction to books has never changed. Very often they will give the book a post-purchase hug. Women will with surprising frequency kiss a book after buying it.

This does not, the women I have asked tell me, happen with the superficially more sensual purchase of clothing. Perhaps it is books as portals to an infinite past which invites the kiss, a sort of natural reverence for something which silently holds so much. Reactions to an installation at Tate Modern in 2019 shed some light on this beautifully mysterious behaviour. Icelandic artist Olafur Eliasson placed blocks of 15,000-year-old ice from the Greenland Ice Shelf outside the gallery. To his surprise, faced with this storied ice, many women kissed it.

The secret history of women enjoying books in the round is long. Michelangelo's spiritual mentor, Vittoria Colonna, kissed her copy of Dante, which inspired the forgotten Victorian Caroline Fellows to a poem, 'Book-Song':

> Vittoria kissed the page with sudden, tender lips
> And sighed, and murmured, the beloved name.

In the 1600s the pompous bore Philip Salmuth, in his six-volume medical encyclopaedia, attempted to pathologize a perfectly innocent young girl who 'experienced extreme pleasure in smelling old books'. The Edwardian sexologist Havelock Ellis was in the Salmuth mode, goggling pruriently at what he called women's 'considerable degree of sexual excitement in the presence of leather objects, leather-bound books, etc.' (Ellis, a virgin until sixty who got his kicks by watching women urinating, is perhaps not the go-to authority on female sexuality.)

Sensuality does not have to be orgiastic: in modern times the academic Marina Warner goes enjoyably bonkers over an old *Arabian Nights* she finds in London's Arcadian Library. The book, she writes:

> gives a powerful sense of the way books lived . . . boards softened by handling, pages tattered and torn, in some places patched and edged to stop them falling to pieces – these copies have been read to bits . . . a fusty creaturely smell of human hands and breath rises.

Nineteenth-century Romantics shared Warner's appreciation of old books which had patina, a good history, feel and smell.

Visitors to Dove Cottage were surprised to see that Words-worth's few books, in a recess beside the chimney, were 'ill-bound, or not bound at all, sometimes in tatters'. Coleridge was seen to kiss his old copy of Spinoza, and Charles Lamb shocked the upright lawyer Henry Robinson in 1824 with his tatty stable of comfort books:

> Called on [Charles]. He has the finest collection of shabby books I ever saw . . . filthy copies, which a delicate man would really hesitate touching . . . he loves his 'ragged veterans'[and] throws away all modern books, but retains trash he liked as a boy.

One of those veterans was the copy of Chapman's Homer which he was once spotted kissing. Lamb wrote unashamedly in an essay of embracing his 'midnight darlings', books 'which have been tumbled about and handled'.

Male physicality with books became a little more restrained as Victorianism encroached and men had to be steadily less demonstrative: Thackeray was seen to hold Lamb's writings to his forehead 'and ejaculate: Saint Charles!' – verbal ejacu-lation, but no kissing. As the age of steam transformed printing, new books' smell became a thing, and Dickens loved the waft of fresh paper coming out of a bookshop, as did George Gissing a little later. I have found one lone twentieth-century man showing physical love for a book, but even he was old in 1927:

> When Harry Smith bought at auction the copy of *Queen Mab* with Shelley's inscription to Mary Wollstonecraft, an old bib-liophile came up to him and, brushing tears from his eyes, asked if he might merely hold the book in his hands for a moment.

Neuroscientifically, olfactory book-love is healthy. It is a commonplace that smell is the sense most directly linked to memory, but it signifies much more. In patients with damage to the storytelling side of the brain, language and literalism take over. Such patients 'struggle to understand context, intuitive processing and metaphor'. They 'over-intellectualize and lose the ability to appreciate narrative'. Smell, Iain McGilchrist concludes in *The Master and his Emissary: The Divided Brain and the Making of the Western World* (Yale University Press, 2009) 'grounds our world in intuition and the body'. In the *International Journal of Neuroscience*, Marcello Spinella's 'A Relationship between Smell Identification and Empathy' (2002) underlined the link between awareness of smell and mental wholeness. Women are generally raised to be more grounded 'in intuition and the body', and to love narrative, and so it is unsurprising that they smell, hug and kiss books. Sylvia Plath's first reaction to the news that Ted Hughes's poems were to be published was intuitive: I can hardly wait' she wrote, 'to smell the print off the pages!' This olfactory sensuality – the French for 'smell', *sentir*, means both to smell and to feel – sheds some light on Freud's lament that the one thing he could not understand was what women want. In Freud's writings, David Howes noticed in *Sensual Relations: Engaging the Senses in Culture and Social Theory* (University of Michigan Press, 2003), the nose is 'notably missing'.

It seems that all those book-smelling women and romantics were neither in need of clutter-clearers nor sexology; they were in possession of a healthy love of life's narrative context, as experienced in the aroma of books. Sensing books is animal, and so is where we go to read them.

*

Curling Up

I mounted into the window-seat: gathering up my feet, I sat cross-legged, like a Turk; and, having drawn the red moreen curtain nearly close, I was shrined in double retirement.

Charlotte Brontë, *Jane Eyre*

Where do we go when we curl up with a book? The ability to lose ourselves in a book is spooky, and so is the whole question of where we choose to read. In the right place, we forget time, we forget the room, then the chair, then our very self. The self-educated radical William Cobbett recalls it evocatively. He saw Swift's *Tale of a Tub* in a Richmond bookshop window, bought it instead of dinner for threepence, climbed over a wall into a field at the upper corner of Kew Gardens and there:

> On the shady side of a haystack, I read on till it was dark without any thought of supper or bed. When I could see no longer . . . I fell asleep beside the stack; and then I started off: still reading, I could relish nothing besides.

There are extraordinary stories of this sort of absorption. G. K. Chesterton read through the hansom cab he was in lurching off the road, unaware of any disturbance until he was ejected in surprise on to the ground, and his brother Cecil regularly read standing in a crowded London pub, pint in one hand, book in the other, 'chuckling occasionally'. The Blitz did not stop old Mrs Dyble, housekeeper at Dr Johnson's former house off Fleet Street. While everyone else went to the cellar when the siren sounded, she went to her favourite reading spot in the attic room where Johnson had written his *Dictionary*.

This 'losing ourselves' is a phenomenon of our river-like consciousness. Science remains hazy about this dissociation. The 'stream of consciousness' idea coined by William James in about 1890 remains convincing. Descartes's theatre of mind has been long debunked, and the recent ideas of Antonio Damasio, Daniel Dennett and quantum physicists all point to a consciousness which cannot be viewed mechanistically as having discrete levels. Certainly, the two-level idea of conscious and subconscious has come and gone. Consciousness is more like a stream, or deep river, than a machine or any spider diagram.

It seems obvious that we duck and dive around our river like an Amazon dolphin when we, say, drive habitually on a known route and 'switch off', or when we dream, or start registering background music during a conversation, or tune out aircraft noise. Virginia Woolf's fictive descriptions of being have lasted better than the shifting semantics of much neuroscience. To lose oneself in a book is akin to what booze gave the once-alcoholic writer Leslie Jamison, something she called a 'wriggling-free of the swaddling of self-awareness'.

Whatever one chooses to call the as-yet-unnamed state of 'losing yourself in a book', coming out of it is like transporting back on to earth anew, hence the vividness of re-arrival described by the parapsychologist and classicist Frederick Myers (1843–1901) remembering his six-year-old self reading Virgil: 'It is still stamped on my mind, the ante-room at the parsonage with its floor of bright matting, and its glass door into the garden, through which the flooding sunlight came.'

It happened to Marjory Todd, a Limehouse boilermaker's daughter, with *Wuthering Heights* in a park in 1920:

I experienced that sudden awareness of identity and purpose which I suppose comes to most adolescents. Perhaps to some it comes gradually. For me the moment was caught so that now I can remember the exact angle of the slanting sun, a clump of pine trees, the rough worn grass and a few pine cones at my feet. (*Snakes and Ladders*, 1960)

My son, aged about fifteen, told me of finishing the *Northern Lights* trilogy in his Canterbury bedroom. The Cathedral bell had been tolling for a while but only after he finished the last line did it wash back into his consciousness. The memory of the room, the sunlight and the bell is etched on to his mind.

This occasional awakening of a sense of self happens to us all, mostly in childhood. Bachelard in *The Poetics of Space* calls it a '*cogito* of emergence'. It has a corollary. If we can suddenly become aware of our existence, what is existence when not present in our consciousness? Here we are near Sartre's existentialism, and he was deeply impressed by a childhood '*cogito*' in Richard Hughes's *High Wind in Jamaica*. Emily is lying in 'a nook right in the bows' when 'it suddenly flashed into her mind that she was she'. Emily was not reading, but readers have frequently recorded experiencing such quiet revelation in a sequestered nook.

This finding oneself in a nook is subtle and beautiful, and fragile too. Novelists and poets are congenial explorers of these magical stretches of river. Here is Andrew Marvell in his garden in 1681:

The mind, that ocean where each kind
Does straight its own resemblance find
Yet it creates, transcending these,
Far other worlds, and other seas;

Annihilating all that's made
To a green thought in a green shade.

Marvell's transcendentalism is not for everyone, but everyone does become, around their home, different people, differently conscious. At the front door when the policeman or postman calls we instantly strike poses of ideal citizen, or receiver of mysteries. On the stairs we are between states, becoming public going down, renewing individuality going up. Sometimes a shattering event sends us to a new domestic location, to process emotions undeadened by habit; when I heard that a bookseller friend had died young in Scotland I found myself disappearing to stand in the alley by the wheelie bin. Yorkshirewoman Anne Lister in 1824 went to extremes. To read, she sat in a window seat with curtains open only enough to admit reading light, a high folding screen cordoning her off from the house, two great coats on and a dressing gown over her knees.

Seclusion

Van Gogh painted many nests and wrote in a letter of his hope that his cottage could resemble a wren's nest. Significantly, the entrance to those globe-shaped nests is often hard to find. That extreme outsider Quasimodo found his nook in the belfry, which Hugo called his 'egg, and nest'. Pasternak had a particular partiality to seeing the human-made world as akin to a swallow's nest. The reading nook is I think easily metaphored by the swallow's home, being made from the mud of a nearby river, just as we make our mythic home from the rivers of consciousness.

There is a heroic hidden history of people managing to read books in extraordinary circumstances and against the odds, by what can best be described as inspired pragmatism. So many people can only read in bed, because the rest of the house is just full of jobs, or simply not cosy. 'Cosy', this untranslatable word, derivation unknown, came to us from the Vikings via the Scots, coined by two peoples who knew all about appreciating a warm nook out of the weather. Out of the wind too, for which those connoisseurs of wild weather the people of Orkney have eight words.

In *Nature Cure*, the naturalist Richard Mabey's memoir of crippling depression, he describes roaming the house for the right reading nook and eventually finding it, next to a small corner table with a side light on. In this quest he was emulating animal processes: thus hares find a form, a place in a meadow that is just right for giving birth. (Francis Bacon painted well only in limited South Kensington lodgings: he needed 'to be confined', one critic thought.) We are closer to this animal instinct for the right nook than we might recognize, especially when it comes to the moment when we decide to go and lose ourselves in a book. Octopus studies have got us thinking about how consciousness can be distributed in limbs, which hints at why and how we arrange our legs and arms with such purpose when we settle into reading.

(There is one amusing case of fake-nookery, of someone pretending to absorption in a nook for political reasons. A servant observed Thomas Cromwell, after his patron Wolsey's fall, in a window seat at Esher Palace loudly sobbing over a prayer book. It was, Eamon Duffy remarks, 'a public display of traditionalist picty'.) Back to genuineness: Erasmus had Mabey's problem too; although he had 'a fine house' he spent ages 'finding a nook in which he could put his little body', his first biographer wrote. This process of finding a reading nook is all the more freighted because of what might happen during reading. Often it is a chrysalis experience and we emerge a different creature. We curl up to read, become disembodied, and might emerge re-embodied, changed. Once, Kafka's actual body seemed to counterpoint this metamorphosis. He wrote to his would-be girlfriend Felice in 1913 of reading a poem: 'it rises with an uninterrupted, inner, fluid development – how one's eyes open wide while lying scrunched up on the sofa!'

Landings and staircases can be tempting, free of visible household tasks and possessed of an unowned departure lounge feel. Sir Walter Scott's house was so grand it was almost impersonal, so he often read perched halfway up his library steps.

Away from Erasmus's and Scott's reading issues in their fine houses, working-class readers had more challenging problems to overcome than finding the right spot.

2. Reading in Adversity

Tears on the Machine: Working Readers

For many working people in human history, books have been so hard to come by, and leisure time so scarce, that reading has been restricted in matter and manner. For Cornish carpenter George Smith (born *c.* 1800), maths books had the gift of longevity. As he recalled in his autobiography: 'a treatise on algebra or geometry which cost a few shillings, afforded me matter for close study for a whole year.' Others were more time-poor than book-deprived, such as the London cobbler and future book-seller James Lackington (1746–1815). He devised a truly astonishing regime, by which he and his fellows allowed themselves only three hours' sleep a night:

> One of us sat up to work until the appointed time for the others to rise, and when all were up, my friend John, and your humble servant took it in turns to read aloud to the rest, while they were at their work.

The same humbling commitment was displayed by James Miller, a Highland harness-maker, who usually found people to read to him while he worked, and held readings every evening, often attended 'by two to three intelligent neighbours'. Perhaps unsurprisingly his son Hugh (1802–56) became a significant writer, transforming the study of geology and prefiguring Darwin. Ingeniously, another early Scottish reader, a travelling stonemason, taught his horse his regular routes and read as he rode.

The ingenuity award for readers must go to the nineteenth-century Scot James Somerville. He was an itinerant labourer with eleven children, who were literally clothed in rags, collected and sewn together by their mother, Mary. Their son Alexander started work aged eight, cleaning stables and digging ditches. A determined reader, he would become a politician admired by Engels, and recorded his childhood in his autobiography. So many of the hovels the family stayed in on their wanderings in search of work lacked light, so James carried a window with him, complete with glass, and installed it in each dwelling.

It is hard now to imagine what a problem lighting was for the literate poor. Many workers had to read by the light of the moon, as tallow candles – made from beef or mutton fat – were often too expensive to buy, and wax candles were the preserve of wealthy homes. In some areas, rushes were available that could be soaked in fat to make rush-lights, but, like tallow, this lighting was smoky, smelly and in need of continual trimming. Small wonder that two footmen at St James's Palace in the reign of Queen Anne could found a roaring business by selling palace candle-ends on a market stall after work. Before long they had their own business: Fortnum and Mason.

In book-poor environments, the most unlikely tome could become a comfort book. Millworker Thomas Wood (b. 1822) went to a school where the only book was the Bible, so he joined the Mechanics' Institute for a penny a week and there fell upon the six volumes of Charles Rollins's *Ancient History*. As an old man, Wood recorded in the *Keighley News* how Rollins 'left an impression on my mind which 40 years' wear and tear has not effaced'. Somerset farm boy John Cannon used market trips to slip inside a benevolent gent's house and there he read Josephus's huge *History of the Jews*, followed by Aristotle.

Shepherds' isolation was ideal for reading. The Wiltshire shepherd boy Edwin Whitlock (b. 1874) read the 1867 *Post Office Directory* 'from cover to cover' whilst tending his flock. This got him into importuning neighbours for more books, and by fifteen he had read 'most' of Dickens and Scott, and a twelve-volume *History of England*. In Clackmannan, Scotland, the shepherd John Christie had not only a library of 370 books, but complete sets of *The Spectator* and *The Rambler*.

Coal miners worked in hellish conditions compared to Whitlock and, maybe because of that Stygian life, they had an amazing commitment to self-education from early on. They forged 'one of the greatest networks of cultural institutions created by working people anywhere in the world' (a 2010 analysis). A study of the many miners' libraries has found the earliest in Lanarkshire, Scotland, being set up in 1741. Library books not excluding popular fables and 'penny dreadfuls' would do much to radicalize miners. A Welsh miner recalled that any Robin Hood stories were much borrowed, and loved for their redistributive message.

One book captivated working-class audiences more than any other throughout the Victorian and Edwardian age. Harriet Beecher Stowe was, in sheer popularity and impact, the ancestress of Harper Lee. Stowe's anti-slavery novel *Uncle Tom's Cabin* had an influence hard to imagine in this book-prize age. A North Welsh miner explained that it 'played hell with our emotions. We felt every stroke of the lash of the whip. It cut us to the quick, heart and soul.' A Forest of Dean colliery storekeeper wrote in his diary how he was 'struck most impressively with it'. Elizabeth Bryson

(b. 1880), daughter of an impoverished Dundee family, exclaimed, 'Oh, the reality!' and broadened her reflections to express the essence of the comfort of books:

> Suddenly, blazing from the page, the resounding words that we couldn't find. It is an exciting moment . . . 'Who am I, what is this ME?' I had been groping to know that since I was three. (*Look Back in Wonder*, 1966)

The anonymous 1935 autobiography of 'a common man' told how Stowe's book, read surreptitiously in a factory, caused 'many a salt tear' to fall on to his 'numbering machine'.

Macho fellow workers were a hazard for readers, and sailor Lennox Kerr (b. 1899) found himself 'under suspicion' for reading:

> I had to take up every challenge as soon as it showed: had to swipe a chap's face when I did not want to, or boast about my splicing – to prove that reading books was not making me any less a good sailor.

But, sensitively, Kerr detected that:

> The secret desires in men come out as they feel themselves . . . free from the screen of cynicism men don in public. Their deep creative wish to be more than obedient workers appears . . . men are more romantic, courageous and poetic in the secrecy of darkness . . . I heard a man, the most foul-tongued on our ship, reciting the Song of Solomon to the darkness and rustle of the sea breaking against the ship's forefoot . . . Alone, man becomes what he would be if not forced to a mould. (*The Eager Years: An Autobiography*, 1949)

Bosses seem to have been generally tolerant of workplace literacy. A Swindon train factory worker read Ovid, Plato and Sappho in the original and chalked the Greek and Latin alphabet on his lathe. The foreman initially told him to clean it off, but relented when told what it was. Rowland Kenney (b. 1883) read in secret until his foreman one day recited Tennyson's 'The Lotos-Eaters' 'in a powerful voice with a Lancashire accent'. He was reassured. 'If a fighting, drinking, you-go-to-hell man like him' loved poetry, then Kenney could read openly too.

Nottinghamshire miner George Tomlinson had a similar, rather moving, surprise. Used to reading 'half a mile from the surface', he was clouted by his foreman when he let some coal trucks crash because he was reading a Goldsmith poem. The next day the foreman lent him a pile of his own poetry books with the caveat: '*If tha brings em darnt pit I'll knock thi block off.*' Later on, Tomlinson cringed with shame when a fellow miner picked up his dropped pages of original poetry, but the colleague simply said, 'No good, lad. Tha wants ter read Shelley.'

This is getting almost unbelievable: Lancashire miner Joe Keating (b. 1871) read Greek philosophy at home until 3 a.m. before his gruelling shift shovelling slag out of the mine. Here is an underground exchange with an unnamed colleague, whom I'll call C:

C, with a sigh: 'Heaven from all creatures hides the book of fate.'

JK: 'Are you quoting Pope?'

C: 'Aye, me and Pope do agree very well.'

Keating felt much less alienated after this, and formed a chamber quartet, playing Mozart and Schubert.

Working-class reading history is elusive, under-represented in biographies and in histories of the book. One chance day in the life of Charlie Chaplin in New York invokes a picture richer than existing narratives imply: an African American truck driver introduced him to *Roget's Thesaurus*, a hotel waiter quoted Blake and Marx as he delivered courses, and an acrobat put him on to Burton's *Anatomy of Melancholy* (1621). En passant the tumbler explained, in a thick Brooklyn accent, the seminal influence of Burton on Samuel Johnson.

Surprisingly, when proletarian reading is analysed, it is still sometimes done with condescension. In 2001, one academic, commenting on Chaplin's own reading, which ranged from Schopenhauer and Plato to Whitman and Poe, called it the 'mongrelization of philosophy and melodrama, of high culture and low comedy that characterized the typical diet of autodidacts'. That word 'mongrelization' has a whiff of cultural eugenics, implying pure-bred higher beings who eschew 'low comedy'. Surely innumerable great novelists, spawners of many a PhD, became great by just such eclecticism.

The average person getting direct access to books has sometimes been viewed as a threat, and a surprise. Thomas Burke, the historian of East End life, fumed about 'sleek West End novelists' underestimating and patronizing his Whitechapel co-habitants. In 1932 he wrote:

> One of our 'intellectual novelists' recorded with a note of wonder, that on visiting a Whitechapel home the daughters of the house were reading Proust and a volume of Chekhov's comedies. Why the wonder? (*The Real East End*, 1932)

Burke pointed out that Bethnal Green Library was always bustling with locals. My own father (b. 1913), who grew up in Bethnal Green with his police constable adoptive father between the wars in abject poverty, was very widely read despite having left school at fourteen.

Another academic who took a dim view of autodidacticism was Q. D. Leavis. She longed for a golden age when 'the masses were receiving their amusement from above, instead of being specially catered for by journalists, film-makers. and popular novelists'.

Virginia Woolf struggled to understand the masses' reading habits:

> I often ask my friends the lowbrows . . . why is it that we highbrows never buy a middlebrow book. To this the lowbrows reply – I cannot imitate their style of talking – that they consider themselves common people without education. (*The Collected Essays of Virginia Woolf*, 2013)

There is now a slightly bonkers theory of English literary history that modernists started writing obscurely to fend off proletarian readers who were getting uppity and invading the uplands of literary life. The theory goes on to say that once common people got on to reading Eliot and Woolf, and – dammit – understanding them, postmodernism was hatched to repel afresh proletarian boarders of the good ship Literary Academia. The Svengali of postmodernism, Jacques Derrida, seems to be a democratic figure. He asserted that there was no distinction between low and high culture, implied that a Madonna concert was as good as *Hamlet* because art happens in the mind of the audience or reader. But his own impossibly dense prose has kept the literate masses at bay. As one critic who saw him lecture said, he was more performance artist than logician, playing with words and enjoying a very French mode of free association. He himself fails the democratic litmus test since he is unread outside academia.

Ezra Pound was breathtakingly frank in predicting 'a new aristocracy of the arts' which should be as cynical in gulling the masses as the old aristocracy of blood. After all, he was dealing with 'A race with brains like rabbits . . . and we are the heirs of the witch doctor and the voodoo. We artists who have been so long despised are about to take control.' To sew up this control, Pound's Imagist group tried to patent the word 'Imagist' so that inferior imitators could be excluded from invading the new style. This was 1914, about the time of Battersea postman's son Richard Church's childhood: he lamented in his autobiography *Over the Bridge* that 'the problem with accessibility is that there is no profit in it for the intelligentsia'. Happily Pound's heirs, Poets Laureate Ted Hughes and Simon Armitage, are firmly of the 'rabbit' class, and writers' backgrounds are less of a focus for the writer or the reader.

To close this section I cannot resist a story Macaulay told of a working man's honest reaction to a 'classic', which illustrates the mantra 'you cannot fool all the people all the time'. An eighteenth-century Italian criminal was given the choice of being a galley slave or reading Giuccardini's twenty-volume *History of Italy*. He chose the book, but after a few chapters he changed his mind and became a 'slave of the oar'.

The proletariat, common people, or whatever term one prefers for non-elite readers, have had it tough, fighting for access to books and then for the liberty and light to read them by. They have faced enemies across a fearful establishment. Women readers of every class have faced unique barriers, and circumvented them in inspiring ways, unique ways, with wit and skulduggery.

Hiding Ovid Behind the Bolster: Women Reading

Julia has free access to all her father's books, with the exception of
the book-case; this has glazed doors, and the books are all turned
with their titles inward, so we do not know their names or
contents, but Mr Waldron says they are not suitable for us to read.
Julia looks at them with a sort of awe.

Anonymous, *She Would Be a Governess: A Tale* (Routledge,
London, 1861)

Leah Price, who became a Harvard professor at thirty-one, is
a leading historian of reading. Her observation that 'reading is
a peculiarly feminine source of interiority' seems to be confirmed by the sources I have read, the predominance of females
among bookshop customers, booksellers and librarians, and
by the plethora of paintings of women reading; Gwen John
alone did seventeen such pictures.

Although the Bible makes no mention of Mary reading, in
paintings of the Annunciation from about 1100 or so she is
often reading a book. This is most odd and merits inspection. The Annunciation is when the angel Gabriel comes to
tell Mary, six months pregnant, that her baby is an immacu-
late conception, fathered by God not Joseph, and is the Messiah,
the Chosen One. The earliest pictures have Mary surprised
by the winged intruder, sewing or spinning; a book is sub-
stituted in the period often identified as the twelfth-century
renaissance. By then, reading, specifically women reading,
had become an accepted cultural reference point, or 'a thing',
a meme. Consequently, it became a vivid way to dramatize
her receiving this startling celestial data. What better time

for her to process such news than when she was already in a state of interiority? For men, the image of a woman reading has remained both romantic and threatening; a state of dangerous potency.

Girls and women have faced specific challenges to reading: imposed concepts of womanhood, censorship, husbands, clergy, housework and more. Men have been terrified – not too strong a word – of their being sexually gratified by books, or politically or spiritually liberated by books. Probably the biggest threat though was if they got themselves educated by reading. The reasoning is clear: more reading = less housework, and less devotion to the husband as a source of wisdom and gratification. More subtly, many men felt envy: slaving away at a soul-dessicating job created a natural jealousy of reading leisure.

Women book-owners flash into history from early on. The Roman scholar Melania was described as going through books 'as if eating dessert', until she decided to renounce all possessions and live as a hermit. The book-loving abbess Hilda of Whitby (c. 614–80) had her Arab counterpart in Fatima al-Fihri (c. 800–880), who founded the oldest extant library in the world, in Fez. She was no big exception in Islam: several women in the early centuries of Islam founded libraries and educational institutions. A female scholar made such an impact at Cairo University in the twelfth century that the male students said she knew 'a camel-load' of reading matter. Educated women were admired in Islam, not least because of Muhammad's wives: Khadijah, successful entrepreneur, and Aisha, renowned scholar of the Hadith (the Prophet's writings). More generally, Muhammad himself taught both women and men and enthused: 'how splendid were the women . . . shame did not prevent them from becoming learned.' In those early days women were barred from much formal instruction but were welcome at public lectures and teachings, especially in mosques.

Fifteenth-century Poland was considerably more hostile to the reading woman. In 1480s Krakow a woman disguised herself as a man to get into university. She kept up the deception throughout the course, getting excellent marks and being noted for her conscientiousness, but just before graduation a soldier rumbled her and she was taken before a tribunal. When the judge asked her why she had perpetrated the deception, her simple reply moved the judge to let her off, and moves us still 600 years later: 'Amore studii' – for the love of learning. She chose to be sent to a convent – these were often secret refuges for frustrated female readers – where she quickly rose to be abbess and turned the whole place into a sort of academy for book-mad girls and women.

The Venetian Republic produced a heroic woman reader by a series of happy accidents. Christine de Pizan's father got the job of astrologer to the king of France in 1368, when she was four. He moved to the Rue St Jacques in Paris, and psychogeography swept in: she was at the heart of France's literary and bookselling life, and had access to a royal library of thousands of books, the foundation of the Bibliothèque Nationale. A keen reader, married at fifteen and mother of three children, she wrote that she would have become an unknown stay-at-home mother were it not for a sudden revolution in her fortunes.

When she was twenty-three, a few months after the death of her father, her husband, Étienne, whom she loved, succumbed to the plague. Caught up in a legal wrangle to access her inheritance, Christine was strapped for money. She used her wide reading to good effect in turning to writing to support herself. After initial success with love ballads, she wrote flowery histories of France for aristocrats, cleverly upping the price by offering personalized editions with bespoke forewords. These books were produced by some of the finest scribes and artists of the day.

Pragmatically, when one patron, Philip the Bold, died, she sold the manuscript he had commissioned to his equally modest son John the Fearless, for the equivalent of over €20,000. She was the first woman in the world to live by her writing, which became increasingly personal.

Her attack on the revered *Romance of the Rose* questioned its reductive portrayal of women as seducers, and other works included life-advice to her son upon his emigration to England and her most famous work, *The Book of the City of Ladies*. This tale of a fabled city built by heroines throughout history has a quirk which is typical of her. The city is also the book itself, the chapters representing building-block accounts of great women which form a convincing thesis, an ideal intellectual city, free of misogyny. This meta device means that the book could also be called *The City of the Book of Ladies*. It is a radical world history of women which attacks head-on Aristotle's view that women are second-rate men. She celebrates women's vulnerability as their secret power, but also praises strong women, relishing in particular the Amazons, with a picture of them in battle.

This feminist history is included in the finest edition of her collected writings, *The Book of the Queen*. It was presented to Queen Isabeau of France in 1410, and became one of the founding objects of the British Museum in 1753. This priceless illustrated parchment anthology, 14 x 11 inches, was rebound in 1962 in green leather, at which time protective sheets of paper were inserted to protect the pictures. Although you need a letter of introduction to handle it, anyone can turn its digitized pages via the British Library website. As one of the most-requested books in the library, it was an early candidate for complete digitization.

The book smoulders with Christine's personality: she appears in illustrations and at several points the handwriting is her own. The power of the physical book in chaotic times is a root-message of *The Book of the Queen*, and there are several pictures of Christine writing or reading, and one of her delivering advice to her son – his folded arms were once thought to indicate indifference, but are now known to signify receptiveness.

Charlotte Cooper of Oxford University points out that Christine is always portrayed in a certain blue dress. An allegory of love is illustrated by several ninnies giving away their hearts too readily, whilst the figure in the blue dress, who holds her love thoughtfully in reserve, was deleted in subsequent versions.

The British Library manuscript, with its feminism, and reflections on how men cock up governance, was a comfort book for Queen Isabeau. Like Christine, Isabeau had come from abroad – she was half Italian and half Bavarian – and married in Paris at fifteen. Both women effectively lost their husbands, Christine to the plague, Isabeau to madness. As queen regent, or acting monarch, Isabeau struggled to keep the country stable as her unfortunate husband, Charles the Mad, descended ever deeper into insanity, murdering trusted knights and becoming convinced he was made of glass.

The Book of the Queen's most poignant image is of Christine in her simple blue dress handing the book to Isabeau, who is accompanied by just a dog and her two lifelong German ladies-in-waiting. Contemporary factions vying for power accused Isabeau of being an incestuous, unmotherly Bavarian adulteress; they murdered her supposed lover brutally, starting by cutting off his hands. Even monarchs need comfort books. Isabeau became such a byword for bad womanhood that the Marquis de Sade wrote a horrible novel about her, *The Secret History of Isabel of Bavaria*, later admitting that it was without foundation in fact. The black legend about her life continued in Victorian England with Andrew Lang's *The Little Queen* (1908). Her reputation is now more nuanced, as a cultured woman struggling with queenship whilst supporting her mentally ill husband amid a misogynist court.

Isabeau's book went on an extraordinary journey before reaching the British Library, continuing its association with remarkable women readers. After Agincourt the new Regent of France, John of Lancaster, took it to London, but it is inscribed in four places by his French wife, Jacquetta, who also wrote her motto on two pages. John was called 'well-boked' – a book-lover – in his lifetime, but these inscriptions show that she enjoyed the book just as Isabeau had. Jacquetta too got snarled up in power factions, and was accused of greed and sexual lubricity. There were alarm bells: her fourteen children indicated an almost unnatural fecundity. She was French. How did she get her daughter to enchant Edward IV into bed? Happily for her enemies some images of him made of lead were 'found' in her quarters and she was tried as a witch, but acquitted. Jacquetta's marginalia are intriguing evidence of a silent conversation between this formidable survivor of power politics and Christine de Pizan.

The Book of the Queen was bequeathed to Jacquetta's son Richard, and then crops up in the library of an England-based Flemish diplomat called Louis de Bruges. Louis snapped it up to adorn his notable book collection, of which 145 items have been identified in libraries worldwide. He wrote his motto ornately on the first page.

The book next turns up in Welbeck Abbey, Nottinghamshire, home of the Royalist Henry Cavendish, 1630–91 (incidentally the last common ancestor of Prince Charles and Camilla). Despite his childish scrawl across the cover in big letters, 'Henry Duke of Newcastle His Booke 1676', it seemed destined to fall into the hands of the sort of women Christine de Pizan would have liked.

A chum of Henry's griped that his wife, Frances, simply 'had too great a share in the government of the family [and] expected everything to go as she pleased'. The couple separated over how to split their inheritance between five daughters. The book passed to the third daughter, Margaret Cavendish, and then to her daughter Henrietta Cavendish (1694–1755), a great reader who annotated many of the books at Welbeck Abbey in her own personal code.

Henrietta's independent-mindedness caused some vexation. Swift's judgement is typical: 'she is handsome and has good sense, but red hair' – that is, too damned feisty. She was a book-ish introvert in a time of hard-living aristocrats. Her friend Lady Mary Wortley Montagu defended her to others thus: 'she is not shining, but has more in her than such giddy things as you.' For historian Lucy Worsley she is simply a gloriously vig-orous eccentric. One frosty January day Henrietta wrote from Welbeck Abbey, among her books, lamenting even the limited social duties she had to perform, demonstrating a sort of strange solidarity with many a working-woman reader: 'I live as retired here as I can in this country where my ancestors have lived so long but must see more company than I chuse.'

The book's last private owner was Henrietta's daughter, another Margaret, and in her hands Christine's great dream-narrative, *The Book of the City of Ladies*, seems to be eerily coming to pass after 300 years. Margaret was a founder member of the

Bluestockings, an informal society which has given its name to intellectual women who refuse to be defined by motherhood or wifely duty. She was a pioneering scientist, sought out by Enlightenment intellectuals. When most women in her position were spending on curtains, she bought the Portland Vase (AD 20), while others were swooning over Gothic romances, she preferred the ground-breaking *Cecilia* by Fanny Burney, and in a time when twiddly landscaping was all the rage, she studied the life cycles of bees and hares. Whilst she might have been expected to sit demurely in salons, she went hiking in the Peak District with Rousseau, and insisted he take refuge in her house.

From Margaret's library *The Book of the Queen* came to rest in the British Museum. De Pizan's work was widely published in the twentieth century, and Simone de Beauvoir cited it as an inspiration. A society dedicated to Christine holds annual conferences. She is still out there: the secondhand paperback I bought last week in Lancashire of *The Book of the City of Ladies* has a McDonald's salt sachet as a bookmark. She defied gender expectations and her bright image, reading in her blue dress, still shines at us through the arches of the years.

What happened to Christine de Pizan in old age? She retired to a convent, where she pursued her reading peacefully into her sixties. She stopped writing, but not hoping, penning a sudden last poem when she heard about Joan of Arc's first victory. Prefiguring Larkin's historical-moment line 'sexual intercourse began in 1963', she exclaimed, 'the sun began to shine again in 1429'.

Soon after Christine's death a Frenchwoman in her mould arrived at court. King Francis's sister Marguerite of Navarre (1492–1549), 'the first modern woman', read widely and uninhibitedly, with a team of readers to keep up the literary input even when she was making her beloved tapestries. Her reading bore fruit in her poetry, which theologians of the Sorbonne condemned – one monk wanted her sewn into a sack and thrown in the Seine. More discerning critics were vocal in their admiration: Elizabeth I, as a girl, translated her poetry; Erasmus called her a great philosopher; and Leonardo da Vinci came to stay in her house. She had two lifesaving strokes of luck: she was offered as a wife to Henry VIII just before he became king – he declined – and her *Heptameron*, stories of seduction and cuckoldry which would have landed her in prison, was only made public after her death.

The English Renaissance counterpart to Marguerite was Lady Anne Clifford (1590–1676) – five feet tall with waist-length brown hair. She amassed a huge library and, unlike many of us, she remembered what she had read. John Donne loved conversation with her, because she could discourse on anything 'from predestination to shea-silk'.

There is evidence of many other early modern noblewomen with large personal libraries: the Duchess of Suffolk had 'a chestful of books' in 1580. Lady Anne Southwell moved house in 1631 with 'three truncks of books'. She was free of any sense of womanly inferiority: the Kings of Bohemia and Sweden enjoyed corresponding with her as did politicians and poets at home. A keen religious debater, she said the greatest heresy of all was 'That females have so little wit, to serve men they are only fit'. Her life should be filmed, but until then her memorial is her poetry and a small grave plaque in the badlands of Acton, on the road to Heathrow from central London.

Male worries about all these women reading printed books started early. Edmund Spenser's *The Faerie Queen* (1590) is now generally only read as a set book, but was the most influential poem to come out of Elizabethan England after Shakespeare's

Venus and Adonis. Spenser was a thoroughly establishment figure, still hated in Ireland for his advocacy of a scorched-earth
policy in that 'diseased part of the state'. He was terrified of
the effects of unrestricted printing on womanhood. His female
monster in *The Faerie Queen* is 'loathsome, filthie and foule'.
She seems half serpent, a dead giveaway for sexual power.
When a knight fights her she vomits up books, showing the
danger of voracious and ill-digested reading.

Censorship eased in the following century and bookshops
and libraries proliferated, but the main enemy of women reading was then closer to home: their husbands. Although women
hoovered up astonishing forgotten epics such as the sixty-volume
L'Astrée (1627), and although Pepys did not feel challenged by
his wife staying up after him to finish books such as the ten-
volume *Cassandra* and five-volume *Polexandre*, many wives had
to affect a maidenly vacuity. In his play *The Rivals*, Sheridan
amusingly has Lydia and her maid detected reading too widely:

> Here, my dear Lucy, hide these books. Quick, quick – fling
> *Peregrine Pickle* under the toilet – throw *Roderick Random* into
> the closet – put *The Innocent Adulterer* into *The Whole Duty of
> Man* – thrust *Lord Aimworth* under the sofa – cram Ovid behind
> the bolster – put *The Man of Feeling* in your pocket, so – now
> leave *Fordyce's Sermons* open on the table.

Even women writers warned their sex against off-piste reading. According to the 1777 *Letter to a Newly Married Lady* by
Hester Chapone, a wife should learn to like her husband's reading tastes because she must 'beware of all things . . . his growing
dull and weary in your company'. For every Hester Chapone
there was a woman to give pushback, such as Jane Collier, whose
wonderful 1753 *Essay on the Art of Ingeniously Tormenting* gives tips

on interrupting husbands reading aloud when wives want to get on with their own books, tips which are so good I must confess I would not want my wife to see them. That men were regularly beaten back is shown by an 1863 article in *Macmillan's Magazine* which warned that 'a lady who differs in opinion from her lord and master will not uncommonly retire behind a book'.

The American Founding Father Alexander Hamilton's wife Elizabeth hid Lord Kames's *Elements of Criticism* under the chair cushion ready to whip out if discovered at her preferred reading, which she had been warned might make her seem 'a pedant'. Or perhaps somehow prey to a stimulation which rivalled her expected role? In *The Tenant of Wildfell Hall* Anne Brontë treats of this, portraying a husband who only reads newspapers but stops his beloved reading books.

The trouble was, even after women's reading was accepted, it had to be edifying, often husband-chosen. John Marsh, an early Victorian Chichester gentleman, shamelessly said he 'usually read to the Ladies for an hour after tea whilst they worked'. As the Victorian feminist Harriet Martineau fumed, a woman was: 'Expected to sit down in the parlour with her sewing, and hold herself ready for callers. When the callers came, conversation often turned naturally to the book just laid down, which must be carefully chosen.'

Lady Lugard was so desperate to read off-piste in a High Tory household that she regularly read up an apple tree: 'she went up the tree a Royalist and Tory, she came down a passionate democrat,' lamented *The Times*. Carlyle's wife, Jane, rather enjoyed the unfaithfulness of her novel-reading in the house of 'the Sage of Chelsea': 'I felt I was having an illicit affair.' Ironically her letters are now more read than his great tomes.

In a way, the lower orders were less surveilled. Jane Eyre was only a governess, but at least she could vanish into her curtained window seat, rather than have to be seen to be reading *Fordyce's Sermons* or be read to by the master of the house. An awful lot of surreptitious reading was going on among household staff, more than we will ever know. Edith Wharton portrayed a house where, despite a grand library, nobody read except a maid who set her bed on fire with an illicit candle.

'The hour of hair-dressing' was regarded as a torment of boredom for rich ladies without someone to read aloud to them, and such sessions benefited domestic staff. A maid in 1749, hearing *Clarissa*, 'let fall such a shower of tears upon her lady's head' that she had to leave the room and compose herself. Her mistress gave her a crown for being so sympathetic. A disapproving gentleman in 1752 entered a house in London to find 'the mistress of the family losing hours over a novel in the parlour, while her maids, in emulation, were similarly employed in the kitchen'. The Old Bailey's records of book thefts almost entirely concern maids nicking books. In 1761 Londoner Mary Gaywood went to her maid's lodging and found twenty years of filched books and – this seemed to infuriate her the most – 'my cream pot'. Some servants secreted books they found whilst dusting the library, perhaps deducing expendability from neglect. By the mid nineteenth century the more enlightened aristocrats provided special servants' libraries, an acknowledgement of their duty of care slightly marred by the presence of so many instructional tomes.

Working women were reading enough for a vicar to moan in 1715 that these days 'every Country Milkmaid can understand the *Iliad*'. Clergy aside, as working women's reading staggered forward there is evidence of continuing peer resistance. The break-time reading habit of Glasgow's 'Factory Girl Poet' Ellen Johnston (born *c.* 1830) aroused a toxic mix of impotent anger and envy: 'The girls around me did not understand, consequently they wondered, became jealous, and told falsehoods of me . . . I suffered all their insults.'

Ellen still had it easy compared to African American slave women. Their reading history has only been uncovered as their own stories emerge. Harriet Jacobs' *Incidents in the Life of a Slave Girl Written by Herself* (1861) stood alone until 2002, when Hannah Crafts' *A Fugitive Slave Lately Escaped from North Carolina* was first published in book form, although written in the 1850s. Using her owner's library, Crafts had read *Jane Eyre* and *Rob Roy*. Her surprising knowledge of *Bleak House* by Dickens has helped to date her narrative. The book was so good that it was at first suspected of being ghosted by abolitionists. It demonstrated, according to the doyenne of women's reading history Belinda Jack, 'that women slaves read widely and with considerable critical insight'. Another moving scrap of evidence is an early photograph of an Alabama slave girl reading.

Nearly-forgotten Hannah Crafts had her heirs in six women who got together to found the Aurora Reading Club in 1894. This, the oldest known African American women's reading club in the world, held a party to celebrate 120 years recently. The guest speaker was a direct descendant of Solomon Northrup, the author of *Twelve Years a Slave*.

Two wonderfully atmospheric moments evoke women finding a room of their own to read in peace, moments which would have warmed the heart of Christine de Pizan.

Eleanor Butler and Sarah Ponsonby lived together in domestic bliss for forty years in Wales. They had eloped together dressed as men, with pistols. Their unusual lifestyle attracted admiring visitors, from Wordsworth to Wellington, but for most of the year they lived in seclusion. Reading together was at the heart of their intimacy; they jointly initialled their books. Eleanor wrote in late autumn 1781:

Reading Rousseau to my Sally . . . incessant rain the entire evening. Shut the shutters, made a good fire, lighted the Candles, a day of strict retirement, sentiment, and delight.

You can almost hear the Welsh rain outside and the occasional page turning.

Here is another quiet breakthrough about a century later, a story from a train in Italy in 1874. Two American girls astonished the archetypal patriarch of the arts John Ruskin on the service from Venice to Verona. They pulled down the blinds the minute they entered the carriage, sprawled among cushions and got out two much-loved books:

They had French novels, lemons and lumps of sugar . . . the novels hanging together by the string that had once stitched them . . . densely bruised dog's ears . . . from which the girls, wetting their fingers, occasionally extracted a gluey leaf.

The really historic moments slip by unnoticed in human history: the first glance of mutual love, the moment of conception, the last time you read a story to a child, the moment a fatal disease takes hold. History's milestones and crossroads are not only battles and regime changes, they are these quiet triumphs too.

Overflowing Emotions: Blubbering and Shouting

The curious history of emotional responses to reading tracks our psycho-history. For most of human history stories have been read aloud. Silent reading only became widespread after the Middle Ages, partly because religion fostered a more individual relationship with God. Ancient Greeks and Romans often had a special slave whose sole responsibility was to read aloud. And the Spanish thinker Isidore of Seville (*c.* AD 560–636) was radical in recommending silent reading, which he said made you remember more of the text. Reading silently mirrored the rise of a sense of self. Just as painting developed perspective, and sculptures of people became more individual and less stylized, humans became more self-consciously individual.

The rise of print made private reading more possible: book ownership among householders in Canterbury, for instance, rose from 8 per cent to 34 per cent in just the forty years after 1560. Then came Canterbury's engagement with the age of nineteenth-century steam-drive printing presses, and of the steam train. Soon the city had four railway stations with all the attendant train reading, a big university, then two more, plus several bookshops, then A. S. Byatt cut the tape and opened a chain bookshop there in 1990 which has since sold £50 million worth of books.

We all read more, but we might not feel as much as early readers unless we find our true comfort reads, and the right reading nook. Modern culture enables both variegated opinion and a sort of herd-like consensus. Psycho-diversity is worth protecting as much as biodiversity.

The rawness of reader reaction in the past is thought-provoking. Unlike today, men were almost as susceptible as women to public weeping over books. The eighteenth-century poet Thomas Gray recalled that in his Cambridge days *The Castle of Otranto* 'made the undergraduates cry and . . . afraid to go to bed 'o nights'. In 1749 two sisters in Colchester, 'sensible and accomplished women', were found 'blubbering at such a rate one morning' over *Cecilia* that they had to postpone lunch to recover from 'red eyes and swollen noses'.

Even volume three of a German novel – she had not seen the first two volumes – awakened 'a germ of melancholy', which Ann Lister in 1830 'thought had died forever', so that she 'cried a great deal'. One lady in the 1820s noted this loss of affect, recording that a friend had thrown aside Rousseau's once notoriously moving *Julie, ou la nouvelle Héloïse* unread: 'If she, the same she, had lived fifty years ago she would have been intoxicated and bewildered and cried her eyes out.'

The astronomer Sir John Herschel (1792–1871) recorded an almost unbelievable tale of reader response from his Buckinghamshire youth. A village blacksmith, reading out the happy denouement of Richardson's *Pamela* to a gathering, made the audience 'raise a great shout and, procuring the church keys, actually set the parish bells ringing'.

Dickens wrote to his sister-in-law about a man who attended his reading of *Dombey and Son* in Yorkshire:

> After crying a good deal without hiding it, he covered his face with both his hands and laid it down on the back of the seat before him, and really shook with emotion.

Samuel Richardson's epistolary novel *Clarissa* (1748), the tale of a young woman's virtue under siege, was the single most tear-jerking book for many decades, as the maid who wept while brushing her mistress's hair has already shown. A lady wrote to Richardson about its effect: 'In agonies I would lay down the book, take it up, let fall a flood of tears, wipe my eyes, read again, not three lines, throw away the book, crying out.' It provoked an equally raw response in male readers. In 1852 'an old Scotch doctor' was too ill to attend dinner from crying over it. Even the intellectual Macaulay 'cried his eyes out over it' in 1850. In the Athenaeum Club library in Pall Mall he once met Thackeray and they compared notes over the *'Clarissa* effect'. Macaulay got up, and started walking up and down to act out the reactions of various members of the Indian government to the book. As he enacted the Chief Justice collapsing in tears he himself began to weep at the memory.

Tolstoy, a sober bearded mystic in the popular imagination, shed tears like a baby when reading Pushkin. Even grave Archbishop Cranmer was an epic weeper. In 1872, a British Museum curator called George Smith was so affected by reading *The Epic of Gilgamesh* 'that he began to tear off his clothes, crying out for joy'.

Although recommendation is human and warm, unmediated discovery of a book can give it great emotional power too: Donegal navvy Pat McGill (b. 1890) left school at ten and saw no literature until a page from an exercise book with poetry written on it fluttered out of a carriage window. It grabbed him, he bought *Les Misérables* and sobbed as he read it.

What was going on, a heaving Yorkshireman, a weeping navvy, a blubbering Chief Justice?

Public emotion was not only OK in the past, lack of it was seen as odd. People, for most of history, knowing that only werewolves and vampires didn't weep, would support Joey's line in the *Friends* episode where Chandler says he does not cry, even at *Bambi*: 'You're dead inside, man!'

Going far back I cannot find tears – of joy or grief – being a problem for readers. They even kicked off the first epic: Odysseus' tears at recalling the fall of Troy prompted the start of Homer's tale. After classical times, Bible stories made tears more than acceptable, a badge of engagement, and many statues sported real and magical tears. 'By the waters of Babylon we sat down and wept' is a line made resonant by many musical settings.

Moving forward through history, crying was approved of within the eighteenth-century cult of sensibility. Just imagine the general climate then: this was a time when Edmund Burke and Charles James Fox, two weighty intellects, wept openly and simultaneously on the floor of the House of Commons. Goethe and Rousseau made the expression of individual emotion part of a revolution in thought, and in Britain the massively popular novel *The Man of Feeling* was about a man who went around identifying, and crying with, oppressed minorities. As the French Revolution unlocked a wave of hope, and the age of industrialization loomed, the Romantic movement cherished emotion, and nineteenth-century novels took us to previously unimagined heights and depths of feeling.

Reading had assisted the growth of a complex sense of self, but shows of emotion were less acceptable as the nineteenth century progressed. The challenges of Empire sent us back to imagined virtues of Sparta, and the 'stiff upper lip' became part of public school education, and weaponized: 'the battle of Waterloo was won on the playing fields of Eton,' in Wellington's view. In mid-Victorian times a mocking satire of *The Man of Feeling* was published. As late as 1958, when Anna Neagle broke down in tears on television, the press excoriated the episode of *This Is Your Life* as if hard porn had been screened. The late Victorian stiff upper lip reigned right down to the end of the age of the bowler hat.

Amazingly, although weeping is now the cheapened currency of reality TV, and although we now have films to cry at, comfort books still move us, if we find the right ones and curl up in the right nook, like Jane Eyre in her window seat.

Instead of censorship and scarcity of books there is a new challenge to finding a comfort book which customers talk about a lot in my bookshop – too many books. This was complained

of as long ago as the seventeenth century, when Sir Thomas
Browne (1605–82) fantasized about burning down a library. John
Ruskin (1819–1900) felt deluged by books and said that in the
resultant swamp we must find our 'little rocky island, with a
spring and a lake on it'. In the first fifty years after Gutenberg
more books were made than in the previous thousand. Paper
production in Great Britain alone went from 2,500 tons in 1715 to
75,000 tons in 1851.

In addition to the greater volume of books, vocal commen-
tators are ever ready to disdain our reading habits. In Victorian
times the politician Henry Brougham sneered at the 'steam-
intellect society', the philosopher Frederic Harrison slagged
off the 'promiscuous, vapid reading of garbage' and the Tory
Critical Review blamed booksellers, 'those pimps of literature'
who sell to those 'not capable of distinguishing good from
bad; female readers in particular have voracious appetites, and
are not over delicate in their choice of food'. Those damned
eclectic women.

The official classification of 'good literature' can still make
bookshop customers apologetic about their purchases. I feel
like reminding them how fickle the official classifiers are –
that novels were regarded as a vice for centuries, that Dickens
was once seen as trashy, that James Bond ended up in Penguin
Modern Classics. What, one wonders, is wrong with the ever-
popular but critically ignored Georgette Heyer?

For book-lovers of any gender or level in society, it's been a
long struggle to get reading freedom, freedom in effect to
explore ourselves. What architecture we are: such rooms,
attics and secret passages known only to us, and dimly. There
is so much to discover, from the safety of our favourite reading place, book in hand.

Published Weekly.   NOW READY.   Price One Penny.

NOS. I AND 2 (TWENTY-FOUR PAGES), SPLENDIDLY ILLUSTRATED, IN HANDSOME WRAPPER.

The History of this Remarkable Being has been specially compiled, for this work only, by one of the Best Authors of the day, and our readers will find that he has undoubtedly succeeded in producing a Wonderful and Sensational Story, every page of which is replete with details of absorbing and thrilling interest.

3. The Strange Emotional Power of Cheap Books

Noël Coward's observation that it is 'extraordinary how potent cheap music is' has a bookish equivalent: the magnetic pull of a rollicking read. Many of us have an object of secret shame we enjoy curling up with. Why only relax once a year with a 'beach read'? Perhaps we spend too much time reading what we 'should' be reading. In thirty years of bookselling I have seen it a lot: people apologizing for buying comfort books, and ploughing glumly through the Booker shortlist. There is a slow-motion mass hysteria that causes all to agree that the latest craze is wonderful, ignoring the fact that history is littered with Hugh Walpoles: once highly esteemed, now unread. A. N. Wilson told me that he was walking through London with Iris Murdoch once and she pointed to a blue plaque on a house commemorating some Elena Ferrante of the day, now utterly forgotten except by the ineffectual dons on the Blue Plaque Committee. But we all still feel Booker shortlist FOMO. It is hard to be honest and like what you like.

One of the character traits of enduring writers seems to be an eclectic ability to take stories for what they are: reflections of human weirdness. This is why fairy tales and myth keep crashing back into mainstream culture like a minotaur charging into a genteel restaurant. As I write, examples are Madeleine Miller's *Circe* novels, Stephen Fry's *Mythos*, Neil Gaiman's *Norse Mythology* and the phenomenon of Marvel films becoming mainstream. 'We're all geeks now', claimed one headline about this latter phenomenon; but no, the truth is we've always been geeks, dreaming of the forest, of half-beast men, discarnate entities, ambiguous Loki-types and messed-up families; it's just that contemporary highbrow novels don't seem quite grown-up enough for our quaking collective unconscious. Ancient tales were orally sculpted and tweaked over the centuries to service the whole range of our psychic needs, hence there are some 395 variants of *Cinderella*.

When great writers such as Kazuo Ishiguro and David Mitchell do suddenly write otherworldly tales, they confuse publishers, who fear the words 'sci-fi fantasy' as they might a cheap Chardonnay. Yet groundbreakers such as Angela Carter and J. K. Rowling shamelessly plundered myths and fairy tales. Respected novelist A. S. Byatt, who lovingly edited *Grimms' Fairy Tales*, recalled that, 'as a child, I never really liked stories about children doing what children do – quarrelling and cooking and camping. I liked magic, the unreal, the more than real.' She admits that 'It is very odd – when you come to think of it – that human beings in all sorts of societies, ancient and modern, have needed these untrue stories,' but, she observes, they continually explode all over the internet. Since most adult booksellers don't cater much to our need for the fantastic – we all pretend to a Hobbesian rationality these days – our need bursts out in online clicking. Freud would say this is because of wish-fulfilment fantasies, Jung would say that going into the forest of all those fairy tales is simply a natural drawing upon the collective unconscious to get us through what Nietzsche called 'the horror of living'.

So why the distinction between 'the novel' and the chapbook tale? As early as 1929 the Russian philosopher Mikhail Bakhtin thought it was rubbish to say the novel 'began' with Defoe: it existed way before 'traditional literary history'. He pointed out that early novelists such as Cervantes and Sterne built their books on parodies of 'lower' literary forms: the cracking fairy tales in chapbooks. 'Novel', he thought, is just a name; what he called 'novelness' (probably sounds wonderful in Russian) is timeless. He quoted the Basque philosopher and Chico Marx lookalike (even down to the hat) Miguel de Unamuno: 'anyone who invents a concept ["the novel"] takes leave of reality'. With typical boldness Bakhtin said Socrates was the first known 'novelist', or practitioner of novelness, simply by pursuing the message 'know thyself'. Door-to-door chapbook sellers, then, were to a degree selling novels and psychotherapy.

Some of literature's great leaps forward, or sideways, have happened because of new writers who embraced timeless tales zestfully. Dylan Thomas, for instance, loved reading Westerns; John Betjeman religiously watched TV soaps; and Umberto Eco particularly enjoyed *Spiderman* films. Hazlitt surprised the literary world by writing an essay about boxing. Much of Chaucer's appeal was bawdy fun in street language. Shakespeare's street bawdiness was excised by the Victorians. All through history, prudery and cultural elitism have tried to edit out fruitiness in the name of God or good taste. Tried, but failed: Orwell knew that, however much the more educated classes pretend to deride examples of sensationalist culture, they were all enjoying it, even if it was edited out from dinner party conversation:

> They remind one of how closely knit the civilization of England is, and how much it resembles a family, despite out-of-date class distinctions. If you look into your own mind, which are you, Don Quixote or Sancho Panza? Almost certainly, you are both. Your unofficial self . . . punctures your fine attitudes . . . It is simply a lie to say it is not part of you. ('The Art of Donald McGill' in *Essays*, 2000)

For over 300 years, from about 1550 until the late nineteenth century, millions of Europeans, rich and poor, loved a now mostly destroyed sensational form of book: the chapbook. This was a short, cheap book, often cheerfully illustrated. Chapbooks were a Europe-wide phenomenon: they were called blue books in France, folk-books in Germany, string-sheets in Spain and Portugal. Studying in Germany in the 1520s, Mark Edwards found 'a market flooded with 6 million "folk-books"', and pointed out that it is in the nature of such disposable literature that they often had multiple readers before their re-use in the kitchen or lavatory. Many of us have a dim folk-memory of the English chapbooks sales line: 'penny plain and tuppence coloured'. Being coverless and made of the cheapest paper, they have mostly disappeared back into the biomass, often via a spell as pie-paper or worse. In the seventeenth century John Dryden described a London clogged with chapbooks destined to be 'martyrs of pies, and relics of the bum'. As late as the 1920s the sole reading matter for a miner's daughter in the Forest of Dean was torn-up books in the privy. A further reason for their near-obliteration is that they were derided or ignored by the (mostly male) arbiters of taste. Librarians saw no reason to collect them.

They were tales of ghosts, crimes, knightly quests, sleeping princesses, star-crossed lovers and misdemeanours, miracles and wonders. Like social media today they could be immoral, irreligious and subversive, but not merely crude: they contained world news, pirated poetry, abridged novels, lost folklore and much useful information.

They were read by high and low – Pepys collected 215 of them. Sam Johnson was still carrying one around – *Palmerin* – as a comfort book when he was sixty-three. For Boswell, a chapbook printing-house was a shrine which he revisited in elegiac mood: in Dicey's, Bow Churchyard, Cheapside, he was awash with 'a kind of romantic feeling to find myself where my old darlings were printed . . . *Jack and the Giant* . . . *The Seven Wise Men of Gotham*'. The magic of childhood flooded back to him in a way which happens to all of us unexpectedly – those days of imagination are really, behind all the costumes we wear in life, where our visionary selves live. As he left, he bought two dozen chapbooks.

Even the philosopher Edmund Burke confessed half-seriously in the House of Commons that his favourite study was 'the old romances *Palmerin* and *Don Bellianis*'. William Morris did not wholly disown his own taste for 'naïf and gross ghost stories read long ago in penny-books'. At the household of the High Sheriff of Norfolk, Sir Nicholas le Strange (1511–80) remembered 'a gentlewoman often used this short Ejaculation; God love me, as I love a Pedlar'.

Among poorer folk, John Bunyan confessed to the 'sin' of preferring chapbooks to Scripture, and the poet John Clare, in his humble rural household, was 'very fond of the superstitious tales that are hawked about the streets for a penny'. He saved up all his pennies to buy them and thought that 'these have memorys as common as Prayer Books with the Peasantry'. His favourites were *The Seven Sleepers, The King and the Cobbler, Jack and the Beanstalk* and *Robin Hood*. Robin Hood crops up in most pedlar inventories, and his appeal was surely grounded both in the atavistic lure of the forest and in the alienation most people felt from central government (which some of us still might be able to conjure).

Victorian East Ender Walter Southgate loved Dick Turpin and Buffalo Bill chapbooks but recalled that they were 'confiscated by my teachers, who were all from middle-class backgrounds'. A prescient postmodernist, Southgate reflected that those tales had generic similarities to Defoe, Scott and Dickens. Another cockney, George Acorn, 'read all sorts of books, from "Penny Bloods" to George Eliot', with the same appreciation of style. He eloquently pointed out that *Treasure Island* (now considered a classic) is 'just the usual penny blood sort of pirate story, with a halo of greatness about it'. Chapbooks were both a gateway drug to literary classics and in themselves contained shards of greatness.

Apart from the sensational tales, chapbooks were often abridged versions of 'great' novels. Within a month of *Robinson Crusoe, Moll Flanders* or *Gulliver's Travels* being officially published, there were multiple pirated and abridged versions for sale. An astonishing 75 per cent of surviving eighteenth-century copies of *Robinson Crusoe* are chapbook abridgements, 'forcing us', historian Abigail Williams says, 'to ask what was the "real" Crusoe for Defoe's contemporaries', an observation applicable to all classics. She also points out that 'substantial evidence of gentry reading chapbooks suggests that an apartheid in print culture between popular and elite cannot be sustained'. The fact that chapbook versions of classics had such a society-wide appeal implies that literary critics' studies of how such novels landed in the contemporary consciousness are seriously flawed.

The fullest study of chapbooks, written in 1882 by John Ashton, is 500 obsessive pages long, out of print, but a rich source of titles:

> *The Witch of the Woods*
> *Strange History of Dr Faustus*
> *Dreams and Moles*
> *The Lovers' Quarrel*
> *The Travels of John Mandeville*
> *A Dialogue between the Blind Man and Death*

Largely uncatalogued, chapbooks still turn up all over the country; they were never London-centric. Remote towns with no publisher such as Newton Stewart or Hexham had back-room chapbook-makers using worn upcycled type, and children to do the hand-colouring. Only recently have historians of popular culture studied this secret river of culture – with difficulty. In Scotland, for instance, nearly 20,000 chapbook titles are known about, but Edinburgh's National Library has managed to collect just 4,000. Robert Louis Stevenson, arguably the most enduring Scottish writer, was reared on chapbooks, which gilded his childhood like today's sometimes snobbishly derided graphic novels, manga or Enid Blyton books ('Read a proper book, darling!'). Stevenson even wrote his own chapbook, in homage to the genre. Dickens read 'penny dreadfuls' throughout his childhood and had 'the very wits frightened out of my head'. *The Mystery of Edwin Drood*, his unfinished last book, reverts back to a grim tale from that childhood reading. Coleridge's childhood chapbook version of *The Arabian Nights* so haunted his dreams that his father burnt it. Goethe regarded tales such as *Melusina the Snake Woman*, 'on hideous paper and barely legible', bought from itinerant chapmen, as indispensable to his philosophical development. G. K. Chesterton defended such sensational tales as 'tremendous trifles', which contained all the themes of the 'great literature' which they fertilized.

Oddly, South Carolina University – not somewhere in the UK – has a centre studying these ephemeral productions. It estimates that eighteenth-century British sales ran at about 4 million copies a year, at a time when the population was only around 7 million.

Chapbooks are beginning to take an honourable place in cultural history. They increased literacy and reading hours among the poor, and fed both social change and the development of the novel. Their descendants, after about 1860 when steam-driven presses replaced cottage-industry chapbook-makers, were the 'penny dreadfuls' and 'shilling shockers'. These in turn paved the way for cheap paperbacks. The spirit of chapbooks lives on too in the graphic novel, an art form which now wins literary prizes.

4.   'Heigh-Ho, the Wind and the Rain': Book Pedlars

Many corporate retailers atavistically seek the human warmth and engagement of the street market. Just as all art aspires to the condition of music, all shopkeepers aspire to the immediacy of the stall-holder. Chain retailers speak of the need for a sense of theatre, a concept which trickled down from business schools and is now the go-to means to lure the public back to high-street chain retail.

Retail theatre cannot be dictated, but comes naturally to outdoor traders. Chain retail devices such as window displays, special price offers, a special greeting script – all of these are the anaemic offspring of the ancient practice of outdoor selling from a stall or out of a basket. The outdoor market is where selling, and so much human interaction, began. The Stonehenge complex was, apart from its ritual purpose, a huge mart. London's open-air Borough Market has been going over a thousand years. Outdoor sellers are the original shops: low-rent, quick on their feet and engaged with passers-by in a way shops behind glass windows cannot be. They don't need to aspire to a sense of theatre: much of their daily existence is improv.

The Mos Espa street market in *Star Wars*, full of wholly accepted inter-galactic freakishness, gives the feeling of liminality and possibility which markets everywhere possess, a space full of opportunities for discovery and evasion, like the souk where Aladdin can hide, the bazaar where *Bladerunner*'s Deckard can buy illicit android skin-scales. The myriad voices of the market-place invigorate society. In the words of the Russian literary theorist Mikhail Bakhtin, outdoor markets 'counter the artificially monologic tone of industrial commerce'. It seems natural that Jimmy Porter, the alienated young hero of John Osborne's revolutionary play *Look Back in Anger*, should run a market stall rather than work indoors in a shop.

The marketplace is the arena of humanity, the happy hunting ground of the storyteller. Bakhtin proposes that:

> Folk culture is the culture of the lower orders, a healthy anti-dote to all that is overweighty. In the marketplace and square, poet, scholar, monk, knight are parodied in irreverent repartee. Hierarchy is put to rout. There are found, in the three heroes – rogue, fool and simpleton – the beginnings of the novel.

On the day I was writing this section I heard the extreme opposite view on BBC Radio 4. The Director of Creative Writing at the University of East Anglia, challenged about the purpose of his department, explained that 'University literature departments are custodians of literary form in a way that the commercial world of publishing and the marketplace cannot be.' Custodians of literary form? What does that mean? That good stories would die out without academics to put them into ephemeral genres? Gentle reader, if the book in your hands ever descends to such sophistry, please consign it to the correct recycling bin.

The often-censored Bakhtin had a marketplace-loving soul-mate across Europe in the German Jew Walter Benjamin. When he committed suicide on the run from the Nazis, he left a suitcase of notes about Paris culture and commerce, notes later published as the vertiginous and unclassifiable 1,000-page *Arcades Project*. In 1926 he had given a Radio Berlin talk about Berlin's outdoor street trade. The recording is lost but the typescript was confiscated by the Gestapo, then seized by Russian troops, then moved in 1960 to East Germany, where access was denied until 1983. The talk was finally published in English in 2014:

> Is not the street market thrilling and festive? Even the most ordinary weekly markets have some of the magic of oriental markets, of the Samarkand bazaar. The market talk, the back-and-forth of goods is rich and sumptuous. [Seller and buyer] are like two actors sharing a stage. The book peddler himself is featured in many of the books he sold. Not as the hero of course, but as the wily old man, the warner, or the seducer. The book-cart seller is unfazed by people rummaging through his wagon, he knows people buy books from a cart they never would have dreamt of buying when they set out in the morning.

I once sold the new *Harry Potter* off a stall in Canterbury High Street, and it felt as different from sitting in my bookshop as sea-swimming does to swimming in an overheated municipal pool.

Market theatre and ancient tradition were demonstrated to me during a book signing which I organized at Waterstones Canterbury with Steven Berkoff. Eastender Berkoff, a very physical and 'in yer face' actor who was a noted Bond villain, became impatient with the slow take-up of his books. He stood up and started a market-trader patter as if selling the last fruit of the day on a stall, rapidly gathered a crowd and flogged great handfuls of books.

From the dawn of print until about 1900, these chapmen or book-hawkers wandered unlicensed. Only a fraction of them in England bothered to pay £4 for a licence in 1696 when an Act of Parliament attempted to regulate them, so the 2,500 who did purchase one in that first year indicates just a tiny part of their number. Many were of no fixed abode, so were ineligible for a licence anyway. Of the 2,500, over 500 gave London as their domicile.

Victorian book-hawkers were memorably described by Henry Mayhew in his *London Labour and the London Poor* (1851). Mayhew, one of seventeen children, was a teenage midshipman on an East Indiaman before a rackety few years in Europe evading creditors. Returning to London, he struck gold when he co-founded *Punch* magazine, which celebrated and satirized all levels of society. Mayhew's four-volume epic record of London life is testament to his sheer love of humanity. It has acres of priceless reported speech and remains a historians' goldmine.

Mayhew noticed that book pedlars frequented busy thoroughfares such as the Old Kent Road, Stoke Newington High Street or Commercial Road. The clustering of chapbook publishers along the Strand (the road to the West Country) and around Smithfield (handy for the road north) demonstrates London's role as exporter to country chapmen.

Pedlars and their suppliers had stuck to such arterial routes for centuries. Chaucer lived for a while in rooms above the city gateway known as Aldersgate. Peter Ackroyd has pointed out that he would have noticed a daily stream of varied humanity pass under his windows, and one can also imagine the vocal hawking of vernacular literature being part of the soundscape outside his windows. At least four chapbook publishers and sellers are known to have existed on old London Bridge, the route to Dover in the seventeenth century, when the bridge was a street with houses. Here is the ad for one of them, Josiah Blare:

> Bookseller, at the Sign of the Looking-Glass on London Bridge, Furnisheth Country Chapmen or others, with all sorts of History Books, Small Books and Ballads.

One imagines these bridge premises to be quite small but chapbook publisher John Tyus, 'At the Sign of the Three Bibles on London-Bridge', stocked 90,000 books, overflowing up his staircase and into the attic. They included, for instance, 375 copies of *The Tale of Guy of Warwick*, twopence each.

Apart from the main arterial routes, one chapman told Mayhew, 'If there's what you might call a recess, that's the place for us, where you'll often see us with flower-stands and pinners-up [sellers of ballad-sheets].' They sold a huge range of books: *Don Quixote* in Spanish, odd volumes, classics and chapbooks.

Mayhew recorded the following sales pitch for various books of poetry, and if you care to say it out loud as he heard it 'very rapidly, with words clipped', you will hear the voice of Dickensian London:

> Byron! Lord Byron's latest and best po'ms. Sixpence! Sixpence! Eightpence! I take penny bids under a shilling. Eightpence for the poems written by a lord – Gone! Yours, sir' Coop'r – Coop'r! Published at 3s. 6d., as printed on the back. Superior to Byron – Coop'r's 'Task.' No bidders? Thank you, sir. One-and-six, – your's, sir. Young –'Young's Night Thoughts. Life, Death, and Immortality,' – great subjects. London edition, marked 3s. 6d. Going! – last bidder – two shillings – gone!

One pedlar remembered two regulars: essayist Charles Lamb, 'a gentle stuttering man', and the chaplain who had been on HMS *Victory* with Nelson, 'a pleasant old gentleman with white hair and rosy face, who loved to have a little talk about books'.

An indicator of these nomadic sellers' role in history is how many of them sold radical literature. One veteran recalled how Tom Paine's *Rights of Man* sold well in the Peterloo Massacre era, but he sold it 'on the sly', covered up by anti-revolutionary tracts. And there are several references to court cases involving pop-up bookstalls which lined the walls of the Old Bailey when big cases were being held, and of Westminster Hall, when Parliament was sitting.

Big blank walls provided a ready opportunity for pop-up bookselling, and so did wasteland. Moorfields, west of Bishopsgate and just north of London Wall, was a marshy, inhospitable zone, skirted on the right by the Walbrook River before it was redirected underground. Its anomalous administrative status helped: it was presided over not by the City authorities but by the Prebendary of Finsbury, as reflected in its legal name, the Liberty of Moorfields. Londoners displaced by the Great Fire camped out there; it was later drained but remained one of London's badlands, indeed the underground vaults to drain surplus water became a criminal underworld refuge. From 1680, to add to the otherworldly atmosphere, at the southern edge of Moorfields sat the Bethlehem Hospital for the Insane – Bedlam. Over the entrance it bore two colossal statues of *Melancholia* and *Mania* (now to be found in the Museum of London). The police frequently attended the area to confront 'unruly assemblies of apprentices', much of the violence of the Gordon Riots erupted there, and it was London's chosen destination for fences, muggers, pickpockets and 'sodomites', a sort of Hampstead Heath-meets-Whitechapel.

Book-pedlars dominated the Moorfields stall-holders, especially along the long blank wall of Bedlam. The 'lunaticks' of Bedlam ranked with Westminster Abbey and the zoo as a visitor attraction, so footfall was guaranteed. Booksellers were also attracted by the unregulated atmosphere, and partly they were spilling over from the old bookselling centre of Little Britain a little to the East – still a street today – the only bookselling street which had escaped the Great Fire. Typifying the eclectic nature of street bookselling, a late-seventeenth-century browser in Moorfields found the specialized multilingual book collection of the late Robert Boyle, the father of modern chemistry, 'laid out casually'. At the close of the eighteenth century, on Finsbury Pavement, a raised dry thoroughfare by Moorfields, a slight, bookish boy, doomed to die at twenty-five, lived at the Swan and Hoop inn. It is surely not too fanciful to assume the nearby bookstalls were being browsed by young John Keats.

Moorfields' badlands were built over by 1812; Finsbury Circus covers part of them. Over time, a more regulated London finished off many street traders. But booksellers found a new long, unregulated wall to replace Bedlam's. In 1869 the new thoroughfare of Farringdon Road was constructed near St Paul's Cathedral. Immediately down its eastern side was a long wall bordering a new railway. This became the only London book market which could be compared, in type if not extent, to the great bookstalls by the Seine in Paris. A former hot-chestnut seller called James Dabbs was one of the most successful traders, with five barrows selling thousands of books. These traders sold ancient manuscripts and books as old as printing itself. Journalist Mary Benedetta wrote in 1938 of the browsers there:

> rain drips on their shoulders from the canvas stall covers, but they never notice. Time means nothing to them. They are under the spell of the romance and glamour of old books.

Dickens had put such a Farringdon Road browser into *Oliver Twist* as Mr Brownlow:

> He had taken up a book from the stall, and there he stood, reading away, as hard as if he were in his elbow-chair, in his own study . . . for it was plain, from his abstraction, that he saw not the bookstall, nor the street, nor the boys, nor, in short, anything but the book itself: which he was reading straight through.

Such absorption allowed the Dodger to steal Brownlow's handkerchief and return to Fagin's den a few yards away on Saffron Hill, a lane which still exists.

In the 1950s my father, who worked at nearby Smithfield Market, used to browse books at lunchtime in Farringdon Road. As a low-paid father of eight, he was always wary of his wife seeing him bring home old books we could ill-afford, but he was excited to find Agnes Strickland's three-volume *Lives of the Queens of England* (1848) in original red cloth. He went back to work but the book haunted his thoughts. He phoned the *Daily Worker* (later the Communist Party newspaper the *Morning Star*) and asked, as their offices were just opposite the market, would someone cross the road and put a deposit on the book for him? They did, and my brother still has the books.

Later regulars of the market were John Betjeman, Trinidadian legend C.L.R. James and Spike Milligan but the Council rent for pitches – nothing was charged in the early days – went up steadily and in 1994 the last stallholder, stentorian George Jeffrey, died after a bookselling career only interrupted by his time as a paratrooper at the Battle of Arnhem. I remember Jeffrey's stall, an extraordinary cornucopia, presided over by Jeffrey with his thermos flask and blue overalls. One browser found a Thomas More manuscript there (sold later for £42,000), another found manuscript letters from Byron in a book. Psychogeographer Iain Sinclair, who ran a bookstall in Camden Passage not far away, browsed the less-valued piles of books – 25p each – on the tarmac, in search of outré twentieth-century fiction. There he found the rare *Opening Day* by the surrealist David Gascoyne. Jeffrey took unwanted books from London auction houses such as Sotheby's, often by the thousand, and bought institutional and private libraries, and the stock of the great poetry bookshop Turret Books when it closed down. His stall was fed from a low-rent warehouse which held most of his stock. His father and grandfather had sold books in Farringdon Road before him, so George was a real link to Dickens' London and the world of *Oliver Twist*.

Magically, London's outdoor bookselling spirit has relocated yet again, to the South Bank. The market spiit in humanity is irrepressible. The South Bank book market is now buzzing seven days a week, in a happy pedestrian riverside space sheltered by the underside of Waterloo Bridge. Gareth Thomas, a principal stallholder, says he would never go inside for an office job.

Outside London, footfall has been historically harder to come by for itinerant booksellers. For centuries in East Anglia executions drew big crowds (what else was there to do?), so book pedlars clustered there. Fairs were the other attraction. Norwich, England's second city for much of the pre-industrial era, had the second-largest market in provincial England, and a printer who specifically advertised books for 'Booksellers, Country Chapmen and Hawkers' (1706). Norwich's market is still vibrant but it used to be only one of many in the city. *Jarrold's Almanac* for 1822 lists an extraordinary 204 fairs per year in Norfolk and Suffolk.

Forgotten Stourbridge Fair, by the River Cam near Cambridge was between Tudor and Hanoverian times perhaps the biggest fair in the world. The original 'Vanity Fair', it sold pretty much everything, a precursor of Minnesota's 'Mall of America'. Stourbridge was notorious for sexual liaisons and libertinism. Like Moorfields in London, the unregulated sleaziness of what was colloquially called 'Stir-bitch Fair' attracted booksellers. The low-life chronicler Ned Ward noted a section called 'Cuckolds Row, from the great number of booksellers there' (presumably books console cuckolds). Twenty years later, a plan of the fair has the section genteelly renamed 'Booksellers Row'. The patter of one regular, Ed Millington, was recorded in 1700:

> Here's an old author for you! Judge his Antiquity by his leather jacket, herein is contained for you scholars the Knowledge of Everything, by that profound author who thro' his wisdom discovered that he knew nothing. I'll put him up at Two Shillings, advance thruppence. What, Nobody? . . . Fye for Shame! sure you men of learning will not suffer such an author to be undervalued? He's worth more to a Powder Monkey to make cartridges with [a common reuse of book pages]. Nobody advance three pence? I tell you, you'll find learning in here to puzzle both universities.

For lack of the usual inventories and wills, any detail of Stourbridge's book stock is lost to history, but to Daniel Defoe it was even more extensive than the ancient Frankfurt Fair. It was at Stourbridge that Isaac Newton bought the copy of Euclid which he used to teach himself mathematics (he later returned and bought the prisms he used to demonstrate the spectrum). We can assume that the proximity of Cambridge made the booksellers of Stourbridge far more culturally significant than their absence from mainstream history would indicate. Newton was an outsider at Cambridge who did not stay in touch with any other students, and something of an autodidact perforce, since he was pushing back the very frontiers of knowledge.

Open-air markets served the ill-connected oddball autodidact well, with their unstuffy accessibility and stock which included odd volumes, manuscripts and what Shakespeare's lovable chapman Autolycus in *The Winter's Tale* called 'unconsidered trifles'. In the 1960s I knew people who thought Hatchards bookshop in Piccadilly, with its royal warrant as the Queen's bookseller, might simply be too posh to enter. And I still see parents in Waterstones Canterbury actually whispering, as if it was a church. Stalls and hawkers presented no class barriers.

Scotland is one of the greatest nations on earth for autodidacticism, of necessity and by nature. This tendency, and the remoteness of so many communities, made travelling booksellers much appreciated there. Two of them even published their memoirs. Like the Seine booksellers of old, chapmen dressed flamboyantly, to charm and to embody the promise of fabulous characters in their tales, just as clowns and mime artists dress to show us our other, mythopoetic selves. Here, about 1870, is a typical Highland chapman, 'Old Dauvit': 'Always clad in a large blue frock coat with big metal buttons, a huge broad bonnet with a red top, and round his neck a green and yellow Indian neckerchief.' Dauvit, like most rural Scottish chapmen, never knocked but walked straight into the crofts he visited; he had to hope for a bed there, somehow. He arrived always:

> with a rustic bow and some compliment such as 'I needna ask if ye're weel the day, for ye're the very picture of health', or, seeing a daughter in the house, 'Ye're a comely lassie, I haena seen your match i' the Highlands'.

If the farmer came in, Dauvit would assay, 'I ha'e seen nae pasture to compare wi' your ain.' If these lines all seem transparent sales patter, they were, but Dauvit was welcome everywhere, a pure 'actor on a stage', like those in Benjamin's Berlin street market. The crofters also knew that Dauvit had detailed gossip from settlements near and far; his visit was like logging on to Facebook (or whatever new forum fulfils Facebook's function by the time you read this).

Usually the chapman, after his pitch and the showing of his wares – Dauvit did well with 'Shetland-hose', woollen nightcaps, ribbons, pins and such books as *The Arabian Nights* – might get a bed for the night in a byre, 'at a cow's ouxter' [elbow]. This was particularly tough because many chapmen had a physical disability which unfitted them for physical labour or military service; there was a noted hunchback bookseller in the Highlands, for instance.

Surprisingly, there were at least five Scottish societies of chapmen, with great names such as 'The Fraternity of Chapmen in the Three Lothians', which met in 1837 and, in the tone of *Dad's Army*'s lugubrious Highlander Private Frazer, lamented:

owing to the late practise of opening so many retail shops, the number of respectable Travelling Chapmen is become small, and old members of our Fraternity are fast dropping into the grave.

Damned shops! This thoughtful society elected a Lord, and ran a widows' fund.

The mill-worker Alexander Wilson (1766–1813) of Paisley, near Glasgow, was imprisoned for writing a satirical poem about his exploitative employer. The poem was publicly burned. On his release, he became a chapman. He told of the life in a poem:

> I've carried packs as big's your meikle [large] table
> I've scarted pats [scraped porridge pots] and sleepit in a stable

Falling once on a snowy slope, he had to cut his pack free to save his life, and spent a fraught quarter of an hour retrieving it. Abandoning Scotland for Pennsylvania in 1794, this unstoppable autodidact wrote the nine-volume work on American birds which has earned him the title 'the Father of American Ornithology'.

William Nicholson (1782–1849) of Galloway in south-west Scotland stuck at his horse-borne book-peddling with mixed feelings. In his memoir he mused that 'Aeblins [maybe] he might warsle [whistle] up a shop', but, then again, would he really want to 'vegetate tranquilly behind the counter'?

William Magee's *Recollections of a Tour through the North Highlands in 1819–20 by an Itinerant Bookseller* (Edinburgh: 1830, published by the Author) gives a rare and fascinating itinerant bestseller list, indicating a vigorous Scottish nationalism at grassroots level: Ramsay's *Gentle Shepherd*, *The Life of Sir William*

Wallace, The Life and Prophecies of Donald Cargill, The Life of Alexander Peden, A Brief Memoir of Bonaparte and 'Dream Books'. Just as Laurie Lee in the 1930s got beds for the night in Spain by playing his violin, chapmen often augmented their visit musically. Magee had that rare accomplishment, the ability to play two Jew's harps at the same time. Alexander Wilson had a fine singing voice, and William Nicholson played the bagpipes to charm buyers – but often, he confessed with a charming image, on a remote rest-stop simply 'for the edification of the birds and beasts around me'.

Penniless crofters were thought to have one highly prized possession: notably beautiful hair among the women. This was commonly bartered for goods, to be sold on to city wigmakers and adorn pallid urban ladies. This barter is itself like something out of a myth or fairy tale. For the mystically minded Highlander who believed in seers and healers, selkies and ghosts, chapbook literature, in stories such as *The Arabian Nights* and *Grimms' Fairy Tales*, reflected their own world as surely as the novels of Ian McEwan and Elena Ferrante reflect our own more Cartesian chattering society.

From about 1750 to 1850 the Highland Clearances removed many of the chapmen's customers, and from 1850 all 'hawkers' had to be licensed by law. The business moved to towns and fairs, but chapbooks were still being printed in Aberdeen until the Great War.

Poignantly, an anonymous *Dundee Advertiser* journalist writing as 'A. Scot' met a late survivor in 1913 'on a lonely Highland road'. Of the chapman as a profession, this veteran said, 'He's aff the road athegither. You'll meet an anterin' yin [odd one] at the back-end o' the year.' And then the chapman demonstrated his conspiratorial bookselling coquettishness, a style as timeless as it was theatrical:

He turned to his battered box. The strap that held it was mended with cord. He revealed his stock-in-trade [cotton, ribbons, paper and nibs], and then there was disclosed an under-apartment or secret place. He looked at me with a sidelong glance, his eye closing in a wink that was pawkily 'knowing'. Instantly I was on my knees beside him. He brought forth 'The Comical Adventures of Lothian Tom', 'but they are no' much in demand. Man!' and his eye glistened at the recollection, 'I've seen the day when I could sell them by the dizzen.' Cheek by jowl with Lothian Tom were 'The Exploits of George Buchanan the Greatest Scot of his Age', and the diverting 'History of Buckhaven', which ridiculed the Fifeshire town. It was strange to find these chapbooks. They are known to nobody but collectors, and are not to be had for love nor money. Walter Scott had a few, which he treasured. Today's collectors include Keir Hardie [co-founder of the Labour Party].

All over the world, the hidden history of wandering booksellers is being uncovered. Professor Jeroen Salman at the Utrecht Research Institute for History and Culture in the Netherlands has cast light on book peddling in the Low Countries, and runs the EDPOP project (European Dimensions of Popular Print Culture). Although I cannot afford his 2017 account of Dutch book-pedlars (£117), his 2007 conference paper on such pedlars shows them as soul-brothers to British chapmen.

Professor Salman overturns the myth that Holland was so sophisticatedly well-bookshopped that pedlars were rendered superfluous. Drawing on tax records, criminal cases and a Napoleonic audit of occupations, Salman says that 'itinerant bookselling . . . even in the Dutch Republic . . . played a crucial role in the distribution of print'. In 1765 the

Amsterdam booksellers' guild complained that 'nowadays the number of market stalls is easily the same as the number of bookshops', and Salman adduces evidence for similar situations in Leiden and Utrecht.

Amsterdam had a publisher who specialized in chapbooks and subversive editions: in 1715 the firm of Van Egmont published *The Behaviour of the Duke of Ormond (A Catholic Rebel)* in Dutch. The several pedlars who were prosecuted for selling this illegal work stated that Van Egmont was a regular supplier of illegal books to the itinerant trade. Salman thinks that an understanding of the pedlar trade will change our whole view of how cultural change occurred in Europe.

Echoing this, Diarmaid MacCulloch's 800-page *Reformation: Europe Divided, 1490–1700* (2003) cited unofficial literature as one of the ways to explain the detonation, at village and peasant level, of Luther's bombshell. In Germany, the fiery pastor's oeuvre not only appeared in 390 different formats in 1523 alone, but by 1525 had spawned over 3 million *flugschriften* ('flying books'). These were cheap and often graphic: *On the Origin of Monks* bore a picture of the devil crapping out monks. How to describe this grass-roots print-efflorescence of revolt against papistry? Leipzig historian Franz Lau has coined a potent one-worder for it: *wildwuchs* – wildfire-growth, as in a jungle or abandoned garden. As vividly, in 2016 Yale University's Carlos Eire compared anti-papist unofficial literature to 'saturation carpet bombing', something which Pope Sixtus V's hasty and belated establishment of the Vatican Printing Press in 1587 could not have hoped to combat.

Book pedlars across Spain and Portugal were also mixing religious revolution with folk tales in their packs, and – a powerful development – selling literature in the great vernaculars of the peninsula: Catalan, Castilian and Galician.

Clive Griffin, Spanish Fellow at Trinity College Oxford, has pioneered chapbook study for Iberia. Griffin has tracked the elusive Spanish book pedlars through records of the Spanish Inquisition, which burned several booksellers, or sometimes their wicker effigies. They congregated in Salamanca and Seville, prestigious centres of learning and population, and at the great fairs held in Spain's pre-modern financial centre, the now-sleepy town of Medina Del Campo. One pedlar, Borceller, was multilingual and probably from Lyons. He spent his life shuttling between Germany, France and Iberia, and the Reformation literature he distributed merited his investigation by the Inquisition. Another Lyonnais, Pierre d'Altabel, got into trouble for selling translations of the Psalms – banned by the Pope – in Portugal. Once rumbled, he turned to hawking devotional Books of Hours in the Portuguese countryside, a good business because such books were believed to have talismanic powers if carried about the person. Pedlars frequently changed their names to escape detection. A Belgian book-hawker rather uninventively called himself Pedro Flamenco. Suspected by a fellow chapman of having an affair with his wife, he flashes into history in a village near Toledo in 1570, having a punch-up with his rival at an inn; tragically both would later be burnt at the stake for selling seditious literature.

More detail of hawkers' stock in Spain comes from the inventory of an anonymous pedlar who died near Valladolid. Apart from his donkey, he left copies of *The Fair Maguelonne*, a Provençal love tale which was to inspire a Brahms song cycle, some saints' lives, books of ballads and a play about Agamemnon. Pepys found Spain a good hunting ground for his chapbook collection: in Cadiz and Seville he picked up seventy-five chapbooks of traditional Spanish vernacular poetry and song. Pedlars in Iberia often sang their ballads as a way of selling them.

Spain exported the chapbook and ballad-book tradition to its South American colonies and the Australian traveller Peter Robb experienced an eerie timeslip, recorded in his *A Death in Brazil* (2005). In the old colonial Brazilian city of Recife, he saw a man singing a ballad to the sound of a guitar wired to a car battery. The accompanying tales and ballads were displayed around him. Robb bought a story about a girl turned into a snake. Incredibly, a Brazilian printer was still issuing this tale of the water-nymph Melusine, one which had poured off European presses ever since the fifteenth century but goes back deep into the universality of myth. Sir Walter Scott heard it being sung by Scottish pedlars, and it was to be reworked by Goethe and set to music by Mendelssohn, and it crops up today in video games.

Although nomadic book pedlars seem to have died out, their market-stall cousins flourish worldwide. The broad pavement near the Flora Fountain in Mumbai is home to the most refulgently chaotic street book market the world has ever seen. In a neutral space, near a noisy traffic intersection, book piles totter like a Manhattan skyline, office workers buy *Freakonomics*, students buy Dostoevsky, and backpackers trade in old reading material for new. A local reporter marvelled that browsers seem to 'lose themselves in a world of ink and pages, creating their own library silence'; like Mr Brownlow from *Oliver Twist* but 150 years later and on the other side of the globe.

I met the Sikh saviour of Delhi's Daryaganj book bazaar, the late Khushwant Singh, in 1981 when researching the history of the Punjab. He had survived Partition and written the novel *Train to Pakistan* about that terrible time. As a dedicated browser of the fifty-year-old book bazaar, he was central to the successful campaign to stop Delhi's council closing down the market, a campaign which went all the way to the Supreme Court. Today there are 250 stalls at Daryaganj. All Indian cities have on-street book stalls, the biggest gathering of them all being along College Street in book-loving Kolkata.

In Myanmar, Yangon's Theinbyu Road book market still has 70 stalls; Orwell and Neruda used to browse there. In nineteenth-century Cairo booksellers found a neutral space along the wall of the Azbakeya Gardens and the book bazaar there is still going strong, with 130 wooden stalls. The bazaar attracts official disapproval for its willingness to sell pirated editions of, for instance, *Fire and Fury*, the anti-Trump memoir. I wish I could have promptly got hold of such editions, since supplies of the title dried up in Waterstones Canterbury soon after publication, and I had to turn away scores of customers. Istanbul's outdoor book bazaar, pleasantly situated in the court-yard of the Beyazit Mosque, dates back to Byzantine times. In Baghdad, the old weekly Friday book market in Mutanabbi Street is now pedestrianized, after the 2007 car bomb which killed twenty-seven.

Outdoor booksellers have faced wind, rain and snow. Authorities have regulated and licensed them, arrested them and even burned them. But for 500 years they have propagated books to passers-by and remote communities. They had an unwritten role in the Reformation, the Enlightenment and in many revolutions. Perhaps as importantly, they have provided comfort books for a troubled world. They have used the gamut of theatrical skills to sell their wares: costume and humour, speech and music. Their airy trade is simple: as Shakespeare's Autolycus said 'I understand the business,' it is simply 'to have an open eye, a quick ear, and a nimble hand'.

5. Library Dreams

As a student in the library of London's School of Oriental and African Studies I once fell asleep at my desk. I had been up late the night before, finishing an essay, and early-nineteenth-century Sudan can be wonderfully soporific. I slept face-down on the desk; I can still feel the soft leatherette covering. Waking up was one of the most wonderful library moments of my life, for, when I emerged from deep sleep, I was in the inter-galactic reality of hypnagogia. That slippery state, neither awake nor asleep, is curiously connected to the world-soul, as evidenced by the appearance of mythical beings there: incubi, succubi and happier creatures too. Thinkers as diverse as Newton and Beethoven drew ideas from hypnagogia.

As I drowsed awake I had a real Library of Alexandria feeling about that multicultural SOAS library, a disoriented impression of being in infinity. For Jung, the library-subconscious connection was made explicit in his dream about a recently deceased friend: the friend conducted him to a red book on the top shelf, with an indistinct title. The morning after the dream, Jung visited his friend's widow and, for the first time, entered his library. There on the top shelf was a red book called *The Legacy of the Dead*. Jung found comfort in the title's apparent message that his friend's work would in some way be lasting.

Where do we go in dreams if not into a universal library? Such an infinite library would be brain-like, characterized by labyrinthine passages where firing synapses distantly crackle, mythic beings appear and vanish, all is limitless but obscurely connected: *Pan's Labyrinth* meets *The Master and Margarita*. It is interesting that two labyrinthine writers, Jorge Luis Borges and W. G. Sebald, were not only quintessentially inclusive and internationalist – a blind multilinguist and a German exile – but both lovers of 'the orphaned fact', and both authors of stories about libraries with universal resonance. Borges' *Library of Babel* was a universe in itself, and Sebald's Paris Bibliothèque Nationale in *Austerlitz* sat atop a Holocaust site. I saw this infinitude wash over someone once: in 1996 a veteran Siberian academic, Olga Kharitidi, was about to give a talk in my four-floor bookshop, but as she went upstairs to the events space tears started streaming down her face. She replied to my solicitations with some difficulty. 'It's the books . . . so many, all free to look at . . . everyone.' I think 'everyone' referred to the authors and the customers, the books and the universe. This deep feeling of connectedness to everyone is mystical, beyond words, but accessible among words. Breathing out in a library is one thing, breathing in is another, then breathing out again is new again.

This infinity might be overwhelming, were it not for our latent faculty for serendipity. This gives us the fins to swim in the infinite library with whimsical indirection. Serendipity in the library or bookshop seems random and chaotic, but customers of my bookshop often speak about it as the natural way of browsing. Why? A psychoanalytic journal article I read recently noted that our unconscious is 'slippery and promiscuous', not adjectives we would want applied to our personalities, but applicable to our library selves. It seems that browsing mindlessly is somehow browsing mindfully. Unmooring the calculating part of the mind in a many-chambered storehouse of books is quite natural to the many-chambered mind, with its subconscious and conscious, its stacks and upper floors, its attics, its treehouses and seldom-visited bothies. Library stacks mirror the undiscovered self.

Free-browsing, like free-diving and free-climbing, are activities unmediated by official interference; they are responses to an over-regulated and commercialized world. Browsing a library is to browsing online (jerked around by algorithms) what free climbing is to a coach tour.

In Leslie Jamison's memoir *The Aftermath*, a guard at a right-wing drug rehab 'facility' in Kentucky says of an inmate in maximum security, 'Maybe he's had a couple of infractions, made a couple of bad choices, but we still believe he's programmable.' 'Programmable' is how society sometimes wants us to be, a victim of that societal tendency to conformity which New Zealanders call 'the clobbering machine'. In the library you can escape down a random aisle, be unprogrammable for a while, untraceable, explore other ways of being. You might even emerge having decided to be just as society expects, but thanks to the library you got there yourself. The idea that you can crack open society's secret mechanisms of control in the library pops up in such sci-fi films as *Zardoz*, *Soylent Green* and *Logan's Run*.

Unprogrammable eccentrics in libraries are, like many of the strange creatures on a reef, almost expected inhabitants. When I worked at the small Golborne Road public library in seventies Notting Hill, it was a haven at the foot of the then-violent, impoverished Trellick Tower flats. All the windows were heavily barred and some days it felt like *Assault on Precinct 13*, when people ran in to escape knife attacks or, once, after being stabbed. The place was also a haven for tramps and the mentally exotic.

De Quincey biographer Frances Wilson, writer in residence at the New York Public Library, actively celebrated this aspect in 2018, pointing out in the *Literary Review* that, whoever comes into the NYPL and whatever they do, 'the books have a sanctifying quality':

> One woman comes in every day and puts her shopping on the
> table in the Catalog Room, then takes out her knitting.
> Another orders up all twenty-four volumes of Freud and then
> plays *Candy Crush* for six hours. A perspiring man in a trilby
> solves chess problems. One morning, as I passed by the restroom, I happened upon a naked man, as shiny as a porpoise,
> splashing around by the sink. There was nothing uncomfortable about the encounter. It was as though he were Adam, the
> library Eden, and self-consciousness had yet to be invented.

Power reasserted itself in the next issue of the *Literary Review*
when a professor wrote in primly to despair of *Candy Crush*
types desecrating the study space.

Wilson's view will prevail, not the professor's: the NYPL is
probably the most inclusive public lending library in the world;
New York will keep it that way, as will the continuing stream
of films, books and video games which use the library as a setting. It is now so frequently used in films that one studio has a
permanent NYPL mock-up.

The 1932 Senate House Library of London University has a
Stalinist monumentality, utilized in films such as the 1984 *1984*
and the vampire film, starring David Bowie, *The Hunger*. As a
lonely undergraduate in the seventies I used to work late there
on the upper floors of its imposing tower, the small, square,
deep-set windows showing London's populous nightscape,
silent this far up. The wind around the tower was the only
noise, and it howled clean out of Berkshire and across Gower
Street. Its mournful moans seemed to speak to the special
side-room housing the donated library of ghost-hunter and

all-round bullshitter Harry Price (I suspect the University never wanted his books).

But oh, that wind: it made the library feel like a ship on the ocean, and maybe that is one of the best metaphors to get at what a library can be. You feel it in the great bulk of the new British Library, and in the packed rows of desks where people work all day there is a consensual below-decks warmth. The soundscape is nautical in the clean, big lavatories with handles of brass and heavy doors. The roar of the hand driers is like a steady gale and the slammings and bangings of fellow readers, with their snatches of conversation in many languages, evoke a crew as motley as on the *Pequod*, all on quests of uncertain end.

Whatever the library means to us, we hunger for it imaginatively. We know we are more than the one, the person here and now bearing a given name. We are products of great migrations, we speak invaders' polyglot. No wonder we itch to read stories, and need periodically to wander like native Australians going 'walkabout'. We know that trees connect and support each other via mycelial threads underground, and every breakthrough in ecosystem research or neuroscience shows us our interconnectedness more and more.

We reach reflexively towards each other in imagination, across oceans and across centuries. We feel more rounded in a library because we all harbour that 'No man is an island' feeling. The library is a dream of connectedness. Ideas dreamed en masse come true. Paul Fussell's seminal *The Great War and Modern Memory* shows how we once eerily summoned up the coming conflagration, prefiguring it in fiction and essays. Physicist Paul Davies explains this in quantum terms: because of infinite parallel universes, everything imagined can be true, and frequently imagined ideas are mathematically more likely to come true. So, after millennia of imagining a universal library, we manifested the internet, that etheric Library of Alexandria.

Ancient Libraries

For much of humanity, especially in the West, the Library of Alexandria has been the founding library myth, the building in which we vest a lot of our library lore. Universal, compendious and cataclysmically burned down by the Romans or, depending on how the West is feeling, Arabs, or Jews. The 2019 film *Agora*, starring Rachel Weisz, is part of our long mourning and celebration of that library. The story that Homer led Alexander the Great to choose the site for the city of Alexandria in a dream adds to the library's glamour. It represents the idea of a storehouse of ancient wisdom. It is the ur-library.

Surprisingly, the library may not have existed in its imagined form, and there is no evidence for its burning down. The actual library at Ur in ancient Sumer – many thousands of excavated clay tablets – has more claim to be the ur-library than Alexandria. One might say that the Ur Library is the ur-library. Certainly, Alexandria had a great academy of learning and was always a cosmopolitan city, a cultural melting-pot of Egyptian and Classical Mediterranean learning, but its library myth is way bigger than its history.

This uncertainty about the library adds to its potential. As classicist Edith Hall wrote in 2015, 'the myth is more generative than the reality.'

Alexandria is the inspiring breath of fresh air: the idea of a hall of knowledge, spreading out in every direction, the polar opposite of the library of that dry old pedant the Reverend Edward Casaubon in *Middlemarch*, dedicated to a patriarchal quest for a Christian syncretic theory uniting all mythologies. Alexandria's collection still gives us an ideal that is liberating and global, diverse and holistic. If we had more information about it, that ideal would be cramped and more hijackable. It might even be popularly unknown, like the extraordinary library in medieval Arab Cordoba, Spain, with its 600,000 volumes, or the oldest working library of all, established in AD 859 by a woman, Fatima al-Fihri in Fez, Morocco.

The need for a holistic library of diversity is in all of us. The Islamic world has the 'House of Wisdom', or Grand Library of Baghdad, the fabled library founded by the Caliph Harun Al Rashid, who figures in *The Arabian Nights*. What could be more attractive than a library founded by a book character, one who has entranced Western writers as diverse as Tennyson and Yeats? This library really existed around Harun's time, the Islamic Golden Age, and, as with Alexandria, Baghdad was a luminous centre of avant-garde internationalist learning. A wonderful Arab saying implies this: 'What's written in Cairo is published in Beirut, but read in Baghdad'.

Whether or not Harun himself founded the House of Wisdom is less important culturally than the fact that it is the sort of thing he would have done. In the same way of seeing things, I once heard two historians arguing about whether Churchill really ordered troops to open fire on striking Welsh miners at Tonypandy and one, the anti-Churchillian, ended the debate by saying, 'Look I don't care whether he did or not . . . but it's the sort of thing he would have done.' Similarly when Regency-era orientalist John Malcolm toured Persia to write its history, he realized after a while that the locals were giving him a mix of fact and fable. More than this, he realized they did not care about the difference; the important thing about history in old Iran was its utility in the inspirational collective conscious.

G. K. Chesterton stood up for this strange idea of the historicity of myth: 'Fable is more historical than fact, because it is the story of a thousand, not one.' So, on yer bike, Caliph al-Mamun, probable actual founder of the House of Wisdom, and let's ignore for now the thirty-six other major libraries in medieval Baghdad and inhale the myth like the scent of incense.

Not only did Baghdad's House of Wisdom represent a golden age in a golden place, like its Alexandrine counterpart it ended in a mythopoetic cataclysm: the Mongols destroyed it in 1258 and, so the chroniclers tell us, 'the Tigris ran black with ink'.

That myth, however, was of little use to Shia Muslims, who blamed Harun, a Sunni, for much persecution, so they conjured their own Alexandrine storehouse: the 'House of Knowledge' in eleventh-century Cairo, the glory of the Fatimid Caliphate. Founded by Abu Ali Mansur, with his memorable gold-flecked blue eyes, it had its nemesis when Berber troops brought down the Fatimid dynasty late in the eleventh century.

Of course, all these stories of 'barbarian' destruction – by Romans, Arabs, Jews, Mongols or Berbers – are partly ways of bigging up the civilization writing history at any given time. As writers like Edith Hall and the Palestinian Edward Said have shown us, 'civilization' depends for much of its credibility on inventing 'barbarians'. And if they burn your semi-mythical library down, they give your civilization an added glamour.

The reality of libraries through history is even more exotic than these ultimate-storehouse-destroyed-by-orcs myths. For a considerable period in the ancient world, they were dedicated more to goddesses than to politics.

The Goddess in the Library

The widespread dedication of ancient libraries to goddesses contrasts with the later, male-created library. Just as one justification for monarchies is that they prevent a dictatorship, so a goddess-dedication limited the perennial problem of libraries becoming just instruments of state power. Anciently, goddesses were more associated with wisdom than gods: Saraswati in India, Athena in Greece, Minerva in Rome. It's as if humanity dimly grasps the fact that, through all the ages of male dominance and male philosophers, women are good at peace and men are good at war: maybe women are on to something.

In the seventh century BC Assyria had library goddesses, a fact somewhat occluded by the famous library of Ashurbanipal, a power-project for that Assyrian king, its contents littered with inscriptions praising him. A more interesting library was the one at Sultantepe, the one-time Assyrian capital, now in Turkey. The library there, including medical works, poems and several versions of *The Epic of Gilgamesh*, doubled as a temple to the goddess Ishtar. When Babylonian soldiers attacked the complex, library tablets were heaped up on Ishtar's altar in a last-ditch offering.

Equally unknown is the ancient Iraqi city of Uruk, by about 3000 BC half the size which Imperial Rome attained three millennia later. At the centre of the city, as late as 300 BC, were two gigantic library-temples, both dedicated to the goddess Ishtar. Hundreds of inscribed tablets, now slowly being translated and displayed on a dedicated website, were unearthed there during a period extending from the first, illicit raids after the First World War to German excavations in the late twentieth century.

The main reading room of the ancient Greek Library of Pergamum, also now in Turkey, was dominated by a colossal statue of Athena, goddess of wisdom (its remaining plinth is nearly three metres square) – particularly apt since a noblewoman called Flavia seems to have been the *éminence grise* behind the library.

Bath-houses and Books

Not only did ancient libraries often have a presiding goddess, they were places of leisure and entertainment. Many ancient Greek and Roman libraries were housed in public baths, which were general relaxation centres, 'always the focus of social and aesthetic life in the Roman Empire', as Tony Rook put it in *Roman Baths in Britain* (2002). Rome's huge Caracalla Baths contained a large public library, divided into Greek and Roman rooms.

Bath-houses often doubled as temples, partly because of their attendant spring and the Roman enthusiasm for water goddesses. This letter from Seneca vividly evokes the Roman bath-house – not just a place for a wash, but a riotous complex of buildings:

> All kinds of noise: the grunts of musclemen exercising and jerking, their sharp hissing as they release pent-up breath. If there happens to be a massage I hear the slap of hand on shoulder, or flat or hollow . . . a ball-player calls his score . . . add to this the sound of a fellow who likes his own voice in the bath, plus those who plunge in the pool with a huge splash . . . now add the mingled cries of the drink peddlers and the sellers of sausages, pastries and hot fare, each hawking his own wares with his own particular peal.

It was a striking instance of psychogeography when a Roman bath-house floor was discovered under the lower floor of my Canterbury bookshop. A large plinth near the Philosophy section indicated, the chief archaeologist told me, the presence of a devotional statue; my bookshop, too, had perhaps been a temple-library like a mini-Pergamum. A perennial damp patch on the back staircase from the basement indicated the spring – possibly a sacred one as at nearby Lullingstone, which may have attracted the Romans to the site.

At the Roman bath-house in Chassenon, France, members of the public would once have come to sleep, then have their dreams interpreted by on-site experts. Before I knew this, back in 1991, I think I had Chassenon-style experiences in Waterstones Canterbury's basement – the academic floor. I worked epic hours in those days, but I had picked up from some business guru a belief about it being more natural to cat-nap rather than slog through the day with declining efficiency. I installed a hammock above the bath-house floor – it was in a handy storage room – and took my lunch hour there. Drowsing in that hammock, I could hear conversations through the stud wall in the History section which merged with the afterglow of the remarkably vivid dreams I had there. Being surrounded by books and bath-house memories seemed to give rise to almost druggy dreams. Groggily, I once answered a customer query through the wall: I suspect they thought this was a preternatural event.

A picture is emerging of ancient libraries as nodal public spaces, both rowdy and sacred, commercial and eventful, frequently presided over by goddesses. We are slowly evolving back towards ancient ideas of a more open-ended library, the forum rather than the cloistered fastness. The modern world's two great open-ended libraries – the New York Public Library and the British Library – bristle with outreach events, from talks and concerts to film screenings, or exhibitions as inter-active as the BL Manga exhibition, at which hundreds of people created their own Manga personae.

Libraries in the Age of Print

The buzz of ancient libraries transferred into Renaissance establishments, after a medieval interlude of principally royal and monastic libraries. The monks of the Swiss alpine monas-tery of Admont, however, resisted the Renaissance zeitgeist. When a Venetian professor, Antonio Graziadei, was imposed as abbot in 1483, he imported forward-looking books and ancient classical texts into the stock – some of them are still there, marked as his accessions. He had worked as a tutor to the Habsburg emperor and studied in Paris; he was way too urbane to rule a community of Alpine diehard traditionalists. The monks accused him of squandering money and so, unable to bear the snowbound valley and their hostility, he surrepti-tiously left for Italy. 'Those bastard monks' – to quote the tramp in a Harold Pinter play – tracked him down and put him in their prison – of course every good monastery has a prison – where he died 'of sorrow and wretchedness'.

When the spirit of the Renaissance invaded Italian libraries, they became power stations: Machiavelli was one of many authors who read out his work in libraries. Eminent book historian Andrew Pettegree of St Andrew's University is a sur-prisingly outspoken voice in favour of such lively, inclusive libraries. 'The Renaissance library,' he says, 'was a noisy place – a place for conversation and display, rather than for study and contemplation.' It was only in the seventeenth century that the library began what he calls 'its long descent into silence, emerging as that new phenomenon of the nineteenth and twentieth centuries, the library as mausoleum, the silent repository of countless unread books'. Libraries, he thinks, with their 'descent into obscurity and irrelevance' have not always helped their own cause. He is cross, too, about the way many great libraries today hand over their old books with reluctance to readers: 'this is of course the greatest nonsense', as old books, unless really wrecked, benefit from being handled. Interaction with the hand is, after all, where they got their wonderful patina. He touchingly describes visiting one of the modern French 'ideas-space' médiathèque libraries:

> Some of the happiest reading experiences of my career have been in these libraries, where sixteenth-century books are often delivered to the general reading areas, with infants toddling through, and alongside war veterans with their daily papers. One of the pensioners kindly stopped by my desk to assure me that I would get far more enlightenment from his illustrated magazine than the text I had in front of me.

Renaissance libraries, however wonderful, were few; it was the eighteenth and nineteenth centuries that saw an explosion of accessible libraries. This was the golden age in Britain of over a thousand pay-as-you-borrow 'circulating libraries' – vigorously commercial operations with a big social side, dotting the nation from Bath to Margate and Plymouth to Aberdeen, and mirrored in Europe and North America.

Advertisements for circulating libraries actually invited people to come and enjoy conversation and discussion there. The Tunbridge Wells library in 1780 promised a space 'triumphant over prejudice' where, typically and unlike most coffee houses, women were welcomed. An anonymous poem about Bath tells us about the liveliness of Leake's Library:

Now, with motley throng, resorts the fop
To kill an hour, in Leake's fine spacious shop

These circulating libraries, private businesses derived from bookshops, were the start of widespread access to books for many women and the working to middle classes in eighteenth-century Europe and North America. As such, they were the preliminary artillery barrage which cleared the way for all classes to storm the cultural establishment, via those free-at-the-point-of-lending public libraries, which were so much to the credit of the industrial age.

In Britain the pay-to-borrow model was adopted by W. H. Smith, who set up a lending library in 1860, taken over in 1961 by its long-standing rival Boots the Chemist. Boots' shield-shaped green sticker can still be found on the cover of old books. Boots' customers, for most of their history, were predominantly the poorest of society; the company started off bulk-buying stock in cash, enabling them to brashly undercut the traditional bespoke pharmacies. Their library, therefore, has an unsung role in popular education. It was started in 1898 at the altruistic urging of Florence, the wife of Sir Jesse Boot and the daughter of a bookseller (she also revolutionized staff welfare at the company). Dedicated library staff took special exams in literature. Four hundred and fifty Boots' stores had libraries, which often contained sofas, pot plants and even specially designed stained-glass windows. Boots' libraries only closed down in 1966, after the Public Libraries Act required all councils to provide free libraries. In 1938 Boots' libraries were lending an astonishing 35 million books a year and they were sufficiently part of the national psyche in 1940 for John Betjeman to list books from Boots along with democracy and proper drainage as defining features of British civilization.

Betjeman happily coupled a library with democracy. In modern times this seems reasonable, but libraries have a sinister side too. If knowledge is power, librarians, especially cataloguers, have a hidden wire-pulling power which has subtly guided societal attitudes and leached into the way internet algorithms work.

Classifying Books, Classifying Staff

Washington's Library of Congress, the biggest library ever seen, was founded with impeccable intentions. The first librarian, Ainsworth Spofford, was a Civil War battlefield reporter and anti-slavery campaigner appointed personally by Abraham Lincoln. Spofford presided over the library for thirty years, retiring in 1897, and oversaw its exponential expansion. Under Spofford it was housed in the magnificent Jefferson building, with a dome which, to some protesting politicians, seemed to rival the Capitol's. The rivalry was more than symbolic, for this library more than any other became an instrument of state power.

'LoC' cataloguers, in naming and grouping radical thinkers and sexual minorities, both expressed and propagated their own opinions, opinions which have been as much of their time as the 1890 decision to adorn the library façade with statues of nine great white men.

Of course, libraries need to be organized to be accessible, but it is odd how most people don't organize their books at home by classification and subject. Often we go by colour, format or usefulness. I seem to have mixed-genre comfort books together. At home, many of us are the opposite of Ruskin, who actually used a saw to make all his books the same height.

Library classification is like language itself, both an enabler and a limiter of authentic connection. Libraries reflect the division of departments in universities, but those divisions are over-reductive, more rigid in their world-view than our minds are. Universities themselves recognize this in their continual renaming of departments. Wittgenstein ended up so exasperated by language's limitations that he thought poetry often got closer to perception than prose. Even poetry can be so flowery, wordy, concepty, that it gets between you and, say, the mountain. In 2011 the novelist Max Porter interviewed Alice Oswald for the *White Review*. As I write, Oswald seems to be increasingly regarded as the greatest living British poet. In the interview she spoke of Homer as a poet who could describe a leaf with immediacy, and referred to a Ted Hughes quote which I have not found anywhere else, and which struck me all the more because I found the *White Review* in question on a sofa in a hotel amid a wintry moor in Scotland, all nameable features blanketed in snow: 'Hughes says . . . that thing about if you burn down the library, the language that would be left. I love that. The courage of that.'

Libraries have to be organized, but the act of organization limits beauty in the way language sometimes can. As Kentucky Librarianship professor Melissa Adler says: 'Imagine a time before any classificatory apparatus took hold, before the universe of language absorbed our sexuality, denatured it.' Life before language, libraries before cataloguers. To catalogue is to confine and define: sexual minorities have been roughed up by Library of Congress cataloguers. From 1898 until 1972 the category 'Sexual Perversion' included homosexuality and a range of preferences now in the mainstream. That category's replacement, 'Sexual Deviation', was as judgemental and was itself replaced in 2007 by 'Paraphilias', a pathologizing term which alienates by its very obscurity, effectively concealing what it catalogues.

This old-fashioned cataloguing has had worldwide reach for over a century: 72,000 libraries still mimic Library of Congress classifications. This reach goes way back in time: in the bygone age of library index cards, the library itself sold 60,000 pre-printed cards a year to libraries globally.

So the HQ71 to HQ76 classifications have shot out all over the world from the Jefferson Building, with their oddly named sub-category, 'Women, Special', which included women as sex criminals and lesbians. HQ71–76 runs smoothly from paedo-philia and incest to bisexuality and homosexuality, via fetishes which are, these days, now neither eyebrow-raising nor illegal.

The library today has tidied up much of this, but only after much LGBTQ campaigning, and imperfectly: for instance, a smattering of books on sexual orientation still live in RC620, the 'Moral Insanity' section.

The tradition of Library of Congress policing goes way back. The FBI's J. Edgar Hoover thought the 'degenerate sex offender' a greater threat to America than organized crime, and so in 1937 declared the ancestor of the War on Terror, the 'War on the Sex Criminal'. Hoover's language on the threat of communists and perverts was a seamless argot of penetration and infiltration, infection and cleansing. Like many moral cru-saders, his passionate policing was an operation partly driven by his own demons.

Even if the widespread accusations about his cross-dressing are untrue, his covert homosexuality seems incontrovertible.

A reliable witness, the *Sophie's Choice* author William Styron, saw him painting the toenails of his longtime friend Clyde Tolson, surely an activity requiring proper cataloguing.

The library was not exempt from Hoover's moral crusade, and his power was extraordinary – President Nixon was to admit that he never fired Hoover for fear of reprisals. The restricted-access 'Delta Collection' expanded in the Hoover years to include not merely works such as *Venus in Furs*, *Lolita* and *Ulysses*, but also books on birth control and heterosexual sex, and volumes of subversive propaganda. Not for Hoover was Freud's observation that 'we are all perverse', nor Hamlet's: 'Use every man after his desert, and who should 'scape whipping?'

As customs officers sent increasing numbers of books to the library's Delta Collection, the keeper struggled to catalogue it. His 1956 diary questions the time spent cataloguing 'large quantities of unprocessed filth'. Burning was increasingly the solution for these 'perverted' books – the word was used for both political and sexual ordure. The body politic must be cleansed. In May 1963 alone, 123 'burn bags' were filled.

Staff had to be cleansed too: the Orwellian-sounding Library of Congress Loyalty Review Board was established to seek out perverts, political or sexual. Standard Form 89, issued to all employees as part of a medical history questionnaire, asked 'Have you ever had or have you now any homosexual tendencies?' In 1950 the board charged fifteen unfortunate Library of Congress employees with 'sexual perversion'. Most resigned under pressure, the rest were quietly sacked.

In 1953 thefts from the Delta Collection were reported. Since it was kept locked, a staffer had to be culpable. Additionally, pages had been cut out of *Erotic Prints of the Ming Dynasty*. The personnel director thought the thefts 'the work of a sexual pervert'. The FBI investigated and homed in on Phillip Melvin because he seemed 'highly emotional' and, more conclusively for Hoover's sleuths, he displayed 'effeminate characteristics'. Poor Melvin, a mere microfilmer, protested in vain that he had often asked to be transferred from the Delta Collection, and had been cleared as wholesome by the Loyalty Review Board back in 1948. The FBI records on Melvin are heavily redacted but they seem to have suspected him of being a communist as well as 'effeminate'.

After two FBI searches of Melvin's apartment yielded no evidence, the case was closed. As late as 1962 another library employee was detected in perversion: Nevin Feather was asked by the library's personnel director to sign a notarized statement that, contrary to rumour, he did not enjoy homosexual fellatio.

Today, the library's HR department no longer spends time on fellatio, and has implemented many changes suggested by an active staff LGBTQ campaign group. The library still has a national political role – and an actual tunnel to the Capitol – but nowadays it reflects a broader political platform; in 2016 it even abolished the 'Illegal Aliens' category as derogatory. There was a Republican outcry and, for the first time in history, the House of Representatives ordered a class-mark change, reviving the aliens category.

Dubious Dewey

The much-loved Dewey Decimal System never caught on at the Library of Congress, but it remains the most successful library classification system globally, still used in 135 countries. The 'DDS' went viral quite early on; Dewey was Director of

New York State Libraries from 1888 to 1906, and President of the American Library Association for much of that period. But DDS is a child of its time, with homosexuality only completely removed from the 'social problems' section in 1996, and minimal space for non-Christian belief systems. Dewey's general Eurocentrism has led libraries in Holland and parts of the United States to move to more flexible and nuanced systems, usually closer to the way a bookshop is organized. 'Done with Dewey' is the concise title of a recent article in a Dutch librarianship journal.

If the truth were widely known about the Dewey system's creator the migration from his system would accelerate. Appropriately, my tattered biography of him, ex-Panama City Library stock, is boldly stamped in red on the title page 'DISCARDED'. Dewey must be admired for the gargantuan achievement of his system; back in 1577 Madrid's royal librarian, Arias Montano, tried to make such a universal system, with sixty-four subject zones and handwritten labels. It was of such infinite complexity that only Montano himself understood it. When the king's secretary, Antonio Gracian, tried to find a book he was reminded of 'the original Chaos of Hesiod', but Montano was too concerned with ascetic practices and writing mystical verse to care what Gracian thought. By 1855, when the British Museum Librarian Frederick Madden visited, this huge library was scarcely more accessible, open only three hours a day, but not on saints' days. Inside, he found only 'an ignorant monk' as librarian. Terribly, in 1935 when the library was being professionally run, Franco 'systematically executed' the entire library staff.

Dewey did for knowledge what digitization has done, some say, to recorded music: encoding it in numbers and thereby imposing a mathematical mediation between ideas and their audience. This expressed his obsessively domineering persona. The number 10 was his lodestar; he organized his mother's kitchen jars in tens, got ten hours' sleep and preferred to write ten-page letters. He was left-brain dominant, interested in language and linearity. From his twenties onwards he wrote in a contracted phonetic sort of baby language, a system which he arrogantly hoped would catch on worldwide; it is infuriating to read ('Fyn vu from golfhous', for instance). In later years he claimed to have had the decimal classification idea in church during a sermon ('I jumt up and neerli shoutd yooreeka'). In fact, as one of his many enemies, Ainsworth Spofford, Librarian of Congress, pointed out, Dewey got the idea from Nathaniel Shurtleff, a Boston librarian who had self-published *A Decimal System for the Arrangement and Administration of Libraries* back in 1856. (Shurtleff was another left-brain compulsive systematizer and purifier, prominent in a secret society dedicated to ridding the United States of immigrants and Catholics, an aim prosecuted through the tarring and feathering of several priests.) Spofford's accusation is relegated to a footnote in my battered Dewey biography, a book which valiantly attempts to present him as a half-decent human being. Its author, Wayne Wiegand, has to admit that his subject was 'regularly duplicitous'.

As early as 1878 there was 'great exultation' at Columbia College when Dewey left its employment as librarian. As a lifelong evangelical, at the New York Library Service he appointed a Chief Inspector of Libraries to ensure that only redemptive literature was promoted – no copies of the *Decameron*, for instance, were to be loaned out to women. As co-founder of the American Library Association he broadened this baleful influence, holding its 1894 Annual Conference at his Lake Placid country resort. This estate of over 100 acres, with its wholesome library, farm, golf courses and boating lake, was founded by Dewey and his wife Annie as a place to preserve and celebrate 'refined family life'.

Group hymn-singing was *de rigeur*, and 'no profanity or vulgarity' would be tolerated, so dancing cheek to cheek was banned, women had to ride side-saddle and could not smoke in public. When Dewey spotted a Cornell professor's surname on a guest list he had to regretfully informed him of the resort's 'no Jews' policy. When enforcing this rule, as when he told Jewish New Yorker Albert Harris to cancel his family holiday booking at the resort, he always avoided telling the truth – that he was the source of the policy – regretfully saying that other members would be offended. African Americans were only allowed in the servants' quarters, working-class people were banned, and no Cubans or 'new rich' were admitted, since they would display 'a lack of refinement'. The mind boggles at the resort's atmosphere; an odd photograph of Dewey there shows him dressed completely in leather ('apparently in costume for an event', the biographer Wiegand speculates innocently and somewhat desperately).

This selective admission policy required Dewey's systematizing genius, so he designed a sort of Dewey Decimal System for humans, ranging from Category A, fully acceptable Wasps, through to C, possibly admissible after background checks, to D, definitely requiring investigation, and E, utter no-no's.

The 'no Jews' policy at Dewey's resort lasted until well after 1930, surviving several challenges by New York's Jewish community, whose members particularly objected to a public employee of the city library service holding such views. Pragmatically, in 1930 Dewey described a 'new Jew attack' on his policy as a great PR opportunity for the resort. He even invited black rights leader Booker Washington to his home – but not the resort – as part of a PR operation.

Dewey's resignation from public office was finally occasioned by his egregious behaviour towards women. Ever since the 1900s women had endured his unwelcome advances, but his public eminence and self-assurance protected him. By 1930 at least nine library employees had bravely gone public with accusations. Dewey seems to have indulged in more than just inappropriate groping; the victims were all too genteel, or protective of their own privacy, to go into much detail but one referred to 'a vicious type of sexual depravity which is criminal in the eyes of the law'. She warned investigators of 'his essential falsity'. (Like that other delusional fantasist Hitler, Dewey's doublethink manifested itself in lifelong constipation and piles: coincidence?)

Dewey retired from public office and evaded any official rebuke or prosecution. The establishment closed ranks. A $50,000 lawsuit brought by his female secretary was settled out of court with a $2,000 pay-off. Mrs Dewey defended her husband's 'unconventional manner with women' as part of his individuality. Here is Dewey's own defence, which I found I had to read several times to grasp both its meaning and its breathtaking arrogance:

> I have suffered for thirty years from my conceit that I was so different from most men and had so much more trust in women. Pure women would understand my ways.

The American Library Association still awards an annual Melvil Dewey Medal for 'creative leadership of a high order'. I suppose Dewey's level of hypocrisy was pretty creative, but it is probably time to rename that medal.

The Erotic Library

Despite all the relaxed bath-house and Renaissance libraries referred to earlier, and the unease we feel at Hoover and Dewey's invasions of library culture, I doubt if we would want libraries to be completely unregulated, or utterly absorbed into a leisure-centre culture. Library rules can be good. The British Library and SOAS regulations offer a fair starting point for building a utopia:

> Treat all staff and fellow users with respect and courtesy
> Turn all phones on to silent mode
> Talk quietly
> No blades of any sort
> Turn the pages slowly

And they have flashes of mysterious poetry, such as

> Always use the snake weights [sinuous metal weights for holding large books open]

There is something reassuring about a safe, silent public space with arcane small-print regulations. It seems extraordinary that many library staff have a statutory right to open and inspect one's personal possessions, and that special New York Library patrolmen have the legal right of arrest. For some, control can be erotic. It was so for Lillian Faderman, a veteran of gay rights from the Bronx. She remembers how the thrill of reading *Sex Variant Women* in her local library was intensified by the danger that she would be spotted reading it. And Melissa Adler, author of *Cruising the Library* (Fordham University Press, 2017), suggests that some users find the library erotic, either as a forbidden space or as a masochistic experience; in submitting to rules, some find a special freedom. Theorizing that masochism is cultural and imaginative – suiting library users – whereas sadism is systematizing and controlling, she is unsurprised that the one job the Marquis de Sade applied for was librarian.

Sado-masochism aside, there is excitement in transgressing library rules in a more mainstream way: Emperor-designate Marcus Aurelius wrote a letter in AD 145 about the thrill he would get from sexually fondling a young male librarian in order to illicitly borrow a reference book. More recently, an anonymous female Cornell University student has been posting a highly successful monthly blog called *Sex in the Stacks*, much to the gloom of university authorities. The New York band The Pains of Being Pure at Heart celebrated making out in the library in 'Young Adult Friction':

> Between the stacks in the library
> Not like anyone stopped to see
> We came, they went
> Among the dust and the microfiche
> Don't check me out [this line repeated 25 times]

Unconsummated love in the library sold even more records for Californian punks Green Day: 'At the Library' sings of the feeling of longing you get in the library for another reader, before their annoying standardized inamorata lopes in to take them away.

Librarians

Where do librarians fit into this psychosexual landscape? Traditionally, they are forbidding figures. Many of us can sympathize with Illinois student Jessica Colbert, writing in her 2017 thesis on library culture:

> I have loved libraries my entire life, but I never knew that being a librarian was something that I could do as a career. Like so many others, I thought librarians sort of sprang out of circulation desks, fully formed at age 60.

To some students, the poet and full-time librarian of Hull University Philip Larkin fulfilled this forbidding stereotype. Expecting 'not to give a zebra's turd' about the job, he found it a wonderful vocation. He housed his large porn collection in his office and hoped that, as a librarian, students would find him simply 'a nice chap to have around'. Not all of them warmed to him: one wrote in the lifts: 'FUCK OFF LARKIN YOU CUNT'.

Librarians are traditionally portrayed as female. They have so often been reduced to either frumps or sex objects that one turns with relief to, say, Bette Davis's 1956 portrayal of a feisty librarian who defies censorship in small-town America in *Storm Center* (1956), or Katherine Hepburn's witty Bunny Watson in *Desk Set* (1957). Barbara Stanwyck in 1932's long-forgotten *Forbidden* magnificently fantasized about an apocalyptic end to the 'patriarchive': 'I wish I owned this library . . . I'd get an axe and smash it to a million pieces, then I'd set fire to the whole town and play the ukulele while it burned.'

This bubbling stream of heroic female librarians has broadened into a river; we are finally progressing from the frump era: Batgirl doubles as Gotham City's hero-librarian, and a happily drunk Rachel Weisz in *The Mummy* stands up in a Saharan landscape to proclaim: 'I may not be a treasure-seeker or a gunfighter but I am proud of what I am, a librarian!'

Detroit Librarian Annie Spence's memoir *Dear Fahrenheit 451* is very funny and full of love for her customers. Librarians, having inspired and guided millions, including many famous authors, make the entire literary ecosystem thrive. Search algorithms only work on past history; librarians live in the present and intuit the future. I think nowadays we can all subscribe to Neil Gaiman's 'Rule Number One': 'Don't fuck with librarians.'

The Spider and the Flea, the Bat and the Bookworm

Soon after the new British Library building opened, the rep for the British Library publishing division paid his regular visit to my shop. Like most travelling book salesmen, Geoff was a great storyteller. 'What's it like?' I asked, since I had loved researching in the old library, when it was housed under the dome of the British Museum. I thought nothing could replace the romance of that space, certainly not a fake-looking building in Euston Road, a building lacking either a memorable shape or a single external feature. How wrong I was.

Geoff explained that the visible part of the library was the tip of an extraordinary iceberg: four double-height sub-basements extend 75 feet below ground. Here, Geoff told me, most of the books are stored in chilled conditions, except for the rarest items, which are in oxygen-free rooms filled with a synthetic argon-based gas called Inergen, a mixture which cannot catch fire. I was agog.

Self: 'But what happens if a fire starts in the non-rare books areas?'

Geoff: 'Ah, in those areas there is a sprinkler system.'

Self: 'What! A water sprinkler comes on all over the books if a power point starts fizzing?' [This actually happened in 2003.]

Geoff: 'They've thought of that doomsday scenario: they've got this thing called a Blast Freeze Wind Tunnel down there. You put the damp books inside and it dries them without heating them.'

Self: 'You are shitting me.'

Geoff: 'I shit you not; staff have special training on using it. They practise on wet telephone directories.'

Self: 'Have another fag [it was the nineties] and tell me more – but is all this for real?'

Geoff: 'Absolutely fucking kosher, I've had the secret tour.'

Self: 'Hold on, if it's all chilled-down and argon down there, how do staff get the books?'

Geoff: 'Robots!'

Self: 'Sounds like a sci-fi movie.'

Geoff: 'Funny you should say that – a French geezer has actually filmed a sci-fi picture down there.'

Self: 'What's the title, could I order it at Blockbuster? [a video rental chain]'

Geoff: 'I'm not Barry Norman, I don't remember that.'

Self (still suspicious): 'So does anyone go down there?'

Geoff (warming to his theme): 'Well, the robots malfunction sometimes and start smashing the place up so then engineers in hazmat suits go down with baseball bats to do battle with them.' [Geoff was indulging in poetic licence here, but staff entering the lowest levels do have, according to library staff, 'special training and breathing apparatus'.]

Self: 'But isn't that area all threaded with tube lines?'

Geoff: 'Yeah, it's eerie – you look across these basement floors as far as the eye can see and occasionally hear tube trains rumbling past as if they're coming at you. You've heard about the audio studios haven't you?'

Self : 'Why have they got audio studios?'

Geoff: 'All those cassette recordings of authors, mate. They're slowly transcribing 'em all digitally: the cassettes are all degrading [stubs out his fag end] – just like you and me. O' course they need complete silence, so the audio studios are built on a giant two-foot thick rubber pad.'

Surprisingly, except for the baseball bats, it's all true: Inergen, wind tunnel, telephone-directory training, robotic collection, rubber pad (I still cannot trace the movie, however).

The tale underlines the fact that, as buildings, libraries are utterly unique, with demands different from other big structures such as railway stations, government offices or churches. The difference lies in two main areas: practical considerations – security, humidity, stacks, etc. – and style: they have to express an idea of bookishness and universality in their architecture and fittings, right down to a certain gravitas in the lavatory design (the paper dispenser in the British Library lavatory is 'The Leonardo').

Practically, the old British Museum library had unique challenges from its earliest days. Before the domed reading room was built in 1857, readers got 'museum headache' in a series of stuffy reading rooms where they might be bitten by the 'museum flea', which a reader said was 'larger than any to be found elsewhere except in workhouses'.

Antonio Panizzi, the librarian who pushed through the building of the legendary reading room, was completely un-British. Although the British Museum library split away in 1973 to become the British Library, its present compendious spirit and democratic outlook derive much from Antonio Panizzi. He had good reason to be radical about the library's public mission, having been a revolutionary in Italy who fled his homeland to escape persecution, and was sentenced to death in absentia by the Duke of Modena.

Borrowing money when he first arrived, he got a job in 1831 at the museum and rose up the ranks to Keeper of Printed Books in 1837. A visitor described him as 'a dark little Italian, sitting like a spider in a web of books', but he was a controversially democratic spider: 'I want a poor student to have the same means of indulging his learned curiosity as the richest man in the kingdom.' This determined attitude bred enemies. His bitterest foe was his senior colleague Frederick Madden, who never got over being passed over as Keeper in favour of the man he called 'the foreigner'. Another librarian, Reverend Henry Cary, also had his eye on the Keepership and fulminated that 'a foreigner should run our National Library'.

Today, visitors take for granted that the library's principal treasures are on display in free galleries; Panizzi pioneered this. Madden fought him every inch to stop books such as the Lindisfarne Gospels, the Diamond Sutras and early Korans being publicly displayed. He felt that they were only for elite scholars to see. The Keeper gathered allies around him, what Madden called his 'Russian Police System', describing one operative as a 'lick-spittle booby' and 'slave of Panizzi'. As for the Italian himself, to Madden he had 'all the villainy, cunning and diabolical qualities of a Richelieu'. Panizzi's attempts at conciliation all failed, including even getting Madden's son appointed Keeper of Coins. (Madden was not innocent of cunning himself, concealing his lifelong visits to prostitutes from both his wife and history, until his private diary became public in 1920).

Panizzi's other main enemy was Josiah Forshall, a vicar who co-produced ponderous biblical works with Madden. As museum secretary, Forshall tried to torpedo Panizzi's popularization of the library by expanding the secretary role to include setting the agenda for all trustee meetings, and then excluding all library staff from such meetings. Forshall was quietly going mad, and his mental problems led to three long sick leaves. When a Parliamentary Commission on the library uncovered his megalomania and opposition to popularization, MPs were horrified and abolished the post of secretary. Forshall retired and self-published a pamphlet raving against the new museum policies.

As Keeper, Panizzi enforced for the first time the library's statutory right to have a free copy of every new book printed; he simply fined non-complying publishers. He made the library's acquisition policy more international, using agents in Berlin, Paris and the USA. He wrote to a US agent, Henry Stevens of Vermont: 'send me everything'. He got the books properly catalogued and even got his ink sketch of a circular cast-iron reading room adopted, built and opened in 1857. It filled the empty square courtyard in the middle of the museum. This masterpiece of Victorian technology – now an exhibition space – was fully ventilated but had foot-level heating pipes for winter. The impressive inner dome had two surprises: book storage fitted into the spandrels (the space between dome curve and vertical courtyard walls), and its material – it is made of papier mâché, suspended on cast-iron poles.

The new room made Panizzi a new and formidable enemy: the then-lionized historian Thomas Carlyle. As a vocally racist, pro-slavery opponent of universal suffrage, made extra-crotchety by his lifelong unconsummated marriage, Carlyle was a natural enemy of both Panizzi and democratic library access. The new reading room, full of riff-raff, was abhorrent; he wrote to Panizzi demanding a private reading space for himself at the museum. When the Keeper politely declined,

Carlyle wrote to his friend Lord Clarendon, the Foreign Secretary, but to no avail.

The dome idea had come to Panizzi 'in the wakeful hours of the night', and was inspired by a Roman temple; it aimed to be a temple of learning and did indeed become a great power station of change. Inside, Virginia Woolf felt she had become 'a thought in a huge forehead'. Marx and Lenin researched revolution there, Gandhi and Jinnah were readers, and Conan Doyle and Oscar Wilde both had passes.

When I used the Reading Room I loved its heavy oak and leather chairs, heated footrests and the extraordinary catalogue: housed in huge books on two shelves in a central ring, each one with a small metal handle on the spine to lift it out. Once you opened it up on a special sloping shelf you noticed interleaved blank pages, where new accession records were glued in by hand. By oral tradition, everyone seemed to know about Marx's habitual seat – G7 – although it was like all the others and had no plaque. Like many others I often used it and imagined his ghost. On joining, he signed the membership register with florid quill as 'Karl Marx, Dr, 1 Modena Villas, Maitland Park, NW'.

The reading room was open until 9 p.m., long after the rest of the museum closed. Leaving at nine and walking through the dimly lit and empty Ancient Egyptian galleries maintained the dream-like atmosphere all the way out to my bicycle.

Other days spent in the museum's windowless manuscript room verged on the hallucinatory. Could I really just write out a slip for Lawrence of Arabia's wartime diary without giving any reason? I did, and turned its sere desert-faded pages. I think the rarest manuscripts could safely be viewed there because readers were all under the basilisk eye of an elderly keeper. When he went for lunch, it closed and we were all turfed out. A surprising condition of using the manuscript room, like some shibboleth, was that fountain pens were compulsory: no biros or pencils, which might mark manuscripts with pressure indentations.

These practical considerations have been addressed throughout library history in ways that would seem bonkers if they were not so completely outcome-focused. The Buddhist library, or Sutra store, in Nara, Japan, is both incredibly clever and old (dating from AD 800). Built on stilts to escape damp and vermin, its walls are made of horizontal logs which dry out in the summer, admitting breezes which keep the manuscripts aerated, but expand and close up in wet weather to protect them from damp or cold air. In ancient China there were beetles which ate not just books, but the actual shelves too; boxes of chosen herbs repelled the beasts and the Chinese dealt with damp from early times by installing gypsum damp-proof courses under libraries.

Such technical solutions are not always obvious to library users. When the English Gothic novelist William Beckford visited the 1730 Mafra Library in Portugal he thought it 'clumsily designed . . . with a gallery which projects into the room in a very awkward manner'. Not as awkward as the insanely tall tower Beckford commissioned on his house near Bath, which collapsed three times within a few years of construction. If Beckford had stayed for a sleepover in the Mafra Library, the secret of the upper gallery would have become clear as hundreds of tiny bats swarmed from their roosting places behind the upper cases to eat insects which might threaten the books. Small portals allowed them to fly around nearby orchards. This efficient and ecological system of pest control seems to have been planned by the architect, artillery colonel Manuel de Sousa, and tolerated. I just phoned the library and after initial communication problems a nice lady confirmed in a matter-of-fact way that the inch-long bats still live there, and that staff cover the furniture nightly to catch their droppings.

What are these library-destroying pests the bats eat? They are 'booklice' in the main, a large phylum generally overlooked by entomologists because of their secretive behaviour and size – they rarely exceed a quarter of an inch (6 mm). Knowledge of booklice, or bookworms, is changing with vertiginous speed. They are not lice or worms, for a start, but more like tiny flies. My 1976 insect guide says there are 1,600 known species, but the revised 1993 edition says there are 2,000 species; a scholarly article recently referred to 5,500 species. By the time you read this they might be running Microsoft.

Their appearance irresistibly recalls some of the scholars who are their cohabitants in old libraries: 'swollen forehead, soft pale body, starchy diet, they prefer dim, neglected corners, where there is a musty smell. Reproductive habits remain mysterious'. They (the insects) are incredibly successful, adapting to books from their more predator-rich homes under tree bark or in birds' nests. In libraries, they feed on tiny traces of mould in paper, and binders' glue is their caviar. One insect book refers to them as 'very cosmopolitan', giving us a vision of tiny flies in Ray-Bans sipping martinis on the terrace of the Cipriani in Venice, but this is entomology-speak for 'highly adaptable to different places'.

Booklice have an answer to their opponents: they clear off if a book is used and handled, so they are entitled to point out that it is only our neglect of a book that allows them to become proprietary with it.

The way that the Japanese Nara and Portuguese Mafra libraries worked with their local biosphere was lacking in the concept-driven 1980s. In this decade the new Bibliothèque Nationale was initiated in Paris. Shaped like an upturned table, with four brutalist tower blocks for legs, it is too hot for books and readers, but succeeded as a vanity project for President Mitterrand. W. G. Sebald's eponymous hero Austerlitz takes a dim view of the building's impracticality.

Another impractical library is the 1984 Seeley History Library in Cambridge: the university considered demolishing it but instead the leaky, over-lit and overheated building has been expensively remodelled.

More recently, library architects have been abandoning both the war on nature and quasi-ecclesiastical floorplans. We have moved beyond the domed reading room, to less intimidating and more organic forms. Freiburg Library broke the mould in 1902 with its triangular shape, and then was radically reborn in 2015 as a huge diamond, solar-powered and heated from groundwater. Its car park was replaced with a 400-bicycle park. Norman Foster's academic library at the Free University in Berlin is shaped like a brain, and ventilated naturally.

The language of library architecture is evolving with exciting speed, unlike the language of corporate headquarters, which remains, with a few gimmicky exceptions, phallic and domineering. The idea of designing a library which actually resonates with both its immediate environment and with the way we think, was quietly pioneered in a Florence backstreet 350 years ago.

'Some New Fantasy'

The Laurentian Library pioneered site-specific, and not merely atavistic, library architecture, with a wackiness generated by a sort of love affair between an artist and a pope. One of Michelangelo's friends said of his style that he always 'broke the bonds and chains'. In the future Pope Giulio de Medici, he had a friend who actively encouraged that approach. Giulio's father was murdered early in his life so he was sent to live with his uncle (Lorenzo the Magnificent), who already had much-favoured children of his own. Into this household, when shy, music-loving Giulio was twelve, came the fifteen-year-old Michelangelo. The two boys bonded as outsiders who shared a joshing humour and love of the arts.

When Giulio became a cardinal and commissioned his childhood friend to paint an altarpiece, Michelangelo asked what the figures should wear. 'You decide – do I look like a tailor?' was the gist of the Cardinal's reply. The lack of formality between the men was startling: as Cardinal, Giulio said, 'whenever Michelangelo comes to see me, I am always seated and I always ask him to sit down, because he certainly will, without asking.'

After Giulio became Pope Clement, he still wrote personal letters to his old friend, using the intimate *tu* form. This was sufficiently remarkable for a secretary to once add a confirmation that the missive was actually penned by His Holiness. One letter ended, 'Never doubt that you will lack work or reward while I live'; a later missive, as Michelangelo approached death, implored him not to overwork, to take care of himself. It was not entirely for economic reasons that the artist once said that, without Clement, 'I would be unable to exist in the world.' As Pope, contemporaries thought Clement too indecisive, a ditherer who was more interested in 'investigating the secrets of craftsmen' than in power. This very indecisiveness indicated a mental fluidity well suited to a patron of new art. Seeing all sides of a question can impart what Keats celebrated as 'negative capability'.

When Clement asked his friend to be the architect of a new library the reply was typically blunt: 'I know nothing about this and it's not my profession, but I will do what I can.' His sketch plan survives, on a banknote-sized scrap of paper with a corner torn off, perhaps for a shopping list. From this scrap came 'his most original contribution to Renaissance architecture' and what Alberto Manguel in *The Library at Night* has called 'one of the loveliest libraries ever built'. For art historian Martin Gayford, it was 'a work of extraordinary originality and surreal imagination'.

It was a passion project for Clement, who wanted the Medici book collection housed for posterity. He homed in on the details, urging comfortable walnut readers' benches to be made to last – they were, and they have. He enquired about the source of the walnut, and how it was to be treated, subjects dear to his friend too: Michelangelo had written a sonnet about wood. Clement got into the marble of the internal detailing too, and here Michelangelo insisted on using local stone of the right *colore et sapore* – colour and flavour – for a library. They even devised the right mortar together.

The door was a really big deal. When the Pope got the letter with a design for the door he read it six times – imagine the silent papal court – then read it aloud, and said, 'not another man in Rome' could have thought of such a door: a simple classical design transformed by a triangular pediment over the top 'jutting forward like two elbows', of a reader, or perhaps the library itself, welcoming readers in.

Clement egged on Michelangelo's idiosyncrasy, encouraging him to invent a new library language in stone. When asked about the ceiling, the Pope said, just do *qualche fantasia nuovo* – 'some new fantasy'. Time and again he told Michelangelo to do parts of the library *a vostro modo*, 'in your own way'.

The building had to work for readers and for books – two priorities often ignored since by architects – so Michelangelo suggested skylights, to avoid overheated readers and damaged books. Clement's practicality and humour surfaced in his rejection of that: 'great idea, and we'll have to hire two full-time friars to clean them'.

Michelangelo was a lover of books too, an accomplished poet who wrote love-sonnets to a lifelong male friend and one celebrating Dante. Dante, the Italian homegrown poet, had shown that Italy could reinvent classical literary culture, and Michelangelo did this too with classical forms in the library. He made the building inside out, so that the heavy historical references – classical columns, sculpted window frames – were on the inside but toned down by the presence of living readers: the columns were sunk into the wall in niches, as if they were statues from the past.

The most obvious innovation was that the library was entirely on the third floor, a practical and a stylistic statement that both kept the books safe from damp and created a clean sanctum above the bustling Florence streetscape.

Books contain order and chaos, like the mind itself: order was represented in the measuring-out of the library, which reflected the golden section, a mathematical proportion dating back to classical times which reflects hidden harmonies in nature. Chaos, in all its suggestive splendour, was represented in the feature which, Vasari remembered, 'astonished' everybody: the staircase.

Staircases populate our dreams, where they lead nowhere, or to heaven, or just flip about as in *Harry Potter*. The Laurentian staircase tumbles down like an unruly river, splitting into two sequences of differing tread heights, whilst side parapets descend in yet a different mathematical sequence. This

Escher-esque illusion was, I think, designed to separate the reader from street reality, to act as a sort of airlock leading to the space-walk among texts waiting above. Asked about where the design originated, Michelangelo recalled 'a certain staircase, in a dream'.

The library sprung a final surreal surprise in 1774, when an overloaded desk collapsed. It revealed under it a few complex geometric designs of interlocking circles and ellipses on the floor, in red and white terracotta. Only after a similar mishap in 1928 was a whole floor-length series of designs revealed. The mosaics seem to have been covered up by an early wooden reflooring. In 'Hidden Inscriptions in the Laurentian Library' (*Proceedings of the International Society of Arts, Mathematics and Architecture*, September 2006) two computer scientists from Cardiff University tried to decode the designs' complex geometry but concluded that 'Computer algebra systems are not powerful enough to give a general solution.'

I tried unsuccessfully to contact the paper's author, an Emeritus Professor, about any updates to studies on the floor but his website says he can no longer be contacted about academic matters as he now devotes himself to rearing cacti and playing complex early music in his Welsh cottage. He appends a recommended playlist. More recently, mathematicians at the Illinois Institute of Technology have found references to Plato, Euclid and the golden section in the floor, which they call nothing less than 'an encyclopaedia of ancient geometry'.

What on earth was Michelangelo up to? An optical illusion staircase leading up to an inside-out room paved with keys to the hidden machinery of the universe? The Laurentian Library was designed to put readers in a freed state of mind, out of time, questioning. To play with ancient motifs using Florentine stone and wood was a divinely inspired display of

Renaissance confidence which seems to say 'we need old learning, but we are Florentines, and this is 1525.' Machiavelli did the same thing with Platonic ideas of politics in *The Prince*, retrofitting Plato's *Republic* with pragmatism and utility for the modern world.

Library architecture is getting connected with the local environment again. Michelangelo has a worthy successor as a library designer in the Japanese grandson of a lumber merchant. Toyo Ito has received several international awards, including one for designing rapid-erection houses for tsunami victims, and he has laid out his philosophy succinctly: nature is fluid, but in the twentieth century architecture migrated to grid-patterns, which produced homogeneous cities and even people. His fluidity delighted Londoners when he designed the Serpentine Gallery Pavilion in 2002, but his two Japanese libraries are his masterpieces. The Sendai Médiathèque (2001), like the Laurentian, has its library on the third floor, up a crazy staircase. Ito's stairs are adorned by swirling tubes in different colours which 'provide a conceptual link between the street and library'. The tubes provide light, heat and ventilation. Ito's Tama Art University Library (2007), 'one of the strangest and most imaginative library buildings of the past fifty years', has a sloping ground floor which flows with the surrounding landscape. Floor-height arched windows, plenty of fountains, and trees all around underline readers' feeling of being pleasantly discombobulated, unmoored and ready to explore ideas in books. Tama must have been a builder's nightmare but, like so many libraries, a readers' dream.

Figure 2.3 'Le Bibliophile d'autrefois,' frontispiece by Félicien Rops for Octave Uzanne, *La Nouvelle Bibliopolis* (1897)

6.   Private Passions: Collectors

A few years ago, a little girl was in a book signing queue for a prolific author – I forget who. She was crying and her distress seemed to increase as she neared the signing table.

Mother, crouching to ascertain cause: 'What is it darling? We're nearly there now.'

Girl: 'I don't want him to crap up my book.'

The girl had a pristine collection, and no desire for it to be defaced. Collectors know what they want and the collecting urge starts early, with toddlers' pockets full of pebbles and coloured things; we begin like jackdaws as we end, chattering apparent nonsense and valuing a few fond objects.

There are all sorts of ephemeral theories about collecting, including mother replacement, mate attraction, nest-building and obsessive–compulsive disorder. Marx saw collecting as commodity fetishism, a symptom of late-stage capitalism, and there are barge-loads of books about that. The Béarnaise philosopher Pierre Bourdieu (1930–2002) introduced the idea of possessions like books as cultural capital, boastful trophies. Book historians have reeled in these paradigms to gain gravitas, but they are all but partial truths.

All of these theories are peripheral compared to the foremost reason for collecting books: a sense of history, of using old books to improve the future of mankind. Notable book collectors of the past explicitly rooted their collecting habit in a desire to use history to make a better future. For all of us, this latent awareness of our place midstream in history is easily aroused. Some say they are not interested in 'History', meaning perhaps a TV historian talking about dates and trying to walk naturally towards the camera, or an uninspiring teacher recycling a syllabus dictated by politicians. Everybody, on the other hand, feels history with a small 'h' in their bones.

In Naples there were street riots when *The Civil History of Naples* was published in 1723, and the clergy said that the blood of St Januarius would not deign to liquefy that year in disgust at that liberal take on the region's past. The author fled to Vienna in fear of his life. Even if we have never taken to the streets, we all express our sense of history by collecting, if not books, perhaps family photographs, and an object or two of doubtful utility but familial significance: Great Aunt Harriet's pin cushion or Uncle Silas's eel-catching fork.

My father was an extreme case as a collector, building, as my brother said, 'a fortress against the triviality of the outside world'. He gathered up from London street markets and war-time souks not only thousands of books and coins but prints, fifteen or so walking sticks (he never used one), telephone books for all over the place (when I tried to throw one away he protested, 'I might want to phone someone in there'; to which I replied, 'The Berkshire directory for 1932?'), many toasters, a knobkerrie, an umbrella-stand full of spears, a Zulu shield of hide which groaned when a storm was coming, an antelope head christened by one of us eight innocent children 'Horny', a sextant (he never sailed), scores of old tools, sash weights, three hand-operated drills (he never used an electric one), different grades of chain, an early intercom, two or three Smurf petrol tokens and all sorts of promotional key rings, a few Roman toga brooches, the hand of an ancient Egyptian statue of Sekhmet (when I took it to the British Museum the Keeper said, 'I think it's from one of ours'), fragments of mummy casing, Hittite cylinder seals, both real and forged, an entire run of the *Journal of the Society for Psychical Research*, rescued from a skip outside the Society's offices in Adam and Eve Mews, a rifle, a Luger pistol, a green glass ball to repel witches, a hand grenade with the pin in, a whole cupboard of clocks and watches he was gradually repairing, a wooden box full of cigarette cards, a magic lantern which smoked when in use, with eerie glass slides, a box of watercolours which I discovered were used on the 1875 expedition of HMS *Alert* to try and discover the North-West Passage, a gilt set of stairs (only two feet high) from his Aleppo war service, hundreds of years old and with some ritual Islamic purpose, a ewer full of desert sand from Palestine (used in our crib every Christmas), a small faint sketch in sepia, sold after his death by Sotheby's for £6,000 as the sketch for a famous Venetian fresco, a four-foot Aboriginal boomerang, two seventeenth-century Persian vases, a vial of incorruptible water from the spring which sprang up on the spot in Suffolk where the head of Saint Osyth landed when she was beheaded by Vikings, two human skulls, dowsing rods and pendulums (he was a noted dowser and edited the *Journal of the British Society of Dowsing*), hundreds of fossils, a Tsarist-era display box of gemstones, with inscriptions in Russian, a tank sight from the Western desert, with a rubber eyepiece so that your eye did not get bashed when going over rough terrain, a dagger donated by a Bedouin sheikh for whom my father had dowsed a well, the *Service of Exorcism*, published by the Vatican in 1890 (Bishop of Arabia's copy), and several crucifixes: both my parents were Catholic converts.

Some 105 billion of us have lived since we started telling stories, but there are only 8 billion people alive. We are a fraction of ourselves, and we all have moments when that knowledge drenches us like a sudden shower of rain.

Once, I was reading an 1821 manuscript letter in the Lahore

archives which ended abruptly with 'I must stop now there's a sandstorm.' It was as if a frock-coated figure out of an aquatint was suddenly in the room with me. Just in my bookshop, I have had conversations with customers about Ian Fleming and Joseph Conrad, Camus and Sibelius, and all of those conversations have suddenly come alive as my interlocutors revealed personal, unrecorded stories of those people, whom they had known. One conversation with a regular, Stella Irwin, really proved the permeability of 'today'. Stella knew Robert Graves well, and reminded me that in *Goodbye to All That* he tells how, as a child, he was patted on the head by Swinburne, who when young met Walter Savage Landor, who as a lad had been patted on the head by Samuel Johnson, who was touched for 'the kings evil' when a boy by Queen Anne. She was close to her uncle Charles II, son of Charles I, Mary Queen of Scots' grandson, whose cousin Elizabeth met Shakespeare. In that conversation with Stella Irwin there suddenly seemed not many degrees of separation between us two old folks chatting in a chain bookstore opposite Primark and the author of *A Midsummer Night's Dream,* that gateway to pagan magic and Ovidian shape-shifting. If you think stories, not dates, two thousand years is just a vibration.

There is an instinctive practical purpose to collecting books, too. Marx warns us that 'history repeats itself, first as tragedy, then as farce'. Keeping our stories close protects us from that cycle, which explains the wise prophylaxis of orthodox Jewry in storing used holy books in a cupboard, the *genizah*, prior to interring them in a cemetery in sealed boxes. Barack Obama's desire to use past stories for a better future was acted out when he chose to be sworn in as President on two books: bibles owned by Abraham Lincoln and Martin Luther King. His critics on the 'dark net' also saw great power in his use of two books at that historic moment, but they weirdly alleged the top book was the Koran, symbolically precedent above a Bible.

Like Obama, collectors get hold of books to protect the future. Private individuals with a defined love of their books, like the girl in the signing queue, have protected our stories through dark times. Ray Bradbury's characters each memorizing a novel in *Fahrenheit 451* are protective collectors, as much as the rebels hiding books behind walls in the dystopian film *Equilibrium,* or the wise Yemeni devotee who, in some unknown war-torn century long ago, hid a seventh-century Koran behind the wall of Sana'a's Great Mosque, a book rediscovered, albeit accidentally, by builders who initially put it in a rubbish sack, in 1974. Collectors are protectors.

If the world's great libraries have helped us to sustain a sort of civilization, we owe them to those private collectors rather than to governments. There are weighty books telling the stories of the world's libraries, but many of the gloriously eccentric collectors who kicked them off, often with a philosophic purpose, lie forgotten in their graves. There is a quiet heroism about their belief in a book collection. We need never cower at the admission desks of our national libraries, for, quite apart from our taxes financing them, they would not exist without us. It is a thought-provoking fact that governments maintain and manipulate state libraries, but rarely originate them.

The collection of the antiquary Robert Cotton, for instance, became the foundation of the British Library, but only because Cotton campaigned via Parliament for the state to acquire his books, which greatly outnumbered the King's collection. Far from being financially motivated, according to one historian Cotton 'virtually gave his books to the nation'. England's other copyright library, the Bodleian, was built up by Queen Elizabeth's determined gentleman-usher Thomas Bodley. An

Aberystwyth doctor gave not only his books but £20,000 to establish the National Library of Wales. The Library of Congress was originally simply a resource for politicians, until Thomas Jefferson's own collection became the foundation of a national library for the people. The millionaires Pierpont Morgan and Henry Huntington founded what are now free libraries of national importance in America. The Bibliothèque Nationale started as a private royal library. Polish National Library? Entirely the creation of two book-mad brothers. National Library of Italy? The Medici family's book collection. National Library of Germany? A visionary booksellers' project, foisted on to parliament amid the fervour of the 1848 revolution. Today's little known library in Aix-en-Provence, distinguished out of all proportion to the town's size, is the legacy of a local, Jean-Baptiste Piquet (d. 1786), who explicitly bequeathed it as a *'depôt publique'* of 80,000 books.

Although Islamic collectors form such a vast constellation that they would merit their own book, I cannot resist including one here, the great Persian scholar al-Sahib ibn Abbad (d. 995). The Emir of Persia offered him the plum job of running the empire's most important province, Khorasan, but he declined on the grounds that it would take 400 camels to move his personal library. Determined to seed books in the empire as civilizing influences, he encouraged the establishment of state libraries in Qom, Isfahan and Tehran, the latter containing 200,000 books.

The Extraordinary Odyssey of the Codex Mendoza.

Empire building was also the instinct which began one book's journey via a rogue's gallery of owners. The Codex Mendoza is a unique survival, an account of indigenous culture written by an Aztec scribe. Looking at it – it is browsable online for those unable to buy the $400 California University reprint – is like time-travelling to sixteenth-century Mexico. Pictures dominate the text, graphic novel style: here are scenes of everyday gardening, cooking, worshipping and fighting, and intimate depictions of child-rearing.

Traditional Aztec books such as this were systematically collected and burned by the Spanish invaders as part of their strategy to extinguish Aztec civilization. The Codex, made in the early 1500s, began its odyssey when the Viceroy of Mexico, Antonio de Mendoza (1495–1552), sent it to Madrid as an intelligence tool: by understanding Aztec culture, it could better be destroyed. Mendoza was a violent bully, so it is pleasing to report that his intelligence plan went awry. The ship carrying the Codex was attacked and taken by pirates in the Caribbean. Here began the odyssey of the Codex, which aroused so many passions that its tale is reminiscent of Tolkien's ring, darkly enchanting its lovers through the centuries and, in one case, wreaking their destruction.

The pirate captain kept the book, and one can imagine him browsing it in his candlelit cabin, a cutlass on his desk. Eventually he sold it in Paris, to André Thevet. Thevet was from sleepy Angoulême in the mid-French flatlands of Charente. His parents had put him into a Franciscan monastery at ten years old, but in adulthood he strayed from orthodox Christianity, developing an eccentric interest in indigenous cultures. The Codex inspired Thevet to conduct his own hazardous exploration of South America.

His personal museum of native art and his passionate curiosity got him a job as Cosmographer to King Francis, and 'Restaurateur des Lettres' – 'Restorer of Literature'. The royal

cosmographer, with his odd interests, was criticized by some
as a fake scholar, but in Paris he gained the friendship of the
Englishman Richard Hakluyt, Secretary of State to Queen
Elizabeth, friend of Drake and Raleigh and celebrator of English voyaging. As a boy in London, Hakluyt had seen 'certain
books of geography' on a table in a relative's house, which got
him hooked on tales of far-off lands. Another great respecter
of other belief systems, he risked his life by openly refusing to
take the Bible literally. Critics saw divine retribution in the red
spot on his face which would indeed grow into a fatal malaise.
Thevet showed the Codex to his English friend and Hakluyt's
admiration quickly turned to desire. He paid a reluctant Thevet the equivalent of about £1,000 for the Codex and took it
home to England.

In 1614 Hakluyt met Samuel Purchas, vicar of St Martin's
Ludgate, the church on the hill just below St Paul's Cathedral.
Purchas, the sixth child of an Essex wool merchant, was
another addict of tales of exotic lands. His book of travellers'
tales, *Hakluytus Posthumus, or Purchas his Pilgrimes, Contayning
a History of the World, in Sea Voyages, & Lande Travels, by English-
men and others* (1625), would be a classic for centuries. Samuel
Taylor Coleridge fell asleep reading Purchas's description of
Kubla Khan's palace, and wrote his famous poem about
Xanadu when he woke up. Soon after Hakluyt died, Purchas
bought up his entire library of travel exotica, including the
Codex.

Samuel Purchas possessed the Codex for six years before his
death in 1626. His son, also Samuel, did not share his father's
interest in far-off lands, having a passion in the back garden: he
wrote the first great beekeeping manual. He flogged off the
Codex to a lawyer down the road in Fleet Street, John Selden.
There is an irresistible contemporary description of Selden:

'he was very tall, I guesse about 6 foot high, sharp ovall face, head not very big, long nose inclining to one side, full popping Eie (gray). He was A Poet.' The scholarly Selden lived a blissful existence in a rambling top-floor flat in the Inner Temple. There, fellow poetry-lovers such as John Donne visited this 'humane, courteous and affable' humanist. There too, Selden learned fifteen languages, including Arabic and 'Ethiopic', and there, when not writing landmark legal texts or pursuing his lifelong affair with a countess, he penned essays defending divorce and cross-dressing. And, up in the top floor flat, the Codex found a happy, dry home for twenty-two years. Selden's respect for all cultures was extraordinary and unusual, so his death at seventy was an uncertain time for his 8,000 books, including the Codex Mendoza.

Fortunately, Selden's executors gave his books to the Bodleian Library in Oxford, where they were received by Thomas Barlow, the librarian. As a 'Reader in Metaphysics', Barlow was enthusiastic about the eclectic Selden treasures – they are still housed in the 'Selden wing' – but he foresaw a personal career problem. Cataloguing the Selden collection would take the rest of his working life: he resigned from the library to avoid that marathon task.

Into the eighteenth century and the more judgemental Victorian era, the delicate Codex was neglected and ignored. Damp, and even frost, afflicted the Bodleian's collections. Founder Thomas Bodley had forbidden any fires in his library for safety reasons; more than one reader died of illness contracted in this freezing temple of learning.

The Codex owes its ultimate survival to the oddest of all its champions. Edward King (1795–1837) was an Irish aristocrat who spent much of his life as a bookish recluse in the tower study of his castle in County Cork. Becoming fixated on the idea that the lost tribe of Israel might be linked to the Aztecs, he visited the Bodleian, where the splendidly named and irascible librarian Bulkeley Bandinel – an ex-vicar and enthusiastic purchaser of ancient bibles – grumpily disinterred the Codex Mendoza. King, for all his eccentricity, is credited with rediscovering the Aztec masterpiece, and it is thanks to him that it has been cared for ever since as one of the library's great treasures. He blew £32,000 on a multi-volume annotated reproduction of the book, hand-printed on vellum (calfskin). It was published in 1848. The venture ruined King, who died of typhus at forty-two, in a Dublin debtors' prison.

After its 500-year odyssey the Codex Mendoza is usually on display in the Bodleian. As a Curator told me in 2017, it is regularly removed and put in a lightless vault 'to rest'. From the heat of Mexico to a dark vault in Oxfordshire in 500 years: few books in history have such a perilously romantic past, dependent on such a gallery of gloriously misfit scholars.

Venus in the Attic

Thomas Isham (1555–1605) made his money in the Tudor wool trade but his heart was in books. In the 1590s he bought, from Leake's the bookseller in St Paul's Churchyard – 'at the signe of the greyhound'– Shakespeare's poem *Venus and Adonis*. In his lifetime, Shakespeare was known first and foremost as the author of this poem and yet few early copies of this erotically charged volume survive. Women loved the book for its feisty female heroine, who initiates sexual advances towards the hunter Adonis. Some feared the book's liberating effect: in the 1608 play by Thomas Middleton *A Mad World My Masters*, a husband confiscates his wife's copy of *Venus and Adonis*, fearing its aphrodisiac effect on her. In later centuries, the poem was often excluded from Shakespeare's collected works. Isham was untroubled by such prudery; he had already purchased Marlowe's translation of Ovid, a book which the church had ordered to be burnt. Both books were taken back to his cosy red-brick home, Lamport Hall in Northamptonshire. The house, now open to the public, is still owned by the Ishams. They were an anciently independent-minded family, who, among other things, opposed King John, and lent Richard III forty pounds, which he never repaid.

As Thomas Isham's poetic interests indicate, the Ishams were an emotionally expressive lot. Thomas's grand-daughter's diary of melancholy and doubt was published in 2016 and his great-grandson's diary, published in 1971, is simply the only known teenage diary of the seventeenth century. This great-grandson, also called Thomas, inherited the passion for books of Thomas senior. An attractive and popular figure, he continually overspent on books, especially on buying trips to Italy. Hoping to salvage his fortunes by marrying well, he tragically died on the eve of his wedding.

By 1654, the family fortunes were restored enough for a later Isham, Justinian, to add the fine classical frontage visible today at Lamport. In the general refurbishment, though, most of Thomas Isham's books, including the extremely rare early *Venus and Adonis*, were stored in the attic. This was a philistine oversight, but, as the frontage might indicate, Justinian was more into outward show than culture. A neighbour, Dorothy Osborne, thought him 'the vainest, most impertinent and self-conceited, coxcomb I ever met'.

Venus and Adonis stayed in the attic for 250 years, resting quietly as the Northamptonshire wind howled outside and long summer days baked the roof. As the Great Fire of London raged, the Bastille was stormed and the age of the steam train arrived, the book remained undisturbed.

It was the 10th baronet, Charles Isham, 1819–1903, who would rescue the book. The fame of this fairy-loving spiritualist and pioneer vegetarian today rests on his introduction of the garden gnome to England from Germany. (The Ishams were never predictable: his gnome-hating daughter celebrated his death by blowing Lamport Hall's garden gnomes to bits with a rifle.) In 1867 the perennially curious Charles Isham went into the attic and discovered the *Venus and Adonis*. It was sold to a London bookseller in 1893, and again in 1919 for £15,000 to the American collector Henry Huntington, in whose Californian library it remains, publicly accessible.

We can be grateful to the 'coxcomb' Justinian for unintentionally preserving this book pristinely in his attic. Like any work with an erotic theme, copies of *Venus* were so well-thumbed that they usually fell apart over the centuries.

Renaissance and Enlightenment Bibliophiles

Private collectors in Europe reflected their times. John Dee's Renaissance blend of mysticism and classical scholarship imbued his library, which was bigger than that of either Cambridge or Oxford University. His lifelong quest to find the philosopher's stone dominated his collecting. With what John Aubrey described as 'a long beard as white as milke', he 'wore a gowne like an artist's gowne, with hanging sleeves', and had a conjuror's reputation: local children were afraid of him.

Dee felt about the dissolution of the monasteries, with their great libraries, as we might feel about the 2015 destruction of Palmyra. As a boy in the time of Henry VIII he noticed the fine illuminated lettering on ancient parchments but 'it was the custom' then to use them as dust-wrappers for printed books, or worse. He used to visit William Stump, the Rector of Malmesbury, a boozer with his own still. Stump used manuscripts from the nearby abbey to plug the 'bung-hole' of his 'ale-barrell'. 'He sayd nothing did it so well; which me thought did grieve me then to see.' The antiquary John Leland made a similar lament to Thomas Cromwell, whom one does not imagine listening with any great sincerity: 'Cuttings from ancient manuscripts are being used by iconoclasts to clean their shoes and candlesticks [and sold] to sope sellers.' You can tell that Shakespeare felt a similar poignancy at the loss of monastic culture from his line in Sonnet 73 about 'Bare ruin'd choirs, where late the sweet birds sang.'

Under Queen Mary, Dee published a *Supplication ... Concerning the Recovery and Preservation of Ancient Monuments and Old Excellent Writers*. Later, under Elizabeth, Dee became the Queen's personal astrologer, and expressed to Her Majesty the hope that his books would one day form a 'national library'. They included important works collected from dissolved monasteries and from his extensive travels. Poverty, however, overshadowed his later years and the collection was dispersed. Some of it did end up in the British Library, though. Dee buried some choice books in his Mortlake garden by the Thames. Robert Cotton, who acquired many of Dee's books during his lifetime, dug more up after his death. An undistinguished block of flats called John Dee House is on the site of Dee's home, but a suspected fragment of Dee's garden wall remains, and there may be more books for the nation under the tarmac where washing now hangs.

Like so many collectors, Dee's worldly career was always secondary to his philosophical life, and it is fair to assume that he partly inspired Shakespeare to create Prospero, that other burier of mystical books, for whom his library 'was dukedom enough'.

An Italian Renaissance polymath had more luck than Dee in leaving his entire collection for the good of the nation. Frederic Borromeo wrote to a friend in the late 1500s hoping, in making his collection public, that 'such crude centuries may not return' as Italy had suffered in medieval times. To this mission, his Ambrosiana Library in Milan has credibly contributed for 500 years.

He was a cardinal, and although part of his mission, as with many contemporary German and Spanish collectors, was to provide a firm base from which to refute heresy, he was passionately eclectic, starting with the childhood discovery of an old book on cosmography in the family home. Determined, like Aerosmith, not to miss a thing, he read whilst being shaved and always travelled in a litter so that he could read on journeys, reading which led him to write about things as various as why birds sing, angels' habits, Egyptian hieroglyphics and cooking in Iceland.

Galileo wrote a covering letter when he donated his own book to Borromeo's collection, saying that it was a selfish gift in truth, because his own self-esteem would go up if his book was in 'your heroic and immortal library'. Other books included an ancient Irish volume which turned out to be a palimpsest, or over-written manuscript. The submerged text was three lost speeches of Cicero. But Borromeo was no precious antiquarian. Refreshingly, when offered a finely bound Cicero he said: 'I would like it more if it were less clean and more used.'

This burly and likeable character, who looked like a mid-life Oliver Reed, was no mere indoor scholar: his compassionate action in the 1627 famine, and heroism in tending to plague victims, became the subject of Manzoni's great nineteenth-century bestseller *The Betrothed*.

Other treasures, all still in the collection, included a fourth-century Homer, a sixth-century biblical codex, numerous Greek manuscripts and hundreds of Hebrew books. He sent agents out to get Japanese printed books and persuaded the Grand Master of Malta to collect books in Arabic from passing ships, to add to those which were sent from a Spanish Arabist in Naples and an agent in Cairo. When he heard about Glagolitic, he added books in that ancient script to his shelves. His books representing the Armenians included the first dictionary of their language. His lifelong frustration was not finding books written in hieroglyphics. As he wrote, 'Even books from other faiths give us benefits and are both beautiful and beneficial.'

The greatest treasure is the Atlantic Codex, a bound book made up of about a thousand pages of Leonardo's notebooks, including his thoughts on maths, flight, parachutes and alchemy. Welcoming such a range of books into a collection was risky in an age of Papal censorship, but the Cardinal had a novel solution, in wording which some of us might be tempted to use in tricky everyday situations. He stipulated in his librarian's contract that no catalogue of the books should be freely shown to anyone 'for certain reasons well known to us'.

The librarian would be kept busy; contractually he had to write a learned work 'within three years of appointment', and the collection was open, free for all, from its inception in 1609. An English visitor in 1670 noted this unusual liberality:

It is not so coy as the other libraries, which scarce let themselves be seen; this opens its dores publikly to all comers and goers, and suffers them to read what book they please.

The library is one of the world's greatest, with over a million books, even after Napoleon's troops stole some (still in Paris), and the RAF bombed Borromeo's original reading room into rubble in 1943. Borromeo's ideal of open access is more alive than ever: the entire Atlantic Codex was placed online in 2019, and the library is still open 'to all over 18' who dress decorously.

Like Dee and Borromeo, Samuel Pepys wanted his books to outlast his life and any career achievements. He juggled a demanding Admiralty job with building a library which he planned to be a public asset, directing that it be kept separately at Oxford, as it still is. Finding himself one day surrounded by piles of books on chairs, he commissioned a dockyard carpenter to make glass-fronted bookcases for his collection, the first bookcases of their type. He chose to make the collection 'different from the Pompous ... libraries of princes', and it included arcana, chapbooks and ephemera. After Pepys' death, the books and the bookcases went to Oxford in a sealed convoy of wagons.

In Italy, soon after Pepys, a less well-known collector amassed such a comprehensive houseful of books that it is still the basis of Florence's state library. In his will, Antonio Magliabechi donated all his 40,000 books and 10,000 manuscripts to the state. His bibliophilia came before all trivial considerations such as dress (he always wore the same old black cloak and doublet) or food (he lived on eggs, bread and water.)

As a boy he was an illiterate backstreet urchin, until his parents found him a job in a fruit shop. He was entranced by the writings on the paper used to wrap fruit, and it was as he sat outside one day, poring over such paper, that the bookseller next door offered to teach him to read. Before long he was fluent in Greek, Latin and Hebrew, becoming famous as a walking encyclopaedia with an almost magical speed-reading ability. To test him, a printer lent him a manuscript to read before he took it to be printed. Later, pretending to have lost it, he asked Magliabechi to rewrite it, which he did, almost word-perfect.

His house in old Florence was soon overflowing with books; they were on the stairs, and, in every room, visitors had to squeeze sideways along narrow canyons between books. Many visitors left astonished accounts of Antonio's house. Once you had manoeuvred yourself into his chamber, you conversed with him as he lay in a wooden cradle which was surrounded by books and connected to them by cobwebs. 'Don't hurt the spiders!' he usually barked. One perfumed visiting nobleman wrote that he lived 'as a savage', but there is something appealing about Magliabechi's spider-respecting simplicity.

His solution to heating was unique. Rather than waste money heating the whole room, he had tiny stoves designed which were fastened to his arms. Singed sleeves and scorched hands were a price he was happy to pay to be able to carry on reading without having to tend a fireplace.

This diminutive Florentine, with his large loose-lipped mouth, shining coal-black eyes and disregard for appearances, was sought after across Europe as a human database. He never wrote a book, but many were dedicated to him, in thanks for his great knowledge. Cosimo de' Medici, who appointed him librarian, once asked for a book, to be told that it was 'in the Sultan's library at Constantinople, right-hand side, the third shelf down'.

Magliabechi was no obsessive hoarder: he knew all his books and several sources attest that he had read them all. He collected for a purpose, for inner transformation, and in this he was a Renaissance urban shaman, known to be fond of the quote: 'It is insufficient to read much, if we read without reflection.' He died at the then very great age of eighty-one, leaving all his money to the city poor, among whom he had grown up.

In this male-run early modern world some notable women book collectors stand out – Queen Christina of Sweden and Catherine the Great, for instance. Less well-known, and with a less privileged lifestyle, was a Mexican, Juana Inés de la Cruz (1648–95). The illegitimate daughter of a largely absent father, she grew up on a peasant smallholding by a volcano with her four siblings, some of whom were step-siblings; details of her early life are hard to come by. Her grandfather loved books, and in his house she taught herself to read and write Latin before she was five. Greek followed soon afterwards and as an adolescent she learned Aztec: writing poems in that language gave her a private outlet. An Aztec linguist has claimed that, on the basis of these poems, 'she was very fluent in spoken Nahuatl [Aztec]'.

University in Mexico City was barred to her, and her mother discouraged her plan to gain entry by disguising herself as a man, so she collected books – more than 4,000 eventually – and continued to educate herself. At seventeen she held her own in a debate with senior theologians, and her beauty and erudition got her a job as lady-in-waiting at the Spanish Viceroy's court, but this life, during which she refused many proposals of marriage, was a gilded cage, intellectually unfulfilling. Like many female book-lovers of her era, she became a nun as the easiest way to pursue a life of study. As she openly admitted, aged twenty, she wanted 'no fixed occupation which might curtail my freedom to study'.

She shopped around the orders and, after a spell with the Carmelites, took her book collection into the convent of the

Hieronymites, an order that valued books and learning in the manner of their founder, St Jerome. There she wrote poems and plays and debated philosophy with visiting scholars, albeit from behind a screen of bars. Even this restricted intellectual freedom was to get her into trouble.

After a letter she wrote criticizing a Jesuit sermon was published, without her permission, she was formally admonished by the local bishop for her preoccupation with worldly affairs. Her response, the *Reply to Sister Philotea*, was a moving defence of the right to books and learning, and an early feminist manifesto. Reading, she argued, should be a habit shared among women as much as activities such as cooking tips and needlework techniques. And those activities need not exclude learning: 'we can perfectly well philosophize whilst cooking dinner'. But, after her father-confessor also rebuked her, in 1694 her book collection was either confiscated or sold off – history is hazy on its fate. She was forty-six, and died next year as a result of ministering to plague victims: she contracted plague herself. Neglected for centuries, she got a beating from male academics in the twentieth century:

'a schizophrenic, mentally disordered' – Ludwig Pfandl (1953)
'her poems are vulgar stunts' – Frederick Luciani (1960)
'a pseudo-mystic' – Gerard Fox Flynn (1986)

She is now widely studied and admired, her poems are published in many languages, her music is performed, a university is named after her, and she appears on Mexican banknotes. Margaret Atwood wrote a poem about her in 2007 ('your exploding syllables litter the lawn'), and a play about her was performed by the RSC.

Another generally forgotten collector lived in eighteenth-century France, and remarkably his collection still exists, for public use. The Bibliothèque de l'Arsenal in Paris is a monument to the collecting passion of Marc-Antoine, the Marquis de Paulmy. Situated in the old residence of the Masters of Artillery, just east of Notre Dame Cathedral, it is a fine, symmetrical four-storey stone building. De Paulmy insisted to Louis XVI that it be maintained as a public library for posterity. Born into a line of politicians, the Marquis showed little interest in affairs of state, although he had a stab at various offices, including Master of the King's Stables. His true love was books, and his excessive spending on them forced him to sell his house in 1769, incurring paternal displeasure. His father, René-Louis, the Foreign Minister – political nickname The Beast – also despaired of Marc-Antoine's vegetarianism and tendency to laugh a lot at comic plays, but not weep at tragedies. 'My son, without being hated, will not be loved,' was his mistaken judgement: de Paulmy is loved today for his books.

In collecting his 100,000 volumes, he was concerned with the text, rather than fine bindings, and he expounded his mission as follows: 'The study of the Human Spirit's progress, even of its errors, and the study of history are the principal objects of attention of someone forming a library.' This embracing of errors meant that, like Pepys, he collected, and saved for later historiography, some real exotica, deploying agents all over Europe to find it. In England, the great bibliophile Horace Walpole was his supplier. Along with the usual Caxtons, early copies of Chaucer and Shakespeare, he bought from all over the world extensive Oriental literature, Croat poetry, forgotten romances, a Chinese life of Christ and the definitive book on Jesus's umbilical cord, an object which some of us will be surprised to hear can be found in a small church near Rheims.

The Marquis expanded his collection by buying the vast library of the Duc de la Vallière, one of the great bookmen of the *ancien régime*. Although humbler folk are rightly celebrated in this book for reading in adversity, the privileged faced their own challenges. Like de Paulmy, the Duc was expected to spend his life in public duties. Made colonel of a regiment at nineteen, and thereafter a provincial governor, Captain of the Hunt and Grand Falconer, he did not feel he could refuse when the king's mistress made him run the royal theatre. Despite all that, he pursued his love of books, and mixed with writers such as Voltaire and Diderot rather than apparatchiks. The Duc's habit of buying entire libraries and discarding duplicates and lesser treasures has led a French writer to diagnose him with '*boulimie bibliophagique*'. According to his librarian, the Abbé Rive, de la Vallière sold 20,000 books each year for several years.

Unlike some vanity collectors, de Paulmy was a voracious reader who had read 'nearly all' his books. Many bear his marginal notes. Sadly his two great bibliographies, one of sixteen and one of seventy volumes, were never finished. He was 'invariably good-mannered', and on his deathbed could tell his daughter that he had 'no dishonest action to reproach myself with', not an assurance many politicians could make.

In 1789 the mob swept towards the Bibliothèque de l'Arsenal from the Bastille but the porter quickly changed his clothes and assured them that the building had no aristocratic connection. Improbably, they left the building alone.

Although de Paulmy wanted the library to be free, it is not now. The Bibliothèque Nationale has taken it over, and the Arsenal website explains, after a mission statement about providing 'the widest access', the recommendation to readers to acquire its €20 'culture pass' (state officials get in free).

'The Leviathan of Book Collectors'

The nineteenth-century author of the 800-page *Bibliomania* bestowed the above title on the son of Thomas Rawlinson, publican at the Mitre in Fenchurch Street. Thomas married Mary, the landlord's daughter at the Devil in the Strand. Their first child was the great bibliophile, also Thomas (d. 1725). Initially pushed towards a career in law by his parents, he discovered that his interest in that was 'minimal'. Books were his thing, because of that sense of their potential for avoiding history's errors, a motive which crops up repeatedly among collectors. As young Thomas put it, the age needs 'Monitors to Goodness', so it was his duty to be the 'foster-parent to orphaned books'. The phrase has the ring of Borges and of Sebald's care for 'the orphaned fact'. His grandfather, Mary's old dad at the Devil, had a soft spot for the boy's idealism and gave him a lifelong annuity, ring-fenced for book purchases.

Young Thomas's collecting determined the shape of his life. He had soon brought so many books to his Gray's Inn rooms that he had to sleep in the passage, so he moved downmarket to a flat in Aldersgate Street, where he frequented a coffee shop. There he met Amy Frewin, whom we would now call a barista, and married her. His friends' criticism of her 'questionable reputation' seems to have been mere casual snobbery. His book spending sunk him in debt and a speculative investment in the government-backed South Sea Company cost him dearly when the 'South Sea Bubble' burst. He died a broken man at forty-four, but there is a happy ending, or at least one which justifies his faith in books.

His father had fourteen more children, and number eight, Richard (d. 1755), also got the book bug, and the sense of a public biblio-mission. These were dark times for history, an era in which the national psyche was riven by civil conflict with the Jacobites, and stoked up by war with both Spain and Prussia. Our relationship with Europe split the nation. Through books, he wrote, 'we must provide for posterity in this ungrateful age'. He made his personal motto 'I collect, I preserve', and, as well as travelling Europe and haunting auctions for treasures, he scoured London grocers' shops and candle-makers' premises for broken-up books being used as pie-paper and candle wrapping. No other civil servant or historian was doing that.

Although most of Thomas's collection had to be sold, in various coffee-house auctions which lasted a total of over 300 days, Richard retained for his own collection many treasures, but only against the wishes of Amy Frewin's new husband, John, who wanted to sell everything. Richard bought back a lot of his brother's books subsequently; he became a comfortably-off bishop who could afford to endow a professorship of Anglo-Saxon at Oxford. The professorship idea was triggered by a desire for his country to know more about its own polyglot roots and stop bickering with itself.

Each year he gave books to the Bodleian Library, including one of its great treasures, the 1092 *Annals of Innisfallen*, an Irish history so important that Republican politicians still ask for its repatriation. As old age loomed he decided to divide his whole collection between the Bodleian Library and the Society of Antiquaries, of which he was vice-president. The Society, however, discovering his Jacobite sympathies, booted him out; so the Bodleian got the lot. The faith of his old grandfather, the publican at the Devil, paid off, and thanks to his imaginative annuity to young Thomas, the open-access Bodleian is enriched by the Rawlinson collection.

Toxic Topham

Naturally not all collectors were dedicated to the public good. The tale of the splendidly named Topham Beauclerk (1739–80) is a useful corrective. He jealously guarded his 30,000 books and would not lend one out, except to an insistent Edward Gibbon. They were housed in an imposing purpose-built library, designed by the fashionable classical architect Robert Adam, in Great Russell Street. It was bang opposite the British Museum which, Horace Walpole observed, 'has put the Museum's nose quite out of joint'.

A spoilt Etonian only child, his unpleasantness was widely recognized, and after his death Samuel Johnson recalled his 'maliciousness' and thought that 'such another will not often be found among mankind'. Boswell found his lewd banter irksome, but accompanied him on 'night-time frisks' in search of sex. His lineage was raffish: grandson of Nell Gwynn and King Charles, and son of a cynical fortune-hunter. With his stacked-heeled shoes, face-powder and towering wig, he was one of those super-affected dandies known as macaronis. They were literally unreliable, as young Miss Anne Pitt discovered when she stepped out of her carriage and leaned on Beauclerk's proffered arm. He staggered under the weight and she sprained her ankle.

Heaving with lice – he once infected the whole company at Blenheim Palace – 'as filthy as a beggar or gipsey', epically constipated, riddled with venereal disease and permanently bombed-out on the 400 drops of laudanum he took daily to counteract it, he was no great catch. One sympathizes with the married Viscountess Bolingbroke, née Lady Diana Spencer, who fell pregnant by him in 1767. The Viscount Bolingbroke, a drunk and serial adulterer, rapidly divorced her, and Topham married Diana two days later, largely for her money. According to Horace Walpole, 'Lady Di passed a most miserable life with him.' She put up with it for twelve years until he died at forty-one, but had to change the sheets daily. A Major Floyd met Topham in this late period and noted that he managed to be 'a torment to himself and all about him'. Diana's daughter Mary Beauclerk inherited the Topham improvidence, and had four sons by her half-brother, Bolingbroke's son George.

There is a pleasing coda: as a widow, Diana enjoyed twenty-eight years of freedom, becoming a distinguished painter, esteemed as a friend by Gibbon and Burke. After Topham's profligacy she was not wealthy, but lived on happily in a cottage by the Thames near Richmond. When visiting Joshua Reynolds' house on Wick Hill, Richmond, Edmund Burke saw the cottage in the distance and, turning to Gibbon, said, 'I am extremely glad to see her placed in that sweet house, released from all her cares.' The whereabouts of her grave is unknown.

What of the great library? To raise some cash Topham had mortgaged it to Diana's father, who sold it all off.

Bibliomania

In Europe, the phenomenon known as bibliomania took hold from the mid-eighteenth century, and really took off after the French Revolution, as aristocratic libraries flooded onto the market. There was a feeling, especially in Britain, that after the horrors of the guillotine, old family collections must be cherished. That view echoed in *Pride and Prejudice*, when Mr Darcy explains his sense of duty in keeping the Pemberley family library going. Book collecting became both fashionable and a fascination. A big library could be a status symbol like a flash car, no longer the mark of a musty obscurantist. For some, like Lord Lonsdale, it was no more than a status accessory: he remarked after his brother died, 'Poor old St George, he was the only one of us who ever read a book.'

Samuel Johnson often told the tale of how he dealt with one such philistine collector. When cataloguing Thomas Osborne's great library, he was ticked off for wasting his time reading and, with an unrepeatable oath, felled his employer with the weighty *Biblia Graeca Septuaginta* (published Frankfurt, 1594). The actual book was still known in a Cambridge bookshop in 1812, but has since disappeared.

Britain's most bibliomaniac collector, a genuine lover of both books and their contents, was Richard Heber (d. 1833), who filled eight houses with 150,000 books. He was a well-liked multilingual scholar, who kept spare copies of all but his rarest books so that he could lend them out freely. His best female friend, whom he considered marrying, was fellow book collector Frances Currer. In her Yorkshire house she quietly accumulated 20,000 books, a collection of global significance which rivalled Earl Spencer's Althorp library and the Duke of Devonshire's at Chatsworth. Like most women collectors I have encountered, her obscurity was self-engineered. Thomas Dibdin wanted to feature her in his 800-page *Bibliomania* but she refused such publicity. He told a friend that 'she has a heart as big as St Paul's Dome and as warm as Volcanic lava.' The financial aid she gave the Brontë sisters at nearby Haworth has only recently been uncovered. Charlotte Brontë's pseudonym, Currer Bell, was a tribute. Many of her 20,000 books are now in Bradford Public Library.

It is not known if Currer and Heber consummated their closeness, but he had a homosexual relationship with a nineteen-year-old man. Tragically, when this was discovered many friends turned against him, including Walter Scott, who expressed his 'horror' at such 'unnatural practices'. The patriotic magazine and whipper-up of cheap emotion, *John Bull* (last issue, 1960) exposed him publicly. Heber had to resign as an MP and died alone in Pimlico, having just sent off one last order for three books. His will was found with difficulty, hidden behind books. Much of his collection remains a significant part of the British Library.

Heber's guru in book-hunting was Isaac Gosset (d. 1812), an obscure figure whose reputation is overshadowed by his father, also Isaac, who boasted an unusual ability to make a lifelike wax head of someone in half an hour. The bookman Isaac has left his mark in the Bodleian with an important range of classical texts. Although no blue plaque marks his house just north of Oxford Street, his death in 1812 was commemorated by a poem, 'The Tears of the Booksellers', such was his reputation. His small, deformed figure wearing an outmoded tricorn hat was a welcome feature at auctions for decades. From his seat just below the rostrum he would utter his familiar cry of 'A pretty copy, a pretty copy'.

Gosset was Oxford-educated, and rich enough to indulge his habit, but his clever contemporary Francis Douce (d. 1834) was capriciously deprived of education and needed to work all his life. His parents, determined that he should not outshine his elder brother, the dim heir, took him out of school and put him in an academy run by an 'ignorant life-guardsman'. Later, they sabotaged his attempts to get into university. He not only educated himself, but wrote still-useful works on popular customs and a brave attack on government repression, informed by his collection of 18,000 books.

His childless marriage to Isabella Price was unhappy, partly because of her mental illness or 'certain peculiarities of her disposition' as one diarist put it. He resented the distraction of work, although he was a much-valued British Museum keeper respected by the likes of Joseph Banks.

When Douce was forty-one his father died and Francis presumed that an inheritance would enable him to stop working, but the evil brother had advised his parents not to leave money to Francis 'as he will only waste it on books'. Courageously, he jacked in the job anyway, and the British Library has gamely put his celebrated resignation letter on their website. It bullet-pointed his reasons for going, which sound consolingly contemporary for anyone in a behemoth-like organization:

> The objectionable organization of the Museum.
> Working conditions, damp and cold, 'an oven in
>   summer, with unwholesome air from sinks and
>   drains'.
> Overwork, but a 'total absence of aid in my department'.
> 'Colleagues far from fascinating and sometimes
>   repulsive'.
> 'Motley and trifling committees', with an 'affected air of
>   consequence'.
> 'The fiddle faddle requisition of incessant reports'.

The kicker was a suspicious staff 'system of espionage', under which he had been asked 'to report on Mr Bean'.

Douce's faith in the universe paid off. Soon after his premature retirement his friend, the childless sculptor and notorious miser Joseph Nollekens, left him £50,000, the equivalent of £5 million today. Douce was always a generous lender of books to scholars, and his will donated the whole collection to the Bodleian.

The Spencers and their Books

I joined Waterstones Booksellers in 1988 and was sent by Tim Waterstone to work in the High Street Kensington bookshop, a short walk from Kensington Palace. It was a beautiful three-floor bookshop on a corner site where you could bump into David Hockney or Van Morrison, Mick Jagger or Madonna. Also Morrissey, as a former colleague recalls, 'before he became a wanker'. Before I joined the company I had loved browsing there late into the evening – it closed at 10 p.m. – especially in the cavernous basement, or on the first floor with its window seats where you could leaf through £90 art books unsurveilled. It was a haven for many, including Princess Diana. It seems extraordinary now but she left her protection officers outside, and nobody hassled her in the shop as she browsed alone. She bought fiction, but also books from the basement on psychology and spirituality.

Diana was brought up with little thought for her education, and found her own way to books. If we cosmically triangulate the princess in that bookshop, the compass points include not only a horrible underpass in Paris but a stupendous library, now lost to her family, created a few boughs up her family tree. The second Earl, George Spencer (1758–1834), collected the greatest private library in the world at Althorp, where Diana is buried. The tale of its fate is Spencerian in both its marbled beauty and its ultimate benefit to an infinitely wide public.

George was tall with an athletic figure, but shy, very unlike his tempestuous sister Georgiana, Duchess of Devonshire. He loved books and their contents. Unlike Diana, dumped in a Gstaad finishing school, George had one-to-one tutoring with the Sanskritist William Jones, a towering Enlightenment intellect, before going on to Trinity College Cambridge. Later on, he was given an honorary degree by Oxford and invited to join Samuel Johnson's Literary Club. His mother, Margaret, a draper's grand-daughter and renowned philanthropist, set him a great example of learning, reading voraciously and punning in Latin and ancient Greek. Her personal filing systems and administrative skills were remarkable, and these methodical traits emerged in her son. His memory and eye for detail were well known: he could recognize a book's printer just by a glance at its type. Every one of his books was marked in the same place with its accession details.

At twenty-four, he fell 'out of his senses' for the 22-year-old artist Lavinia Bingham. Controversially, she had no dowry, but they married and had eight children. She shared his passion for books and ideas, counterbalancing his shyness by turning Althorp into a great salon for cultural visitors.

As his acquisitions from all over Europe grew, he built the 200-foot Long Library, occasioning a servant to wryly suggest his master buy a Shetland pony to navigate the collection. It was so compendious that the historian Edward Gibbon had real trouble leaving once he had started browsing them. Eventually the floor started creaking, books overflowed on to the floor of the picture gallery above, with the result that the library ceiling collapsed.

The collection is routinely called the greatest because of quality as well as quantity: 4,000 incunabula from the cradle of printing, before 1500, including a 1472 Dante. In a famous auction, Spencer lasted 112 bids against the Marquess of Bland-ford to try and get the first edition of Boccacio's *Decameron*. For a long time the £2,260 which the Marquess paid to secure the book was a record figure for a book sale; he sold it years later to Spencer for £900.

George Spencer's determination in getting books was artful. He bought a Gutenberg Bible in Pall Mall, and somehow per-suaded Lincoln Cathedral to sell him several books from the press of Caxton, the father of English printing; he eventually had fifty-five. He collected Europe-wide. An Italian count described as 'a valuable helpmate' by Spencer got him a 1469 Virgil and the first illustrated book printed in Italy. Other suppli-ers included a Bavarian monk, a Munich librarian, an Augsburg professor, an impoverished Neapolitan duke and some dodgy Capuchins in Vienna.

The library's nemesis loomed in late Victorian times, in the form of John, the fifth Earl Spencer, who took more care of his handlebar moustache and celebrated beard, which was bigger than his head, than of the family books. A biographer admit-ted he had 'little claim to intellectual pursuits'. Distracted by cricket at Harrow, he gained scant education and spent much of his adulthood shooting, foxhunting and oppressing Ireland. He once took out a £15,000 loan just to maintain his hounds. As Viceroy of Ireland he is remembered for suspending habeas corpus there. In 1892 he put a notice in *The Times* declaring his intention to sell the whole Althorp library at Sotheby's. It could have so easily been dispersed among a multitude of col-lectors but, by happenstance, the integrity of the library had an unlikely saviour.

The Girl from Havana

Early in Victoria's reign a Liverpool merchant in Cuba married Juana, a local girl eighteen years his junior. When he died his widow took the children to Europe, including five-year-old Enriqueta. Years of hardship followed for the family. When Enriqueta was twentyish she got a job as secretary to a multi-millionaire Manchester textile merchant, John Rylands. This was about 1860 – nobody seems to know exactly when. One account says that her job was as 'companion to Mrs Rylands'. Rylands was a liberal philanthropist but, like many self-made men, frugal. His wine was famously nasty, and he charged for vegetables from his garden: 'the only way to make a garden pay,' he said.

Rylands' wife Martha died in 1875. He may well have been simpatico with Enriqueta before that, because he married her within a few months. He was seventy-five, she was thirty-two, but it was a genuine love-match, if no doubt as speckled with numerical calculations as any. After his death in 1888, she founded a theological library in his memory and one of the booksellers she used is still going, Sotheran's, just off Piccadilly. I recently phoned Chris Saunders, their managing director, to get a copy of their limited-edition company history; they are still doing fine. Saunders' predecessor in 1892, Alexander Railton, saw the *The Times* notice about the Althorp sale and, as a book-lover, he hoped that the legendary library might be bought intact. He cut out the notice and posted it without comment to Enriqueta.

She was interested, and had inherited the bulk of John Rylands' millions, since all seven of his children by an earlier marriage had died young. She contacted the senior partner at Sotheby's, Ed Hodge, who was acting for Earl Spencer. Hodge agreed to reserve the library for a week whilst Mrs Rylands considered the price. Although the New York Public Library then offered more, Sotheby's honoured their commitment and sold to Rylands. Enriqueta saved the collection for the nation, and made it the great free library it is today.

She added to the eighteenth-century Spencer collection another library, 'perhaps the finest private library of the nine-teenth century', that of Alexander Lindsay, the Earl of Crawford. Lindsay was one of many book-lovers to eroticize the acquisition of books, saying that he had 'succumbed to the charms of the bibliomaniacal Circe' (the Homeric enchantress). It is poetic that the pompous Lindsay, whose wealth was founded on the sweat of workers in his coalmines, should have unintentionally helped to set up a great open-access book collection.

To house it all Enriqueta commissioned a huge neo-Gothic library to be built in the slums of Manchester, knowing that it would regenerate the area. It certainly did, and it still domi-nates the great thoroughfare of Deansgate. Enriqueta had definite ideas for her library: she overrode the architect by designing several details herself, and sacked the librarian after four months because he was too interested in the books as antiques. A strong-willed woman, passionately secretive, uninterested in Manchester's social scene and self-effacing, it is typical of her that the John Rylands Library is named after a man who had no idea of its conception. It was declared open on their wedding anniversary.

The Misanthrope's Tale

In the Victorian era, outside the silent libraries of the English aristocracy, the distant whistle of the steam train announced a new age of wealth based on industry. Many old families had railway lines diverted away from their estates, but they still could not escape the Steam Age, and the resultant influx of tycoons into their class. One such magnate, Thomas Phillipps (1792–1872), was as protective of his books as Enriqueta was open-handed, and his pathology caused a legal tangle which was only ended in 1977.

Phillipps was the illegitimate child of a Manchester calico merchant and, driven in part by his father's desire that he should become a 'proper gentleman', a lifelong book collector. He occasionally meddled in the family business, but really never had a job, nor did he need one. No Freudian allegiance is required to ascribe his irascibility and feuding proclivity to his being brought up by his father, a gouty old moaner, after his mother ran off with someone called Fred Judd. Although she lived on until her son was fifty-nine, she had nothing to do with him. I am reminded of my father's compensatory book collecting, connected to his own father and mother abandoning him as a baby to a grumpy spinster. They say 'books do furnish a room'; they make a home too, as surely as moss and twigs make nests.

Phillipps had 110 books by the age of six, and, on more than one occasion as an adult, he strolled into a bookshop and bought the entire stock. He especially hunted out manuscript books, often on vellum, describing himself attractively as a 'vello-maniac'. He hunted down several important books of that nature in gold-beaters' premises. Gold-beaters, then and now, hammer gold until it is gold leaf, so thin that it can be gently blown into position. For thousands of years, until the mid-twentieth century, the only material which the gold could be sandwiched between whilst being hammered for hours was 'goldbeater's skin', a fine vellum made from the intestinal wall of an ox. Its unique combination of strength and smoothness accounts for its use in the condom industry, but it made good book pages too, so gold-beaters would sometimes buy vellum manuscript libraries from house clearances before book collectors got to them. He also haunted tailors' premises, searching for remnants of printed books; they used waste paper in pattern-making. Reuse of paper was extensive, with old books even being used to rebind newer ones. Phillipps's obsessive collecting urge caused him to buy up bulk amounts by weight from waste paper merchants, purchases which continued to yield up treasures for decades, such as the Caxton *Ovid* found in 1964 and sold for over a million pounds.

At forty-two, Phillips was living in a Worcestershire mansion called Middle Hill, under the softening influence of three daughters and a patient wife, who tolerated his overspending on books and underspending on pest control; one rare wifely outburst about her life in the house is recorded: 'I have been booked out of one wing and ratted out of the other.' This uneasy stasis was disturbed by the arrival of a clever young man called James Halliwell, newly graduated from Cambridge, who had written to Phillipps to ask about his books. Invited to stay in the house and assist in their care, he fell in love with Henrietta, his new employer's 23-year-old daughter. The old man convinced himself that James was a fortune-hunter, and opposed the marriage, but the couple eloped.

He never forgave them, but in one of his debt-management wheezes, his house was entailed partly to Henrietta. To ensure that she inherited a wilderness, he adopted a scorched-earth policy. He felled the great avenues and woods at Middle Hill, removed the fittings from the house and moved his whole collection to a gloomy neo-classical vault-like building in Cheltenham, now part of a school, a house so cavernous that Phillipps rode his horse around inside it. The move took over

100 carthorses and 238 wagons laden with books. Some horses collapsed en route. Middle Hill was deliberately neglected. Local ne'er-do-wells smashed windows and doors. Cattle roamed the stately rooms.

As Phillipps's collection grew he became a feared bidder at auctions, often outbidding big museums, and he began to play an endgame to get his collection preserved in one of them. First, with breathtaking arrogance, he said he would sell to the Bodleian Library if he could be made their chief librarian. They refused, so he offered his books to the British Museum Library if they would make him a trustee. They did, but found the many suggestions he made at trustee meetings unacceptable: he resigned in disgust. Finally, he discovered a distant branch of properly aristocratic Phillippses and made approaches to get them to take the library. They repelled his advances, so he carried on obsessively cataloguing his books and increasingly locking them in 'coffin-like' metal chests for fear of fire.

When he fell off his library ladder and died in 1872, his will was found to be an essay in misanthropy. Not only were Roman Catholics and the Halliwells barred from entering his library, it could not be sold, but was to be preserved in its Cheltenham home as if in formaldehyde. After decades of legal shenanigans the books were eventually sold off in batches, the last lot in New York in 1977. In a grim Thomas Hardy-esque ending, poor Henrietta Halliwell fell off her horse and died a few months after her father. Her husband, James, had a happier fate. He went on to become a leading expert on nursery rhymes and the Elizabethan era. He was the first publisher of John Dee's diary, and was instrumental in the purchase of Shakespeare's house in Stratford for the nation. He died at his house near Brighton in 1889 and bequeathed his own library, 'full of rare and curious works', to various public collections.

Upstairs in the Fin de Siècle

A fifteen-minute drive from where I sit in Kent, at St Margaret's Bay, there used to be a hotel with a telescope in the bar. Guests such as Ian Fleming were able to see the time on Calais Town Hall clock from this vantage point. And yet, despite this proximity, Calais remains very differently French, with different values (the humblest shop windows are specially decorated for Easter, for example) and another world-view.

This French difference, whether in films or books, clothes or cooking, has been fiercely protected. Words have mattered a lot. The Académie Française made valiant attempts in the 1980s to stop the use of words such as 'le weekend', and have not given up since. As globalization advanced, an Académie report in 2008 described the language as 'in crisis'. Some recent prohibitions and their official replacements include:

hashtag: *mot-diese*
fashionista: *une femme qui aime l'époque*
LOL: *MDR (mort de rire)*

All cultures dig in when geopolitics threaten their identity: King Alfred did it with his book collection and court culture of writing, to contest influences from both Viking and rival English kingdoms. In France, defeat in the Franco-Prussian War of 1870 and the resultant loss of Alsace-Lorraine grievously wounded French pride. In politics, revanchism or 'revenge-ism' was born under the incompetent but charismatic rabble-rouser General Boulanger, who wanted a return fight with Germany. In architecture, the Eiffel Tower is an essay in industrial prowess. In art, patriotic and mournful paintings abounded. In fiction, Zola wove a whole novel sequence to explain how France had lost its way. In the broader world of book production and collection, wounded national pride merged with three other themes: a fear of educated women, *fin de siècle* aestheticism and a horror of mass production. Walter Benjamin noted 'the withering of the book's aura' in the face of steam presses. For etiolated 1890s aesthetes, that led to a flight to the absinthe bottle and to the bookbinders in search of rarefication.

In Paris, a small group of bibliophiles created a hot-house atmosphere of refined book collecting. This movement also had its punk side, reflecting a desire to renew France by killing off the staid bibliophilia of boringly dressed old men. Like the Middle Ages-loving socialism of William Morris which influenced it, the new bibliophilia was a potent mix of modernism and reaction.

The catalyst for this eruption in Paris was Octave Uzanne, an ex-lieutenant on a mission to revive France through books. This monocled bachelor was often to be found expounding his views alongside the American artist James Whistler in the tiny Café Napolitain, when not in his exquisite attic apartment overlooking the bookstalls of the Quai Voltaire. Visitors entered through a sculpted iron door resembling 'the gate of Paradise imagined by a Byzantine artist'. Upstairs, casket-like chambers were a feature of this movement, which symbolically pulled up the drawbridge against bourgeois conventionality and herd-like consumerism.

Uzanne proposed that making beautiful books more widely desirable would have a trickle-down effect: 'According to the sound principles of humanitarian bakers, the price of brioche will lower the price of ordinary bread.' Those fine words were betrayed by the elitist side of his nature. In 1889 he published 500 copies of a biographical encyclopaedia 'on Vosges paper', of hip contemporaries united by their love of Vin Mariani, a wine

laced with cocaine. But, *quelle horreur*, 'a crowd of surging beggars' clamoured to buy copies. In reaction, he exclaimed,
'Build a dam!' and created a super-deluxe edition.

With a liberal dash of English Arts and Crafts idealism,
Uzanne predicted that new artisan bookbinders would be
'millers of dreams', dreams of a new nation. An early symbolic
act of the group was performed by the bibliophile Henri Vever,
who went to his home in German-run Alsace, exhumed his
relatives, crated them up and brought them to Paris by train
for reburial in free France.

The old guard had to be superseded first, and the 'Société des
Bibliophiles Français' symbolized it. In Uzanne's fevered imagination this old guard was 'a very old monsieur, scrawny, dry as a
mummy, ill-dressed, living peevishly in his old book-den like a
wolf in his lair'. Fellow iconoclast Félicien Rops warned 'archae-
ologicians of the book' to fear for their cosy milieu: 'Tough
luck! . . . We are going to trash and trample all of it.' Rops's masochistic art pictured staid French bores led on leads by booted
dominatrixes. The Establishment had failed the eternally female
spirit of France and must be punished, purged, renewed.

In 1889 Uzanne brought together 160 people whom he
deemed 'Cardinals of the Modern Bibliopolis' in a new 'Societé
des Bibliophiles Contemporains'. This society included, as
well as collectors, a high proportion of book producers, binders, arthouse publishers and writers. In line with the perennial
transfusion of energy from the United States which has fea-
tured so largely in Parisian culture, the 'Biblios-Contempos'
included many Americans. France, Uzanne said, was in need
of their 'lively and avid minds'. 'Always Forward' was the society motto.

A typical outing for the new society was to attend the
funeral of a legendary Left Bank bookseller. The death of

avant-garde craft-artist Aubrey Beardsley was also solemnly mourned, and elaborate editions of urban-chic writers such as Maupassant were commissioned. This was no movement for country bumpkins. The smock and the cigarette-holder simply did not go together. There was one important regional outpost however. The city of Nancy in annexed Lorraine, as if putting two fingers up to Germanic influence, spearheaded Art Nouveau, and that included a radical, colourful group of bookbinders inspired by natural forms, a group much used by the 'Biblios'.

The new Biblios often met in the Bibliothèque de l'Arsenal, where they visited the fount of creativity by looking at books from golden ages past. They stressed utility above beauty, though, and Uzanne described the pristine library of a pretentious collector, with unread books and uncut pages, as 'a mere tannery'.

The movement was noticed in England, where the great children's writer Andrew Lang was not the only one to scent a Jewish conspiracy to drive up book prices. Disappointingly, he noted among the new Biblios a lot of 'the children of Israel'. More positively, the Londoner Henry Ashbee envied the conviviality and liveliness of the Biblios and the similar societies which they spawned. A journalist observed that British book clubs had 'a cold collation and bottled beer', while the French kicked back with 'delightful little dinners . . . followed by curaçao and cigars'.

Out of this milieu, like an orchid in a glade, sprang Robert, Comte de Montesquiou, born in Paris in 1855. This bibliophile, for long an icon of *fin de siècle* decadence, went beyond Uzanne to make aestheticism a way of life. A visitor painted this remarkable vignette:

Tall, black-haired, Kaiser-moustached, he cackled and screamed in weird attitudes, giggling in high soprano, hiding his black teeth behind an exquisitely gloved hand – the absolute poseur.

His clothes reflected his moods, as writer Élisabeth de Gramont explained:

> Leaning on the railing of my upper balcony one bright spring morning, gazing down onto the Avenue I was suddenly struck by the appearance of a tall, elegant personage in mouse-gray, waving a well-gloved hand in my direction. He might, likely as not, have turned up in sky-blue, or in his famous almond-green outfit with a white velvet waistcoat. He selected his costume to tone with his moods.

He might have been 'rather a freak' to a contemporary visiting Londoner, but in this twenty-first century age of servility to market trends he seems to have had a certain something. He inspired both Proust and Huysmans, and counted Verlaine and Debussy among his friends.

He realized that German idea of making your life a work of art: a *gesamtkunstwerk*. Influenced by Edgar Allan Poe's essay, 'The Philosophy of Furniture', he made his upstairs flat overlooking the Seine into 'the mirror of my soul', exotically furnished with *japonisme* and books. Many of us look around our dwelling and see, not a soul-mirror, but a series of shabby compromises, half-loved inherited junk, broken things, lingering Ikea tat, trinkets of long-imploded love – and does anyone, hand-on-heart, have the curtains they really want?

The Comte insisted that interiors can possess what he called 'therapeutic value', but only if they are suffused with friendship and stories. Mass production was out. He explained what he 'instinctively started to search for': that 'grouping of objects, in an association, almost in a conversation' which 'spreads to the soul'. This is all a long way from what millions of us have these days: some Penguins in a Billy next to a fern from Aldi. In that apartment it mattered to be upstairs, away from the hurly burly of the streets. Upstairs as a place to read has cropped up a lot in this book. It's peaceful, even hermetic, and the distant horizons you often see from upstairs free the mind a bit. The Comte's flat was also in conversation with the river below and its raffish bookstalls, and with the Foreign Ministry a few doors away. The atmosphere was never as good after he left the Quai d'Orsay, moving to Passy in the 16th arrondissement, where he built a special greenhouse for his books, or, later still, when he lived on the edge of the city in Le Vésinet, a commune in a bend of the Seine. Even though he hosted great parties there, and built a detached book pavilion called The Hermitage, it was all a bit alluvial, bovine, suburban.

The 1890s spirit succumbed to a cultural marsh-fog which crept across Europe, a toxic mix of cod psychology and militarism which was to be transubstantiated into actual mustard gas in Flanders. In Paris, Jean-Martin Charcot wrote about the 'genital inversion' of fetishistic collectors, then Krafft-Ebing in Germany and Havelock Ellis in London said that these disordered individuals were latent homosexuals. A Hungarian doctor resident in Paris, Max Nordau, weighed in with his book, *Degeneration* (1892). An admirer of German militarism, he attacked aesthetes as displaying a 'pathology of degeneration'. He was specifically disgusted by Oscar Wilde, whose clothes represented 'a pathological aberration', whose writings were 'derivative' and whose sexual practices were diseased.

Nordau's book took off, with seven editions in six months. The English translation came out just before Oscar Wilde's trial and stoked up the appetite for his draconian sentence. Hard labour in Reading Gaol was not just retribution, it was manning-up.

For over twenty years, the book continued to be a bugle call to arouse macho Europe. Dr Nordau, with his gigantic patriarchal beard, seemed to have diagnosed a European epidemic of sissiness. In England, his book was used to explain the failure of the Boer War. Even Nordau's own Jewish co-religionists had gone soft: he prescribed a new muscular Judaism – *muskeljudentum* – and a butch State of Israel, to be founded in Uganda, where it would regenerate the benighted Bantu. This flawed idea had a spirited opponent. In 1903 a Russian Jew living in Paris, Chaim Luban, opened fire on Nordau at close range in an attempted assassination, shouting 'Death to Nordau the East African!' He survived and Luban was classified as mentally ill.

Nordau diagnosed the aesthetes' interiors as harshly as their perversions: 'Everything in these houses aims to excite the nerves . . . the disconnected and antithetical effects . . . all is discrepant, indiscriminate jumble.' Amid this jumble, he wrote, books can be 'anti-social' and 'a corrupting influence on a whole generation'.

Another toxic agent within this Nordauesque fog was eugenics, the idea that effete coves such as Wilde and Montesquiou could be bred out of *Homo sapiens* by sterilization, and with them out of the way humanity could go on to build a super-race of wholesome capitalist warriors. Havelock Ellis was prominent in the Eugenics Society. The dim view of aesthete book collectors as deviants took hold just as a new bogey-word hit the French language in 1891: *homosexuel*.

Montesquiou could not process all this. He fled Paris in 1914 for the d'Artagnan family home – he was a descendant of the fourth musketeer – and spent his winters at Menton on the Riviera, dying there in 1921 a forgotten figure. His books were sold off at auction, and he would give a soprano cackle to hear that the three-volume sale catalogue is now itself a sought-after collectible.

Hidden Women

Nineteenth-century society had barely recovered from the effects of extending the vote and education to the working man when it faced women demanding their rights too.

1875 saw the first woman in the British Empire get a degree (from Mount Allison University in Canada), and a year later American, Dutch and Italian women were admitted to universities. It was 1880 before French women got free secondary education or were allowed into universities; 1910 saw Britain's first woman professor.

There were various male reactions to this. In 1897 one French magazine melded a fear of women cycling with their perceived threat to men's books. It carried an extraordinary cartoon of sweating women cycling their velocipedes over old books. Some bookmen retreated into misogyny, or acted out dominance by sexualizing their books. They wrote about paper as soft as a woman's skin, and compared book-hunting to sexual conquest. In 1904, the Director of Paris's Théâtre Français confessed to stroking his bindings 'like a lover'. Théophile Gautier (1811–72), father of two daughters and once a famous writer, was more unpleasant, enjoying 'The shudder of an ivory knife in a book's uncut pages; it's a virginity like any other, that is always pleasant to take.' Edmund de Goncourt (1822–96), after whom the French book prize is named, admitted to the 'seduction' of a soft binding. The drama critic Adolphe Brisson (1860–1925) got a 'quasi-sensual joy' and even a '*jouissance*', or climax, from handling books.

Women never seemed to view the physical book in this sexually political, misted-over way, and were generally more interested in their contents, to the despair of Andrew Lang in 1886: 'I remember seeing a privately printed vellum copy of a novel in the hands of a literary lady. She was holding it over the fire, and had already made the vellum covers curl.' Four years later a Frenchman lamented how these women would cheekily find a comfortable nook and lose themselves in a book: 'Seated on her low chair, she brings close to the fire the most beautiful bindings.'

By the Seine in the nineties, Octave Uzanne was annoyed by 'female *lycée* teachers', who:

> flip through very thoroughly and quickly all the books on display, monopolizing the stall where they ensconce themselves, even taking notes on their reading, then negligently tossing the book aside.

They were probably on a rushed lunch break, exercising their right to serendipitous browsing and engaging with the text. With the same disregard for his own privileged position, he sneered at them 'haggling over a book as if it were a crayfish or a chicken'.

Folding over a page corner to mark a place is now unisex, but was thought a female vice, part of that interaction with a text which was alien to a vocal minority of male collectors. In 1896 a Parisian journalist wrote of wives 'cuckolding their spouses' by folding down page corners.

The feeling of the decade was, feminist Elaine Showalter says, one of 'sexual anarchy' breaking out. That women did collect books and become experts on book history is both a heroic and a hidden story. In nineties Paris Octave Uzanne described how the policeman's wife and feminist Juliette Adam with her 'grace and *esprit'* cut a welcome figure 'in the midst of black tailcoats' of the Amis des Livres club. Blanche Haggin, a San Franciscan book-lover who had translated the Sufi poet Hafiz from the Persian, refreshed the Biblio-Contemporains by her membership. The young actress Julia Bartet joined too; she lived until 1941, one of the last survivors of the *belle époque*. Another member, the book-loving bohemian Leontine Lippman, was embedded enough in the aesthetics of the decade to become a character in *À la recherche du temps perdu*. It is a wonder that they bothered joining societies which had a quota for women members – as low as 10 per cent in the Biblio-Contemporains.

In true nineties paradoxical style, Uzanne set this quota but still felt that he was radically overturning the sexist previous generation of collectors, those 'crazy old monomaniacal men'. He encouraged his friend, the lawyer Ernest Quentin-Bauchart, to write the two-volume *Les Femmes Bibliophiles de France* (1886), and another Biblio member, Albert Cim, wrote *Les Femmes et les livres*, a celebration of French women book-lovers, and a book about Marie Antoinette's library. Uzanne and his chums are a model of inclusivity compared to the bibliophiles' Grolier Club in New York (established 1884) and Caxton Club in Chicago (1895): they banned women completely until 1976. Britain's Roxburghe Club of book collectors (1812) finally admitted its first woman member in 1985. However, it's not that women have not always loved books – they still make up the majority of bookshop customers – they just do it more quietly and privately, as several women in this chapter demonstrate.

Discovering the Oldest Printed Book

While Western Europe was twiddling with *fin de siècle* notions, a small Hungarian man, tough as a yak, was about to pull off a great book collecting coup in Central Asia. Aurel Stein was his name, but his fame depended on the lifelong labours of a largely unknown Chinese monk.

Wang Yuanlu was born when Queen Victoria was thirty and Britain was entering the age of the steam train. Like many wandering mendicants, he lived by his begging bowl, but in the 1890s his life gained a new purpose. He visited the remote Mogao Caves in the interior desert of China, about 2,000 miles due north of Kolkata. Even now the site is twenty-nine hours by train from the nearest city. Like all visitors, Wang was astonished by the 490 temples cut into the rock which give the site its popular name, 'The Caves of a Thousand Buddhas'. Still a popular destination for pilgrims and tourists, they were in a sorry state when Wang visited, so he dedicated his life to being their self-appointed protector, clearing away the desert sand which had filled some caves, restoring murals, and even commissioning new ones. Periodically he ran out of alms and went off begging, but now his bowl had only one purpose – the caves.

The caves are a palimpsest of Chinese history, in use as Buddhist meditation sites and temples for nearly 2,000 years. In Buddhism the written or printed word is important in quite a different way from its role in other religions. Reciting and writing out the Buddha's teachings are acts which themselves accrue merit. The paper bearing the words then becomes, in the parlance of a cockney fence, 'hot'. A hardcore Buddhist friend gave me an extensive series of letters from assorted *tulkus*, lamas and rinpoches to burn – unlike him I had a fireplace – because such holy papers could not be consigned to the garbage truck. Proper Buddhists will never put a book of dharma (teachings) on the floor or under another book, and reading such a volume in the khazi is out of the question.

The more permanent and widely visible way you can devise to display dharma, the greater the merit acquired. In Ladakh I have seen mantra carvings which extend for miles, and the most extreme site of this sort in the world is China's sacred Mount Taishan. It was here that a monk called Jingwan (d. AD 631) carved four million words of scripture in caves. He knew the caves were good for protection from the weather but he went even further, putting windows on some and sealing off underground carved chambers, marking their sites with pagodas. From a similar karmic motivation, the Japanese Empress Shotoku commissioned a million prayers to go in little chesspiece-sized pagodas all over her kingdom. Just writing out teachings is good karma; doing it repeatedly is better. Print, therefore, was a karmic jackpot.

One day Wang was restoring a cave mural when he realized it was covering up a man-made wall. Some accounts say he noticed fag smoke disappearing into a crack (Boeing's final factory fuselage integrity test used to be done with a fag). Breaking into the wall he saw, by the guttering light of his small oil lamp, another cave about nine feet square, piled ten feet deep with scrolls. It was an archaeological discovery to rank with Howard Carter's entry into the tomb of Tutankhamun: the scrolls dated from the fourth to the eleventh centuries. Wang repeatedly tried to get local officials interested in the cave library, but they were unimpressed, and merely told him to guard it.

This 50,000-document cave library was largely a spiritual archive, including a printed scroll of the Diamond Teachings, or Diamond Sutra, made in 868. This version of the Sutra – originally written in the second to fifth centuries AD – is the oldest dated printed book in the world, and a typical product of Tang dynasty China. Under Tang emperors and empresses – women were prominent in this era – literature and printing flourished, alongside a host of innovations from dental fillings and lavatory paper to air conditioning and the striking clock. The Diamond Sutra's survival is almost miraculous: the dry desert air had left it in excellent fettle. 'Diamond' refers to the sutra's power to cut through illusion and the text is a core document of Mahayana Buddhism. Amusingly, because of the Mahayana cult of the book, Buddhism dictates that wherever this copy of the Diamond Sutra is located becomes itself a sacred site, a sort of wormhole to cosmic reality. So shelf-mark 8210 in the British Library, near St Pancras Station, where the book now resides, could have as big a queue, if it was accessible, as Platform 9¾ a bowshot away in King's Cross Station.

The general Chinese attitude to books at the time the British Library Diamond Sutra was made was very physical. One poet, Li Tsung-Yuan, used to wash his hands in rose-water before opening the poetry of his friend Han Yu.

Other paper versions of the Sutra found in the cave illustrate its perceived power: one scroll was commissioned by a farmer to help his ox attain a better reincarnation, another bore a woman's wish to escape the wastes of the Mogao Desert and get back to the capital, a third was paid for by an official hoping for promotion, a fourth was atonement for eating a clam in the distant capital. It may be a gloomy thought for Richard Dawkins, but print took off because of this desire to repeat and propagate Buddhist teaching, just as the Christian Reformation fuelled the print revolution in Europe.

If the Sutra's rediscoverer, Wang Yuanlu, deserves to be better known, then so does its printer, Wang Jei. He is the first named printer known to history, and touchingly records creating the book 'on behalf of his parents' in 868. He gets no mention in the monumental two-volume *Oxford Companion to the Book* (1,400 pages, £900), even in the China section.

Wang Jei's techniques are only slowly being discovered. Paper was invented in China in about 200 BC, when it was made from rags, roots or old fishing nets, but Wang Jei made the Sutra's five-metre scroll from the more durable bark of the mulberry tree. It used to be thought the paper had yellowed with age, until techniques such as the wonderfully named Fast Acorn Spectrum Bombardment Mass Spectrometry revealed its secrets. It was deliberately dyed with sap from the cork tree. This sap contains a chemical called berberine which, apart from being used in Chinese medicine to cure a multitude of ailments, acts as an insecticide, fungicide and water repellent. Bombardment has yet to uncover all of Wang Jei's secrets: recently two other chemicals have been discovered in the dye, from as-yet-unidentified plants. The long-lasting black ink – you can see the whole document in zoomable detail on the British Library website – was made from lampblack soot. The red ink was from the root of the madder plant, easy to extract from older plants but tortuous to turn into a permanent dye.

All of this artistry was aimed at daily use and durability. The Sutra was not for a collector or a king, so you might wonder why the cave was sealed only about 200 years after the book was printed, just before – to give a Western context – the Battle of Hastings. Your guess is as good as all the scholarly ones I have read, which hint at threats of war or breakdowns of order. If one troubles to read the Sutra it will be seen that the Buddha gives a clue in it, referring to the stages he thinks Buddhism will go through. He expects his teachings to get corrupted, go into abeyance, have all sorts of ups and downs. Surely, especially in the light of the Mount Taishan sealed scroll chambers described above, the idea was to hide the Diamond Sutra in a dry cave, in dry desert air, specifically for it to be rediscovered when and where needed, which is perhaps in messy twentieth-century London. Among its other properties, Thich Nhat Hanh calls the Sutra 'the most ancient text on deep ecology'. The book, enshrined as one of the 'Treasures of the British Library' along with Shakespeare's First Folio and the Magna Carta, might just be a beneficent time bomb.

I had a dream which pointed this way during the writing of this section. The British Library co-ordinates an international research group on the library cave. Working late, reading through the twenty-five years of its research archive online, I came to a section dedicated to the Diamond Sutra in all its aspects, and there the site crashed, so I went to bed. I had read the whole Sutra earlier that day too. Like most people, I dream about boring trivia or anxieties, but at 3 a.m. I was awoken by a vivid dream, in which a nuthatch on a beautiful tree stump turned into a kingfisher, which turned into a baby kingfisher, which turned into a two-foot-diameter ring of interlocked baby kingfishers, upright like a picture, and slowly turning. The most cursory research reveals this to be a mandala, the circle promising wholeness which occurs in every spiritual tradition. The kingfisher, or halcyon, is a harbinger in the West of peaceful days, and a pacifier of nature's storms.

The aforementioned *Oxford Companion to the Book*, like every other account of the Mogao Caves library, mentions a name other than Wang Yuanlu as its 'discoverer': the Hungarian-born archaeologist Sir Aurel Stein. He was 'the discoverer', in the sense that Columbus discovered America and Captain Cook Australia – as if there was nobody about when he arrived. How Stein procured the Sutra and fifty crates of scrolls for £130 is a dark episode for many Chinese. He told Wang, who used the money for further cave restoration, that they were going to 'a great temple of learning' (the British Museum).

The Emptying Cave, 1900–1920

Wang Yuanlu took payment from several other visitors after Stein's visit. In 1908, the young Frenchman Paul Pelliot, who had the command of ancient Chinese which Stein lacked, took away 30,000 books and manuscripts, now mostly in the Bibliothèque Nationale de France. This haul included unique ninth-century Buddhist Jatakas, or parables, in a previously unknown Tajik language, Sogdian. He used his photographic memory to record many of the scrolls he left in the cave. They were so extraordinary in age and quantity that in Paris he was excoriated for a while as a liar and fantasist, and the scrolls he had brought home were thought to be forgeries, until Stein published his own findings in full and publicly confirmed Pelliot's story of the cave.

Scrolls and block-printed books taken by several German expeditions were housed in Berlin's Ethnological Museum but faced many challenges, being hidden across three salt mines during the war, then divided between East and West Berlin, before being finally redistributed, with many losses along the way, across several German institutions in 1989.

The wealthy 27-year-old Japanese Count Otani was an actual Buddhist. He visited Wang just before the First World War and bought 369 scrolls but, becoming embroiled in a financial scandal back home, he sold his collection, splitting it between China, Korea and Japan.

In 1914 the Russian Sergei Oldenberg purchased over 300 scrolls, now kept in the Institute of Oriental Manuscripts in St Petersburg.

In 1915 a Danish telegraphist in Shanghai, Arthur Sorensen, decided to return home to Copenhagen via the Mogao Caves. He bought 14 Tang dynasty cave scrolls from Wang. They ended up in the Danish Royal Library, largely neglected until they were catalogued in 1988.

Even after all these depredations, China holds 16,000 manuscripts from the cave, including 8,000 saved in 1910 by Fu Baoshu, a lone official from Beijing's Ministry of Education.

Wang continued to live at the Mogao temples, in a small dwelling immediately opposite the library cave, until he died there in 1931, aged eighty-three. He is both revered and reviled by historians, just like the little Hungarian who entered his life in 1907. Stein was to go on to achieve his dream of entering Afghanistan, taking a jeep to the capital in 1943. Catching a chill in the icy Kabul Museum, he declined in health and died in the American Legation, aged eighty. His grave in Kabul is overgrown.

Marie the Incunabulist

Incunabula: Books produced in the infancy of printing, before 1500. **Incunabulist**: one who collects or is interested in incunabula.

Oxford English Dictionary, 1933 edition.

I grew up with incunabula, the word, not the things. My father talked about them a lot, though he never found any in his

Saturday trawls down Portobello Road, where he seemed to know most of the dealers. The earliest book he owned, which I now keep in a Freeman, Hardy & Willis moccasins shoebox (kept in defiance of my brother's mockery of those ground-breaking items of footwear) was published in 1543. It is a toddler rather than a true incunabulum, or baby from the cradle-years of printing.

In my youthful imagination, these 'swaddling-clothes books' had a rarefied air, like moon-rock, spoken of, but never seen. Even today I have only seen one or two under glass in the British Library gallery. As a chain-store bookseller I doubt if I have the necessary affidavits to get permission to handle one. My online 'pre-registration' with the BL stalled when it asked me to select my institutional affiliation from a drop-down menu. There was no 'Other' option. The road-safety-themed Tufty Club is the only thing I have ever joined – in 1961 – but this select association, presided over by a red squirrel with peerless hazard perception skills, is not on the list.

For decades after the arrival of print, little interest was taken in incunabula. They were seen as primitive, hand-axes to Sabatier knives. Most incunabula did not come off the press in a finished state, but ready for adornment and illumination. Even then, they were often seen as faux manuscripts. Some major collectors such as the Duke of Urbino refused to have any of them in their libraries. But from about 1650 some cognoscenti realized that they were superb gems, often hand-illuminated, artefacts from an age of wonder at mechanization, an age which held on to many manuscript aesthetics and fused hot metal and quill, type and art. Many were lost or succumbed to time; about 27 per cent of them are known from just one copy. The task of tracking them down was begun in earnest in the 1880s by a woman the Languedoc librarian Guy Barral has called 'wildly passionate', but 'known only to a small number of followers'. Marie Pellechet has slipped out of history, occluded by more flamboyant or talkative collectors, although her scholarly work contributed far more than many of those vain magpies of the patriarchy. She started a process of incunabula collation, and set standards for it which exist to this day.

She is herself part of the reason for her obscurity. Like Enrequeta Rylands and Francis Currer Bell, Marie laboured for the survival of her collection, not her name. A letter recently discovered in Montpellier from Jules Troubat (the Librarian of the Bibliothèque Nationale), written just after her death in 1900, describes her well (my translation):

> Mademoiselle Pellechet was a good woman, very charitable, doing good without ostentation, very modest and simple in her manner, and extremely well-versed in the study of incunabula. It was a vocation for her . . . We hold her in high esteem at the Bibliothèque Nationale.

Troubat is replying to a researcher who wants information about Pellechet. Tantalizingly, he says the library does hold some of her archives, and 'I could get the documents about her, only it is a hassle for me, given that I am down here in the Reading Room.' An obituary notice in *The Times* in 1900 supported Troubat's warm words: 'To those who knew her she was a kind friend and a most delightful and humorous correspondent.'

Her house on the northern outskirts of Paris, now on a main road, is in poor condition these days but was then an idyllic place on the edge of the Marly forest, woodland once painted by Pisarro, now bisected by the A13. Here young Marie became fascinated by science and one day demonstrated her mettle. Her mother, over-worried about Marie having a slight indisposition, sent for medicine. The young girl thought this so unnecessary that she ran to the garden and, sitting on the edge of the well, threatened to jump down it rather than take the prescription. The mother gave in and Marie recovered naturally.

Her correspondence with a local priest got her interested in old books and, wanting to know the language of the first print-ers, she taught herself German. That a teenager could so defy contemporary Germanophobia – Paris had only recently experienced the horrors of war – was remarkable. Soon after this she learned Latin and Italian, and developed a settled per-sonal philosophy of feminism and pacifism.

An only child, she wrote of how her architect father's relentless dedication together with '*l'amour de la France*' inspired her to embark on a project which would dominate her life: a catalogue of all the incunabula in France, and many in neighbouring Germany and Italy. She started with the four big Paris archives, and then visited 178 regional librar-ies. It was for her as exciting as an Indiana Jones quest. She described her growing attachment to reading rooms:

> In the serene atmosphere, a little ponderous, I feel something which French cannot express – a fearful respect, reverent, mysterious – English has the *mot juste*: awe. And when I replace the book on the shelf and go to the door, I almost feel I am leaving a sacred temple.

Realizing that she needed to rapidly record the books, which were in variable condition, she mastered the new art of photog-raphy. With her scientific frame of mind and determination, it came easily to her and she took it very seriously. She invented 'a special photographic apparatus' to capture books, and was so irked when the British Museum charged her 50 shillings for a poor photograph of a book that she sent them drawings of her invention, advising them that 'any carpenter would build this for you at little cost'. Her extensive equipment is at the Musée des Arts et Métiers, the same place which houses Foucault's pendulum, and her atmospheric images, beyond her photography of books, crop up in unlikely places. City views of Aix-en-Provence are on the town's library website: farm wagons frozen in time in squares, forgotten Provençals at upper windows. An Instagrammer has cut up other images to make collages.

Although she struggled for official funding, receiving mainly written encouragement from the Ministry of Public Instruction, she donated many endangered incunabula to the Bibliothèque Nationale. Her odyssey was exhausting. She was prey to migraines and most of her face periodically flared up with a rare skin inflammation. In 1878 a friend begged her to stop travelling 'in rain and snow, fogs and hard frosts' and rest by her fireside. She wrote back, 'Do you think this is *The Benoiton Family*?' In that long-running French farce a domineering father forbids his girls to leave the house by themselves. They reply, 'Oh what a French Papa you are! Why can't we walk alone like in America?'

Marie explained her addiction: 'My daily sojourn in the library is the best part of my day, and I have to be careful it does not so preoccupy my mind and heart that I miss my meals.' Letters from her travels, yet to be published in English, are evidence of a Dervla Murphy-type endurance with a dash of Bill Bryson humour concerning human folly. They are much better than her brother's turgid *Letters From Italy*, which she edited for publication. Unlike some introvert collectors, Marie rejoiced in the pageant of humanity. Her partiality towards '*les petites gens*', ordinary people, was noticed by more than one commentator.

Passing through Aquitaine, she met a villager, Philippe Larroque, who had quietly accumulated 6,000 old books. He became a lifelong correspondent and founded a book club in 1866 which still meets in Bordeaux Library. Larroque became devoted to her and wrote charmingly to tempt her from her criss-cross journeys to revisit him:

Let us meet again; don't go whizzing past like one of those meteors which disappear so quickly to general regret. Give us a good fortnight or, if that seems indiscreet, at least a good week. That is the minimum we need. You will have fresh air here which will do you good, and you can treat my house as your own. You can work here as much as you want, I will give you a special desk in my humble library. We can take little walks together to spur our appetites. Do you like lamb? It is tender like dew at the moment. Do you like chicken? Ours are surpassingly excellent.

Marie did visit Philippe frequently, and consoled him with books after fire destroyed his collection, a blow which cast him down and, he wrote, 'led to atrophy of the brain' and a '*sombre et triste*' last few years. One senses that Marie had brought much-needed wit and vigour into his rural existence.

After finding many incunabula dotted around Burgundy, she approached the Bishop of Beaune to access his library: 'He did not take my abilities seriously, and had a good laugh at my studies and my Don Quixote travels in his diocese.' Undeterred, she found his librarian willing to let her sneak into the collection at 6 a.m. There she found many treasures, mostly unknown because, as she put it charitably, the library catalogue was ' "in a state of becoming", to quote Monsieur Hegel'.

In Zurich Marie made more discoveries, despite an old, deaf librarian, to whom she had to shout her requests. Here, piles of incunabula were brought to her desk while she worked for ten hours straight 'without raising her nose', as sung liturgy drifted in through the open window. In the Swiss Alps she found treasures lurking in high valleys in monastic libraries. Usually, she knew more than the curators she encountered. Getting up at 5 a.m. to reach one cantonal library, she found it guarded by 'the usual functionary, aged, grouchy, an amateur at his job, and deaf to boot'. After a seven-hour walk to the next village, nobody seemed to have the key to the silent abbey. A passing peasant, however, led Marie to an old house where a helpful keyholder resided. He was wearing eighteenth-century-style knee-breeches, black stockings and a frock coat:

> He received me without embarrassment but it was only with difficulty that I could stop myself from laughing at his Lucernois costume. 'What an intrepid traveller you are Madame!' he exclaimed.

Descending to Genoa, she reacted to a less obliging curator with magnanimity:

> Here was an ecclesiastical librarian, with a long pointed nose and white hair, a desiccated and lean figure. On seeing me, and realizing that the grand door of the library was left wide open to the street, he stood up, glared at me, and with a gesture of disdain, indicated the open library door and said, 'Women are not allowed in!' I was at first stupefied by this, but

then burst out laughing, bowed low and left, conjecturing that the poor abbé had been unlucky in love – before entering holy orders of course.

At a second Genoese library Marie met a portly librarian in a cassock who knew only Italian, and found that her gender and age – forty – were threats:

Abbé: But madame, I cannot let you study here!
MP: But why, Monsieur l'Abbé?
Abbé: Because of the young ones.
(I look around and see some scamps on a school trip aged about ten. I reply in an ingratiating voice –)
MP: Oh come now, monsieur, I am no threat to these gentlemen. I am old – look at my glasses! Let me study here, I beg you.
(The little man smiled, but quoted regulations.)
Abbé: Well, I suppose you might make a request to the head librarian, to work when the library is closed?

Although she made this request, she was only allowed to see the library catalogue. Her fortunes improved in Rome, where she was the first woman researcher in the Vatican, welcomed by a librarian with a green taffeta eye-shade; and in Florence, where the kindly curator kept the library open until she had finished her investigations. In Parma and Siena she found more incunabula, before returning to France, where she journeyed on with her cumbersome cameras to the libraries of Lyons, Dijon, Avignon and Montpellier. Her charitable reception in this last city, an ancient seat of learning, sowed a seed of gratitude which flowered much later in the donation of her personal library to the city archives. After a book-hunting trip to Germany she received another plea from her friend Mr

Guignard to slow down and look after herself, because the Lord had only given her a limited stock of health: 'Hercules has nothing on you, such activity! Such train journeys! Such vigour! You are perpetual movement.'

In 1896 she paused to write a polemical article entitled 'The Fire in the Libraries' for a popular newspaper, drawing attention to the sloppy curation of many French collections and excoriating certain universities which were selling off incunabula for profit. The self-funded publication of her *General Catalogue of Incunabula, Volume One* (1897) gained her new respect from even the deafest and most grumpy curators. Now the Versailles Palace Library became one of many European libraries to invite Marie in, keen for her to assess their own incunabula. In 1899, the Education Minister made her an honorary librarian of the Bibliothèque Nationale. In that library, in contrast to the sexist challenges she had faced, she was welcomed daily in her later years:

> All the regulars recognized the lady who, at the opening of the doors, took her usual seat in the reading room, where the delivery boys were eager to serve her and the librarians showed her the fullest respect.

In this more sedentary era of her life, she began an initiative which revived her early scientific interests. Prompted by the ravages of a *'termite mysterieux'* wreaking havoc in Bayonne Library, she instituted the serious study of *'tous ces vilains insectes'* which threatened books. A prize for advances in this branch of science bears her name today. Politically, she was a fiery liberal to the end, writing against the Boer War and fulminating about the anti-Semitism revealed by the Dreyfus case.

In one of her last letters to her old friend Guignard she

shows how all those old books, 'her vocation', far from being dead, softened death's sting. The passage is an elegy for any book-lover to relish.

> Don't worry that my work has dried up my soul. I was never much absorbed in the material side of the books; it's the words alone that touch my spirit. All the perpetual contact with these relics makes me think of the others who have touched these books, read these pages, who perhaps have traced these lines with their fingers. And this makes me meditate on how death is all in order.

On her deathbed, aged sixty-two, Marie was attended by her protégé, the 24-year-old Louis Polain. Polain, a Belgian, learned his trade as a bookseller in the Leipzig firm of Harrasowitz (still in business). He had worked with Marie on the *General Catalogue* and planned to continue it. Marie took his hand and said, 'Can I count on you?' to which he replied, 'Yes, I promise.' He completed volumes Two and Three of her great work by 1909, largely using her notes.

Soon after this, the innocent world of incunabulists was improbably swept up in twentieth-century politics. Incunabula represented cultural excellence, and although the finest examples were Italian, Germany had pioneered printing them. When the Germans invaded Belgium in August 1914, one of their surprising priorities was to begin an inventory of incunabula in that country. Since 1898 a Dresden librarian, Konrad Haebler, had been cataloguing German incunabula and from 1904 he ran the *Gesamtkatalog de Wiegendrucke*, a proposed catalogue of world incunabula. The project had an undertone of cultural imperialism; it was officially sponsored by Frederick Althoff, a Prussian minister of culture who spearheaded the Prussianization of annexed Alsace-Lorraine, setting up the Reich University of Strasbourg. Known for his silky 'secret diplomacy', a rival said he was a remorseless intriguer pretending to be a 'Westphalian peasant'. The incunabula catalogue would be a worthy adjunct to Althoff's huge projected *Encyclopaedia of Culture of the [German] Empire*. In Haebler, Althoff had selected a formidably austere ally. In an oil painting, Haebler looks unapproachably formal, and a recent German historian has described him as 'stern against himself and his employees', a man with 'no room for personal feelings'. Somehow, after the war, Polain got Haebler's inventory of Belgian incunabula and completed it, publishing in 1932, the year before he died, a book recording 4,000 incunabula in his native country.

Heroine of the Rue Serpente

As well as her methods, Polain had inherited nearly thirty boxes of Marie's incunabulist researches, and hundreds of glass negatives. In 1933, he bequeathed all of this, with his own papers, to Eugénie Droz. Droz was as remarkable as Pellechet, and is even less known. A Swiss-born philologist and expert on medieval troubadour poetry, in 1924 she set up a bookshop, Librairie Droz, in the heart of literary left-bank Paris. She was in her early thirties. Sylvia Beach's intrepid establishment of the Shakespeare and Company bookshop in 1919 is justly celebrated, but Eugénie's enterprise at 34 Rue Serpente is worth a plaque, and the building is little changed. While Beach ran her literary crucible of a shop, Droz's bookstore was uncompromisingly scholarly. She also launched a learned journal of Renaissance studies in 1934. Both women had to contend with the Gestapo when war came.

In the summer of 1940 the German army invaded Paris.

Haebler was still alive and his operatives soon got wind of the Pellechet/Polain papers housed at the Droz bookshop, calling there in 1941 to get them. The only press report of the occasion I can find is bizarrely in *The Scotsman*:

> Today comes the news that the [raid on the bookshop] was foiled by a woman. The heroine of the exploit writes tersely to our correspondent in Edinburgh: 'The Germans wanted to take the papers but I stopped them'.

Frustratingly I can find out nothing more about how Eugénie got rid of the Gestapo. In 1947 she moved back to Switzerland, taking the Droz Bookshop to Geneva, where she died in 1976.

Droz came alive for me in a startling way. In my research I kept encountering a great expert on Pellechet called Ursula Baurmeister, Keeper of Incunabula at the Bibliothèque Nationale from 1978 to 1999. Unable to find an email address for her, I sent her a postcard care of the Bibliothèque Nationale. It was a message in a bottle, I did not really expect a reply. Months later, she phoned me on the shop landline, having also struggled to contact me from my handwritten card. I was on the till, she was 'calling from Bavaria', on a bad line, she was 'terribly old', but she arranged to send me Pellechet information, including transcripts of some letters from Marie found in a dusty corner of the British Museum in 1997, when the library moved to its new building. I asked about Eugénie Droz, and Baurmeister began to say how difficult she could be. It dawned on me, as my colleague served a lengthening queue, that she had actually known Droz. I felt a tingling down my spine. The German occupation of Paris, that bookshop on the Rue Serpente, and Marie's amazing life, all became suddenly real.

Droz's publisher, Droz Editions, is still in business. Before

Eugénie left Paris, she sold the Pellechet/Polain archive to the New York bookseller H. P. Kraus, a legendary figure who had survived Dachau and Buchenwald. He generously donated the Pellechet papers almost immediately to the Bibliothèque Nationale. Kraus held on to the extensive Polain archive until 1979, when he donated it to New York's bibliophile Grolier Club, which reports that it is one of their most frequently consulted collections. Kraus carried on working in his Manhattan bookshop until he was eighty-one, in 1988, the year he died. Finally, in November 2018, Kraus's widow donated Polain's diaries to the Club. One day, someone might see them and publish more about Polain. Edoardo Barbieri, a Milanese history professor, has emailed me to say that Polain was 'a little crazy, but very intelligent'.

The last part of Marie Pellechet's *General Catalogue of Incunabula* was published in 1970, and it has fed into the British Library's online database of world incunabula. This complements the ongoing German incunabula catalogue started by Althoff and Haebler, which is today a superbly usable online resource. There are very few unrecorded incunabula now, thanks in large part to the architect's daughter from a Paris suburb, who felt such 'awe' in their presence.

Hunters of Hidden Paintings

In secondhand bookshops with a rambling enough stock, certain customers can be seen, but very rarely, systematically opening the front cover, gripping all the pages between thumb and forefinger and bending them to create a chamfered edge.

They only check books published before about 1910, and they

are looking for examples of a rare book art – the fore-edge painting, pictures painted on to the very edges – not the margins – of
a book in such a way that they are usually only visible when the
pages are bent, or 'fanned'. These finely executed watercolours
are created in the following way: the block of text is held in a
clamp at such an angle that the page edges are offered as a uni-
form surface. Once the painting is dry, the book is closed and
gilding is applied to the outer edge; this is done by applying gold
leaf, using egg white and water as adhesive. The gilding protects vellum or paper pages from dust and insects. In this way
the book appears to be a standard gilt-edged work, but when
inspected at the right angle, a secret painting is revealed. My
father possessed such a book for over thirty years before one
day discovering the fore-edge painting. This was as exciting
(well no, a bit less exciting) as when we discovered that one of
his walking sticks was a sword stick. As so often, the fore-edge
painting was an inspiring pastoral scene of a country house, on
a Book of Common Prayer. It was there to console the owner
during services. Fore-edge paintings often had this guerrilla
function, as distraction for victims of tedious sermons.

A different conversation between the fore-edge and the text
was going on in the copy, now in a New York museum, of *The
Advantages of Solitude* (London, 1805, 2 vols) by Johann Zimmer-
man. A delightful surprise awaited the reader reaching volume
two, with its hidden fore-edge painting of a solitary fly-
fisherman in an evening landscape.

Even rarer and more fiendish to execute is the double
fore-edge painting, where a book displays two different
watercolours as the pages are tilted one way, then the other.
I have only seen one, on Cowper's collected poems, shown
to me by an old man in a medieval house three miles inland
from Dover. I think the trouble is you cannot display such

books in museums without putting them in a clamp, so you can only ever choose to show one of the two watercolours.

Because books in the early modern period were often shelved fore-edge out, edges of book pages contain not only secret paintings but often owners' names or their family crest. This stuff is rare partly because of what happens during rebinding, when binders resew the sets of pages known as signatures. After this resewing the page edges are no longer exactly aligned, so the binder trims them a little. The magnificent book known as the Lindisfarne Gospels, made in AD 715, survived Viking raids only to fall prey to a Victorian binder who discarded some of the original illumination.

Everything, and Nothing: Obsessive Collectors

Like any love, book collecting can be obsessive and mad. At the outer limits of bibliophilia lurk the bibliographers, those who make a whole book out of listing all the books on a certain subject. This strange practice is dying away because of the internet and the sheer volume of works published, but two brave souls once attempted to syncretize all bibliography.

In 1877 the New Yorker Joseph Sabin published his *Bibliography of Bibliographies* but this was to be superseded by the work of Theodore Besterman, a Pole who said he was entirely self-educated at the British Museum Library. A mystery man and world expert on ghosts and Voltaire, whose letters he published in 107 volumes, in 1939 Besterman self-published *The World Bibliography of Bibliographies*, which made him a household name among pre-internet librarians. To attempt this concept today seems philosophically impossible and something which might even cause the universe to implode into a singularity, re-emerging in a parallel universe where you are reading this paragraph in a slightly different chair and with darker eyebrows, as in the *Star Trek* episode where a space-time distortion produces mean versions of Captain Kirk and all his crew. But Besterman was strangely driven, and lacking a certain humanity. His passion for reason led to him living his later years in Voltaire's house in Geneva, and campaigning against God being spelt with a capital 'G'. The historian Hugh Trevor-Roper, as his executor, was one of the small group at his bleak music-free cremation in 1976. He left over £1.3 million to Oxford University, but little to his widow, who clawed some back in 1981 after going to court. As she left court Marie-Louise Besterman said, 'He was very bad-tempered in the last three years.'

There are even wilder shores of book love. In *The Antiquary* (1816), Walter Scott satirizes the collectors of imperfect books, agog at those who pay more for a book without the author's improvements, with still-uncut pages, or with a certain rare title page.

Perverse seeking-after of imperfect copies was imaginatively taken to its logical conclusion in the short story *Baxter's Procrustes* (1904). In 1902 its author, Charles Chesnutt, was refused membership of the Rowfant Book Club in Cleveland, Ohio, because he was African-American, despite the fact that the club had published an edition of one of his novels in 1899. In *Baxter's Procrustes*, Jones, member of a thinly disguised Rowfant Club, sells copies of an exclusive fifty-copy edition of 'Baxter's *Procrustes*' to fellow members. It is said to be a high point of typography, on exceptionally fine paper. The book is sealed in a transparent wrapper, so most members never open it, valuing rarity above content. The book, it transpires, is all blank pages, but, as Jones explains, 'the true collector loves wide margins' so what could be better than a book that is all margin?

This way of collecting books for their look, rather than content, is a perennial cul-de-sac of collecting, observed by Seneca of scroll collectors in Roman times: 'Many use books not as tools for study but as decorations for the dining room! [Some] get their pleasure merely from bindings and labels.'

I have described a few collectors here, but there are so many more shadowy figures of great note. Mysterious Harry Ransom, spotted at auctions until the 1960s in his trademark sunglasses and raincoat, quietly built up one of the world's greatest archives of authors' manuscripts at Austin, Texas. He bought the whole of Evelyn Waugh's library, bookcases included, and his lavish purchases have ensured, Cyril Connolly wrote, that many writers can 'look the milkman in the eye'. On Patmos in the Aegean Sea, a village schoolmaster, Ioannes Sakkelion, found out that some local monks were secretly selling off priceless early books, destroying some they thought worthless. He fought to save many, spent thirty years cataloguing them, and rescued a sixth-century gospel from a damp chest in the monastery basement.

Collectors have risked arrest, hidden books underground and behind walls, rescued them from candle-makers and pie shops, traversed the length and breadth of countries, often blown their whole fortunes, been lonely, shivered at street bookstalls week after week and sweated as auction bids edged higher and higher. They may have been eccentric and sometimes obsessive, but they saw books as doors to other worlds, and to other ways of being, and in this they helped us to be our more extraordinary selves. Very many were idealists who collected, as Cardinal Borromeo did, in the hope that 'crude centuries may not return'.

tendit + parauit illum.

Et in eo parauit uasa mortis: sagit
tas suas ardentibz effecit.

Ecce prturit iniusticiam: concepit
dolorem + peprit iniquitatem.

Lacum aperuit + effodit eum: + in
cidit in foueam qñ fecit.

Conuertet dolor eius in caput ei: +
in uerticem ipsius iniqtas ei descen
det.

Confitebor dño scdm iusticiam
ei: + psallam noi dñi altissimi.

Domine dominus noster:
quam admirabile est no
men tuum in uniuersa terra.

Quoniam eleuata est magnificen
cia tua: super celos.

7. Life on the Edge: The Mysteries of Medieval Marginalia

When Othello remembers falling in love with Desdemona it is all recognizably beautiful, until a part that sends many of us to the footnotes. Othello is narrating how Desdemona was enraptured by his tales of strange wonders:

> It was my hint to speak, such was the process:
> . . . of . . .
> The Anthropophagi, and men whose heads
> Do grow beneath their shoulders: this to hear
> Would Desdemona seriously incline

In *The Tempest*, too, Gonzalo talks of 'men whose heads stood in their breasts'. Reference to such creatures is as surprising as Mercutio's marvellous evocation of a fairy queen's carriage, 'Her whip of cricket's bone . . . her waggoner, a small grey-coated gnat', travelling over men's noses as they lie asleep. This is a lost world of popular fable, hard to recapture now. Happily, it is preserved in medieval art.

Marginalia in medieval books were executed deliberately as part of the intended design, and painted to the same expensive standard as the illuminated text they accompanied. They were a considered part of the textual offering, not mere doodles. They are so extraordinarily varied, obscure and shocking that scholars, both repelled and puzzled, long ignored them. The gryllus, a man with his head beneath his shoulders, appears frequently, as do mermaids, man-animals, animals doing amusing things such as playing instruments, and scenes of every-day life with undreamt-of transgressions. During my research, the more examples I saw, the less ashamed I felt we need to be as a civilization of all those cats on Instagram, and of the stranger things which the internet holds. Medieval scribes, who included monks and secular artists of both genders, seemed to be embracing the outer limits of the imagination, fuelled by the edges of those maps of the known world which really did say 'Here Be Dragons'.

For much of the twentieth century, expert custodians of medieval books at the British Museum had different tactics for explaining away marginalia. Sir E. Maude Thompson, Principal Librarian at the British Museum from 1888 to 1909 and a great champion of public access to manuscripts – he pioneered the photography of early codices – reassured the public that all those strange marginal adornments were not aimed at the devout reader, who would have discreetly ignored them. Eric Millar, the museum's Keeper of Manuscripts in the 1950s, thought that the maker of the celebrated – but wildly adorned – *Luttrell Psalter* (prayer book) had a mind 'which cannot have been normal', and, soon after Millar, a scholar admitted that 'profanity has discouraged full-fledged scholarship of medieval marginal art'. There was one ground-breaking exception.

In 1938 a history professor in Berlin emigrated to the USA with his wife and seven-year-old daughter Lilian. He was part of that diaspora of Jewish academics fleeing the Nazis, including Erwin Panofsky, Nikolaus Pevsner and Ernst Gombrich, which reinvigorated British art criticism, except that in this case it was the little girl who would go on to achieve radical distinction. Married, Lilian Randall became a curator at the Walters Museum in Baltimore. In that role she wrote the pioneering *Images in the Margins of Gothic Manuscripts* in 1966, unflinchingly examining hundreds of examples of medieval marginalia. She had tirelessly sought out these edge-lands in America and Europe, and found in her own museum such gems as a book of Psalms in which tiny construction workers hauled letters into place using ropes and ladders. Randall modestly wrote that she had made a tenuous start on the subject, but sixty years on she remains the authority, much quoted, her book unavailable to order at any price. I called the Walters Museum just now and they remember her fondly – 'Oh yes, she is alive and well, happy and retired.'

Many examples of marginalia remain popularly unknown, but the digitization of early books is changing that every year. We know that they were ubiquitous in the religious books which made up most of early book production, and in law books and histories, romances and poetry. Their frequency is indicated by their modern-day distribution in the libraries of the West. Here is a brief tour by city, but strap in for the ride and expect to see the world slightly anew in a few paragraphs' time. As Kaitlin Manning, a dealer in medieval books said recently, 'It's such a shock when you have this idea in your head of what medieval society was like.' Delicate readers may even experience, as Baudelaire did when he saw an English pantomime, vertigo.

It all started early. The magnificent *Book of Kells* (*c.* 800) in Dublin has a famous chi-ro page on which the very name of Christ in Greek is inhabited by cats, mice and otters; two fluttering moths meet amid it all. Later medieval marginalia moved away from the central text to the edges, but this early style mirrors Celtic mysticism. The natural world was inherent in meditation, which was itself merely resting the mind in its natural state. In those days, extra-textual beasties did not need to be on the margins in literature or in real life: otters warmed Saint Cuthbert's feet, an eagle dropped fish by his cell, a horse brought him bread and he issued the world's first bird protection edict.

Moving into the Middle Ages, in a Cambridge college library, below a crucifixion scene, a monkey musician rides a fox backwards whilst a lion-man lusts after a prim maiden. In Bury St Edmunds, a man with a wooden leg attempts to shave a hare, reflecting a popular saying about doing the impossible. In Norwich, in a bible which was kept on the cathedral high altar, the page about Jesus's temptation in the desert is bordered with animals farting at each other. In the British Library, below Psalm 67, a monkey riding a goose shoots an arrow at a man's rear end: a recent scholar insists the man is Jesus. In a book of hours in the same library – such books were 'medieval bestsellers', ubiquitous as cookbooks today – a winged ape tries to pull *'Deus'* out of the text whilst a gryllus in jester's cap looks on in mock disapproval; a band plays pipe and drums below the text, and a cooking pot and lifelike butterfly fill other spaces. In other devotionals, a monkey eats its lunch sitting on a capital 'S', and mermaids lounge on borders.

Extraordinary things lurk in libraries around the world. In Oxford's Bodleian, a pigeon wears a funny hat, and a courtly betrothal scene is completely demure apart from a huge erection poking out of the man's robe. A knowing gryllus looks on from the wings, an interesting link to Othello's rather cynical romantic account. In Manchester's John Rylands Library a nun suckles a monkey, whilst in The Hague's museum one monkey bares his rear at a writing monk whilst another creeps up behind him to blow a horn in his ear. A breviary in Metz has two men sword-fighting on a tightrope, but both hold their decapitated heads. In St Omer, an archer aims for the rear of a half-fish half-man. In Genoa, cannibals eat genitalia. In New York's Pierpont Morgan Library, below the Office of the Dead, putrefying cadavers do a merry dance and on a prayer book page a naked human couple have sex less than conventionally (*Pulp Fiction* captured the position and sensed the milieu: 'I'ma get medieval on yo' ass'). In another New York collection, below a picture of the flagellation of Christ, a man plays bowls with his own excreta. On a devotional, two goats quietly shag. In a manuscript at Yale, a friar jousts with a nun. Elsewhere a smiling woman rides an eight-foot disembodied cock around like a jet-ski.

In Paris, the Bibliothèque Nationale has a prayer book made by a named female scribe who ran a workshop with her husband and continued to run it after his death. In unmistakable detail and below the word of the Lord, a nun harvests a big cock from a tree of cocks. Little men with vast erections jump on anything passing, be they animals or nuns. According to the medievalist Michael Camille, 'numerous documents attest to the involvement of women in Parisian Gothic manuscript production' and Eamon Duffy tells us that 'remarkably, a high proportion of surviving books of hours . . . were made for women'.

Marginal irreverence went right to the top: the Flemish book of hours made for Catherine of Cleves has trompe l'oeils of flowers, a sitting toad and a seashell on its pages. A little hand even reaches out of a fake hole in the page. A prayer book made for King Wenceslas in Prague had a comic adultery drawn in the margins, and, in Rome, a law book made for Pope Innocent III (1160–1216) is adorned with goat musicians and fox monks.

Some animals have certain associations, so rabbits and hares abound, as signifiers of sexual activity and playfulness.

Monkeys are an easy way to satirize human behaviour. They are so popular that one anonymous painter of the northern Netherlands is known as 'The Monkey Master'.

The biggest puzzle, generator of learned articles and endless online discussions, is the very many depictions of giant snails fighting knights, and usually winning. The joke, buried in some forgotten fable, seems to be on macho posturing, with the slow but armoured snail beating the knight, who bristles with weapons and pride. The snail carried noble associations too, with the moon (its horns come and go), with eternity (its shell a sacred spiral) and with the idea of a steady journey through life. In another piquant contrast to the boisterousness of knights, it was known to be hermaphrodite.

All these pictures of animals, animal/human entities and uncensored humanity show us a world more connected to nature than many of us experience, and more in touch with our animal functions. The body and its functions were a source of more humour than embarrassment. Death was everywhere – even when the Black Death was not raging – and so was crap: ordure had to be carried out of houses, and ran down the centre of many city streets.

I just stopped for a tea break and on the radio a woman was complaining at length about finding a fly inside a loaf of bread she had bought. The BBC interviewer – this is primetime radio amid a constitutional crisis – raised her voice incredulously with a shock which underlines our distance from medieval sensibilities, and said, 'What – inside the bread bag?'

We banish much of nature, death and crap out of sight and shops have whole shelves of killing fluids to banish 'weeds' and execute the humble moth, the pollinating wasp, the storied mouse, the fertilizing slug and even the noble snail. Much of our existence is conditioned, even our air. Our lavatories smell of pine forests, our hair of aloe vera, our crematoria are up back roads. But aloe vera cannot win. Today, as in Gothic times, the more we sanitize, the more storytellers and comedians playfully or outrageously bring out our human-ness. There is an eternal balancing mechanism in the human psyche. Pomposity and affectations of purity have always invited someone to blow a raspberry or, today, create a mocking tweet.

The humour of Rabelais, of Falstaff and Bottom, of Gillray and Alice, of *The Goon Show* and *Spitting Image*, depended on pompous targets, on lecherous vicars and laughable colonels. Pantomime, with its deliberately unconvincing cross-dressing and over-the-top innuendo, like music hall, shows a seamless continuity with the transgressive satire of medieval marginalia. Max Miller resembled a talking gargoyle, taking jokes so far to the edge that the audience wondered, 'Can he really mean that?' Soon after Max, that other gargoyle Frankie Howerd was a medieval figure, perennially finding a marble seat too cold, everyone 'at it' except him and verbally dancing between innocence and profanity. We laugh with relief, because the sacred is meaningless without sacrilege. The border between the two is attractive, magnetized and potent, a source of creativity. Anciently, magic happens there, 'where the froth meets the water'.

That master portrayer of flawed humanity Graham Greene, literary rival of the Monkey Master, professed himself drawn to this antinomy. 'I am interested in the virtuous thief, the bent priest, the saintly prostitute, the corrupt lawyer.' He realized that clowns in particular, expressing the absurdity of our seriousness, have a broader cultural significance than their modern banishment to circuses might indicate. 'Cities and thrones,' he wrote in *Our Man in Havana*, 'come and go.' They have 'no permanence. But the clown [is] permanent, for his art never changes.'

John Cleese said in a *Parkinson* interview that he just cannot understand why the most popular sketch in all of *Monty Python* is the bowler-hatted silly walk he takes into the brass-name-plated 'Ministry of Silly Walks'. It is perennial because, like the arse-kissing priests and fox monks of the medieval margin, it subverts institutional pomposity. This mechanism was at work in medieval manuscripts. Why else did Chaucer's pilgrims tell their bawdy tales, not at a fête or in a tavern, but on one of the holiest pilgrimages in Europe?

Medieval mystery plays were imbued with this same mechanism of 'if it's really serious, we'd better mock it to heat up audience engagement'. Freud's theory of jokes is useful here; they break the tension, provide an 'exhilarating freedom' and are 'socially recuperative'. So in those plays, which Shakespeare grew up with, the men nailing Christ to the cross cracked jokes as they did it, and much fun was had with Joseph's cuckoldry. The plays continued the humour and the limitless imagination of medieval marginalia. As Helen Cooper, Cambridge Professor of Medieval and Renaissance English, wrote in 2019:

> That readiness to stage anything and everything, and to enlist audience complicity in the make-believe that the stage could show the impossible, was the most important thing that Shakespeare and his contemporaries inherited from the mysteries.

The city was filthy but festive too, which the margins reflect. And it came right up to the cathedral walls, even in places which today have sedate precincts with shaven lawns and eagle-eyed vergers, sanctums disturbed only by the clacking of turnstiles and beeps of a card machine at the entrance. Conversely, yesterday I was delivering forty-five copies of *Romeo and Juliet* to the school in the Canterbury precincts when I passed an archaeologist in a pit by the west door; I asked what he had found. He showed me a floor of impacted chalk with cartwheel striations, and explained that the medieval cathedral had market stalls all around it. Medieval records mentioned a barber's shop attached to the cathedral itself for pilgrims' last-minute spruce-up; he said they had just found its foundations. Tat-sellers would have been inside the building too. As on the medieval page, and in so many of the *Canterbury Tales*, raucous commerce was cheek by jowl with sacred space.

Like Marrakesh's main square on a good day, the medieval European city was populated by jongleurs, comedians, quack medicine sellers and acrobats, all probably a bit more multi-gendered than we imagine from movie scene-setting. 'Matilda Makejoy' was a celebrated acrobatic dancer in medieval Paris. An English monk in the 1100s warned everyone about London:

> The number of parasites is infinite. Actors. Jesters. Smooth-skinned lads, Moors, flatterers, pretty boys, effeminates, pederasts, singing and dancing girls, quacks, belly-dancers, sorceresses, extortioners, night-wanderers, magicians, mimes, beggars, buffoons . . . So do not live in London.

Great churches and cathedrals were adorned with marginal art: carved gargoyles and comic figures up to all the pranks seen on manuscripts, and all once painted in bright colours. Canterbury, with all its archiepiscopal gravitas, has waterspouts which are half animal and half human, and, safely tucked away in the crypt built in 1090, a whole gallery of improbabilities from the marketplace and the fabulous realm: Indian acrobats, a Green Man, a chimera, a two-headed dog riding a dragon and, my favourite, a small lizard-like creature known from Persian myth which can turn itself into a wheel and cross the desert at lightning speed. On a fenland church near Cambridge is a man bent over, grinning down at us from between his legs while a water pipe protrudes from between his naked buttocks. All of this art is marginal – at roof level, underground or under seats as misericords – but still in conversation with the sacred, validating the house of God by saying, 'Come in, everything is under God.'

After weeks of research, I went to sleep puzzling over the purpose of these carved grotesques and had a vivid dream which for me got the spirit of what they are for, even if it sounds odd. I dreamed of a great cathedral being completed, but then put on a huge old flat hotplate. As the building warmed up it sprouted gargoyles and grotesques, crypt capitals swirled into life and I got the words, borrowed from technology: 'It's not a cathedral until it's been activated.' Grotesqueries activate the sacred machine, root it in truth. (In understanding them on the page, or in stone, it helps to think of them for a moment without the word grotesque, an early modern invention. Maybe it is just me, but when I do this thought experiment my shoulders relax a bit and human-ness past and present seem more connected up.)

In the Middle Ages, the sacred and profane lived together as if in one centaur, human-headed and human-hearted but satyr-hooved. Or, as the Bulgarian-French feminist philosopher Julia Kristeva said, it's the genius of Christianity to have the profane as the lining to its sacred cloth. Bakhtin too sees adjacency-but-division: 'In medieval art . . . the pious and the grotesque exist side by side but never merge.' Sir John Hegarty, the marketing guru, has said that Christianity is the greatest marketing story of all, with a logo everywhere which every-one knows. It was also sophisticated enough as an organization in medieval times to include our dark side – like much of the most potent advertising – not only in stone, but in speech. Dirty or scabrous fables usually had a moral; they were known as exempla, hence 'exemplary', and medieval preachers often ended their sermons with up to five of such side-splitting or nerve-jangling tales. They were an enjoyable treat after the moralizing sermon but they also addressed the audience's imagination more directly. These colourful sermons were mirrors of the churches aglow with paint made from plants and minerals. They resemble marginalia at the end of a devotional page. In another telling adjacency of sacred and profane, 'carnival' comes from *'carne vale'*, a farewell-to-meat pre-Lenten blowout of bodily indulgence and laughter.

This week in a Canterbury charity shop (the Crooked House, mentioned in Dickens) I got a twelve-page pamphlet with brown rusted hinges and a faded but tactile green matt paper cover: *The Paintings of Canterbury Cathedral* (Price 2/6d). It was printed in a Canterbury back-alley. It is the transcription of a 1935 lecture by Ernest Tristram, the Welsh railwayman's son and Royal College of Art Professor who went around the country uncovering painted-over medieval murals. (The year 1935 was a high point in exploring the wider meaning of Canterbury Cathedral. That year the Archbishop commissioned T. S. Eliot to write *Murder in the Cathedral*.) Imagine this, Tristram's evocation of a medieval cathedral interior:

> Roofs, walls, columns, even tombs and screens glowed with brilliant tints. Wall-spaces were filled with long ranges of subjects, tier above tier, *like the pages of a vast book* [my italics].

We have letters from the Middle Ages so one might think someone, somewhere, would tell us how all the marginal craziness 'landed with customers', as Hegarty might say. But no, it was all too interwoven in the subconscious for such easy explanations. We might have created just such conundrums for historians of the future by continuing to hang on to, say, the monarchy and swan-upping. Two medieval monks did write directly about the grotesque carvings in stone which mirror almost exactly the tropes of contemporary marginalia. They both ranted as we might mentally do about what on earth all those images were doing in a sacred place. They listed the enormities in lengthy and graphic detail, rather like the monk above describing London. They were getting off on it, so to speak; performing the smiling headshake at the obscene clown, for 'methinks they do protest too much'. It is as if the ascetic practices of, say, Becket with his hair shirt, craved and implied their opposite, a celebratory attitude to the body. Most ascetics seem to be sensualists – why else would they bother? The Middle Ages was a world which revered saintliness but also revelled in farmyard humour.

King Edward II opens another window on to this inner world. He had some heavy concerns: war with the Scots, tensions with France and barons so rebellious that they eventually murdered him. He enjoyed mixing with common people, even hedging and ditching with them. He also loved marginalia-style pranks, giving gifts such as an unrideable horse and a chronically lazy hunting dog. And he wanted to be entertained by silly japes too. His accounts record: 'Item paid to James of St Albans the Kings Painter who danced before the king upon a table and made him laugh heartily: 1 shilling.' His cook did even better, getting 20 shillings 'because he rode before the King and fell oftentimes from his horse, whereat the King laughed most heartily'. Heads of state are less publicly amused these days, but paradox and painful accidents thrive in Norman Wisdom and Monsieur Hulot films, in *Tom and Jerry* cartoons and now online.

Margin artists' ability to make monkeys of us was partly the fallout of a revolution in thought. From about 1100, newly rediscovered writers such as Ovid and Aristotle triggered a quiet earthquake under Europe. Aristotle taught the medieval intellect to realize that, as one historian put it, 'the whole process of cognition took place within the ambit of mundane experience'. God and Nature, Aristotle said, 'make nothing that does not fulfil a purpose'. The new way of thinking known as scholasticism, associated especially with Anselm of Canterbury, encouraged dialecticism – truth achieved via exploring opposites – and the incorporation of pagan classical stories into a renewed Christianity. It is no coincidence that Canterbury's scriptorium was one of the most prolific and creative in Europe. Gothic-era scribes were mentally energized by these seismic changes and felt more able to express their humanity and individuality than did their Anglo-Saxon forebears.

Medievalists get cross with Renaissance historians who claim a monopoly on the flowering of self-conscious individuality for their period. Over-extreme positions have been taken. One defender of the Middle Ages has even insisted that medieval marginalia are 'the birth of an artistic self-conscious' – surely nonsense and in turn a diminution of the cave painters' mentality. The truth is less binary, more continuous: hidden in sculptures high up on churches, and in the margins of medieval books locked up in libraries, is a self-conscious comfortableness with ambiguity and wildness which is a stage on from 'Dark Age' art, but continuous with the sixteenth-century Renaissance mentality. Like Hamlet, those anonymous carvers and scribes knew 'a hawk from a handsaw' and enjoyed laying out two such contrapuntal themes just for the hell of it, and the heaven of it.

What happened to it all? Medieval marginalia died off not because we stopped laughing, but because of print, which usually had meaner margins and made the text seem more authoritative. On top of that, print coincided with the Reformation and an era of violent censorship which lasted until after the Civil War. Henry VIII imposed dire penalties for anyone defacing his new editions of the liturgy, and as late as 1661 authorities seemed traumatized by images from Gothic times: one edict ran, 'Print noe Capital Letters with profane pictures.' No more eight-foot cocks, then. When devotion became politicized, the margins stopped being a playground.

Now we bid farewell to those crazy medieval scenes. The pipe and tabor fade, the pageant rustles away with the odd parting fart, the monkeys are still again, the snails put down their lances. With a splash, the mermaid is gone.

PENGUIN BOOKS

BRIDESHEAD
REVISITED

A portrait of an English family
and the fortunes of its
members

EVELYN WAUGH

COMPLETE 3 6 UNABRIDGED

8.   *Signs of Use*

I believe that when it comes to books, conventional morality doesn't exist.

Arturo Perez-Reverte, *The Dumas Club* (1993)

Writing in the Margin

The New York literary agent Michael Stearns has gone from a reverent attitude to books to scribbling in them so much that he buys multiple copies of some ('Moore, Munro, Cheever') 'to find out how they work'. His blog confessing this started a long thread of revelations. I like this one from 'Christina':

> Well, Funny Fivecats, I grew up borrowing books from my brother who would invariably flip out when he detected even the tiniest crack in the spine. As a result of this sibling trauma, I crack spines and write in the margins with abandon (though not library books, Keli, you rebel).

This is quite a rare level of liberation. Most of us are still as confined as 'Reena':

> I want so bad to write in books, but I just can't force my hand to do it. It's like there's some kind of force field surrounding the pages.

Writing on books is a form of guerrilla engagement with the text which has a long history of disapproval but a fine pedigree of approvers. Radical thinkers are the most copious and unashamed marginalists. Rather than reverencing text, they lift ideas off the page, dandle them and then critique them in the margin. The current 'remix culture' where ideas and music are mercilessly sampled and spatchcocked is favourable to dialoguing with the text. For the polymath George Steiner, what signifies a true intellectual is 'quite simply, a human being who has a pencil in his or her hand when reading a book'. Mark O'Connell of the *New Yorker* likes the idea that 'a nicely sharpened HB' can be so powerful, and is funny about it:

> I tend to slot mine behind my right ear, carpenter style; I like
> to think this lends a somewhat rough-and-ready aspect to my
> appearance as I sit reading *Middlemarch* on the bus home.

Interaction with a book changes the experience of it, in the same way that classical Indian music depends on audience reaction for its texture and direction. The reading experience, without interaction, may be more forgettable.

I have heard customers so often say something like, 'Oh yes, it's wonderful, I read it – but I can't remember a thing about it now.' Montaigne forgot whole books he had read too, which prompted him to annotate copiously but also to add a summary of his feelings in the back of the books he read. Inspired by him, last year I did that when I finally finished *Anna Karenina*. Looking back at that summary now, it is already full of reaction I have forgotten.

Henry Miller, in his out-of-print and oddball *The Books in my Life*, pointed out that such forgetfulness implies that humanity cannot remember properly, hence the phenomenon of history repeating itself. Miller observed that Montaigne (1533–92) retreated into his library because his age 'like ours [this was 1952] was an age of intolerance, persecution, and wholesale massacres'. Marginalia combat the loss of our reading memories; they are future-mending, past-restorative. Miller again:

> In marginal annotations of books one can discover one's former selves. When one realizes the tremendous evolution of one's being which occurs in a lifetime one is bound to ask: . . . did I learn my lesson here on earth?

The New Yorker Stearns finds the forgetfulness thing interesting too. Noticing a 'crap!' written by himself long ago in a book margin, he thought, 'Really? Was it that bad?' Margin-writing can be a conversation with the author, and with oneself. We keep holiday snaps and write travel journals, so it seems logical to record the reading journey, not just in some gift-book 'reading journal', or on an Excel spreadsheet as some do, but on the book itself. We are programmed, however, by ghostly authorities, not to 'deface' books, a strangely modern attitude.

Even though print terminated the magnificent exoticism of medieval marginalia, a few early printed textbooks were actually designed for student comments: a 1525 edition of Galen's *Methods of Medicine* had deliberately huge margins for medical observations, as did a 1595 Seneca printed at Padua, whilst a 1580 London law book was actually interleaved with blank pages for textual comments. Usually, though, printed books' narrow margins were restrictive for marginalists, most famously for the mathematician Fermat: he tantalized future centuries with his annotation saying that he had worked out a knotty theorem, but there just wasn't space in the margin for it.

However cramped the edge-land of a printed page, entering

it came naturally to us from the dawn of print right down to the mid-nineteenth century. I've just discovered, in the brutalist University of Kent Library as gusty rain lashes both the third-floor windows and the medieval barque of Canterbury Cathedral visible down by the river, that many early printed books imitated manuscripts, to ingratiate the new technology with traditionalist readers. Early printed books were effectively ersatz, like fake Armani jeans knocked out in Bangkok. One distinguished Italian bookseller closed down in disgust at the sight of such stuff debasing his stock-in-trade.

Making additions in the margins, and pasting in pictures and decorated initials from old manuscripts and other texts, were all widespread but little-documented practices – little documented because hard to catalogue and viewed, in our overlit modern times, as defacements. They have been celebrated by interdisciplinary historians, such as the now retired Mary Erler at Fordham University in the Bronx, pioneer of art/English intersectional studies, who found women cutting, inscribing and palimpsesting throughout the first century of print, as a devotional meditation, an inner practice like lovers putting padlocks on the Pont des Arts. At the Courtauld Institute of Art, Ursula Weekes agrees and has discovered Dutch printed books of hours with pictures artfully sewn on to pages using several colours of thread: needlecraft crashing joyfully over text with all the radicalism of Jackson Pollock or Francis Bacon finger-smearing their pictures. The mystics of the Little Gidding community were dervish-like in their marginalia and cutting-and-pasting of bibles, wielding pens and scissors-and-glue as a gnostic practice. King Charles I heard about their books and called for one. He thought it 'a diamond', better than anything in his 'jewel-house', and started annotating his own bible. According to Adam Smyth, Balliol College Professor of

Book History, cutting and pasting has been 'largely over-looked'. If margin-writing is the poor relation of book history, pasting-in is the disowned love-child, conceived in passion and resistant to categorization.

Were marginalia really widespread before our modern reverence for text? Yes, according to evidence from Heidi Hackel of the University of California. She has ploughed through 150 copies of the 1590 edition of *Arcadia* by Philip Sidney and found annotations in 70 per cent of them. Charmingly, two copies still had pressed flowers in them, and the everyday use of the poem during household tasks was evidenced in one copy by the rust-shadow of a pair of scissors.

Early in the 1600s Anne Clifford, an only child, privately anti-Puritan, vigorously annotated her large book collection and devised a unique way of engaging with her eclectic reading. She pinned up 'sentences, or sayings of remark' on 'her walls, her bed, her hangings, and furniture'.

For centuries, pages marked with marginalia indicated intelligence not irreverence, a questing mind rather than a vegetable passivity. A historian has discovered that 'marked books seem to have been a trope in the funeral tributes of the [early modern] period'. Annotating was not only accepted, its absence hinted at shallowness; a 1606 tribute to the late Earl of Devonshire ran: 'thou hadst not books as many have for ostentation, but for use, witness so many volumes whereto thou hast set notes.'

Bishop of Carlisle, Edward Rainbow's speech at Susanna Howard's funeral in 1649 praised her marginalia at some length, as a mark of her active intelligence. It is oddly moving, in part because she died at twenty-two, knowing that her adored book-loving father had just been sentenced to death by Royalists.

> She had digested her readings of books . . . as may appear . . .
> by the Books marked in the margent. She had marks of several
> kinds in those books where [she] most delighted, with what
> she was most affected, in the Margent.

'With what she was most affected'. Will anyone know what
most affected us? I wish my parents had let rip in their books
rather than left a few neat signatures. Like most of us, they
kept no diary, and most people who start a diary are quickly
disgusted by the panorama of triviality and mean-spirited
bleating into which it degenerates after the initial Prous-
tian entries. But in the warm moment when a book stirs the
heart, what epiphanies can be recorded to the benevolent and
unbigoted gods of reading. Biblia and Intima, I imagine they
are called. They smile on the writers in the margins and the
crackers of spines, their passionate dervish followers. Their
Hades is policed by gimlet-eyed librarians. In their Elysium,
tousle-haired readers lounge in arbours and treehouses, beds
and window seats, scribbling and page-folding, in easy telep-
athy with each other.

Ten years after Susanna Howard's funeral, in 1659, the
Czech philosopher John Comenius would prefigure Steiner
with instructions to deface:

> What is the Study?, a place where the student sits alone,
> addicted to his studies, while he reads Books . . . picks all the
> best things out of them [and] marks them with a dash, or a
> little star, in the Margent.

There was a whole system to these little marks. Robert Grosse-
teste, a sort of medieval Suffolk Stephen Hawking whose science was centuries ahead of his time, had no fewer than 400

marginal symbols, a lexicon still being decoded. These intricate and copious marginal engagements are the hallmark of Steiner/Grosseteste-type polymaths, interdisciplinary pioneers.

The magician-philosopher John Dee, used the margins as a 'sophisticated information-processing' space, according to Bill Sherman of the Warburg Institute, one of the few people to have analysed all of his marginal codes. Dee's pointing arms in the text have different sleeves depending on their place in what Sherman calls his 'cabalistic analysis'. Sadly, Dee entrusted his books to his brother-in-law Nicholas Saunders whilst travelling. Saunders appropriated and sold many, first scraping out or bleaching Dee's name and much of his marginal annotation, a felony only recently discovered by X-ray.

That quintessential Renaissance man Erasmus was not only a margin-writer, he too prescribed the practice, telling us that whenever we see 'a striking word [or] if some argument shows brilliant invention . . . any maxim worth committing to memory, such a passage should be indicated by an appropriate mark', and he enjoined 'a variety of marks'. Luther shared his great antagonist's attitude to annotation, filling his own copy of Erasmus's book on the New Testament with explosive disagreement ('I am not a kind reader and you are not a kind writer'), and picking holes in his punctuation.

Luther was letting off steam, one of several ways that marginal scribbling can be stress-reducing. Another one is in that first encounter with a difficult book. Descartes knew that his *Discourse on Method* was a challenging read. I certainly found it so as I tried to mark seminal passages, but I was cheered when midway through he said – I paraphrase his wordiness – 'Look, don't worry if you're not getting all this. I recommend people to skim read it first, marking good bits with a stroke of the pen, then to go back through it at leisure to see how those parts feel on second attention.'

We have only discovered a tiny part of the world's marginalia; Isaac Newton's are still being deciphered and analysed. As late as 1960 dealers and auctioneers – including the most famous, Quaritch of London – were selling annotated books more cheaply and cataloguing them as 'with some markings' or even 'soiled'. This morning (2019), the *Guardian* has half a page on the probable discovery of Milton's marked-up Shakespeare, found in Philadelphia. Up until the 1960s great libraries were ignoring or bleaching off marginalia. Even now they are understandably ambivalent. If, as they increasingly do, they have exhibitions celebrating marginalia, the catalogue has a version of: 'Enjoy this, but don't you go getting ideas unless you will later become famous.'

Magic Spells and Shopping Lists

Although recording religious dissent on devotional books was illegal for much of the early modern period, the expensiveness of paper made all books repositories for a wide range of needs. The family bible commonly doubled as a register of births, marriages and deaths. Few of us today have a ready place to record cosmic melancholy and quantify our spare bedding but Mary Everard did this during the Reformation, lamenting in a bible the destruction of her local shrine of the Holy Cross near Bacton in North Norfolk, and just below that writing 'in my chest are 12 blankets and a sheet'. Anne Withypole noted day-by-day battles in the Wars of the Roses and such turning points as the future Henry VII's arrival at Milford Haven, in the style of a BBC 'breaking news' line across the bottom of her prayer book.

Others recorded shopping lists and recipes. A Tudor book of love poetry by Boccaccio may have moved its reader, but she used the spacious title page to write a delicious-looking recipe for leek and herb sauce. One notational tradition which cheerfully survives today is that of dialoguing with cookbooks. In 1580 a woman deleted many passages in hers, and wrote 'all these recipes are verye falsly written, but being corrected heer they ar trew'. The poet Thomas Gray tried out a suet-and-pickled-herring-stuffed 'Calve's Heart' and understandably wrote next to the recipe, 'tried, and found bad'. Another refreshing voice, from the very kitchen garden, is seen on a late medieval medicinal herbal, annotated throughout with English folk names for plants, largely and boldly enough to indicate irritation with the stream of Latinisms. 'Basilisca' and 'Artemisia' prompt 'Adderwort' and 'Mugwort', beautifully written. Mention of 'Philomena' is annotated 'Nightingale' and when 'constipatus' is primly mentioned our anonymous writer seems to lose patience: 'May not go to Shit'. Similar independent outbursts in early modern books are found in Welsh, Gaelic and Cornish.

A smallholder in the 1600s blew off steam on the reverse of the title page in Seneca's *Morals* with a 250-word rant about a landowner trying to stop him cutting his thorn hedge for firewood. He seems to have lost the argument, but just wanted to record the injustice for posterity in a timeless book about right and wrong. In the United States, although the entry is only about a terracotta pot, a rare Native American voice from 1698 flickers into a margin-note found in Massachusetts by Heather Kopelsen, who says 'my jaw actually dropped' when she found it: 'Nunnacoquis signifies an earthen pot as [a Nemasket] Squaw tells me.'

The bubbling world of folk magic lived on into Christian times longer than much of the historical record tells us. It appears tantalizingly in marginalia, like a satyr flitting past in a wood. Shakespeare-era people wrote all sorts of spells in book edges: love-spells, magic words for fecundity, charms to write in butter or on an apple to heal toothache, or stop a nosebleed, and many curses on book thieves which call to mind the line on the bard's own grave, 'cursed be he that moves my bones'. A book of hours has a magic spell to quench a fire, and horoscope calculations. Eamon Duffy has pointed out that such charms were 'popular with all classes', and he deduces their 'widespread popularity' from the ubiquity of sermons denouncing them.

These quotidian but evocative edge-comments are perennial. Ted Hughes knew their poetry when he wrote in his blocky, forceful handwriting on the flyleaf of *Ariel*. He explained the long brown stains down the book as 'thatchdrip' from the house he and Sylvia Plath occupied in Devon. They were happy there, until Sylvia felt she was 'turning bovine', and the book's stains held that past, before her darker days at 23 Fitzroy Road.

There is sometimes more poetry in a moment recorded marginally than in a whole book of bad verse or flawed analysis. A recent Oxford student wrote in a dull lit. crit. text she/he was closely annotating, 'Christ, I've left the oven on.' Published authors labour to evoke the heat of human life, while guilty marginalists casually inseminate their pages with the real thing or, as the journalist and annotator Alexandra Molotkow put it, 'I coat the text in my enzymes.' The text is often the dull street plan of suburbia, or of a planned city, whilst the angled marginalia, crotchety or elegiac, take us up earthy alleys or on to the open heath of history. Good marginalia will save many a second-rate book from the dump. No other works of art have this potential to become a new creation: paintings, sculpture and architecture are understandably reverenced in their untouched form. Books can be 'DNA-tagged' by anyone and one day our traces will be analysed to yield up some of our identity to futurity.

For most of us, though, that force field over the page remains. The copious marginalist Hester Piozzi diarized the whole guilt thing in 1790: 'I have a Trick of writing in the Margins of my books, it is not a good Trick, but one longs to say something.' This multilingual friend of Dr Johnson slowly 'came out' in later life and openly annotated in a way that is now a goldmine for eighteenth-century cultural historians. In 1925 many of her jottings were published as a separate book, and they are still being mined. She recorded in margins how people dressed, that a friend cheated at cards using a leprechaun ('a Lypercorn Fairy'), children's reactions to Handel concerts, surviving customs in Wales and that the Prince of Wales's courtiers joked about '*Ich Dien*' standing for 'Dying of the Itch', venereal disease. We all have stray nuggets like this, but Hester's recording of them happened because of her 'Trick'.

An unlooked-for discovery made in the course of writing this book is that, throughout history, women especially seem to engage in the most uninhibited physical way with their books, from smelling, kissing and hugging them, to reading them up trees and by fires (to the despair of dilettante collectors) and copiously inking them. Perhaps women are more instinctive than men. To physically engage with a book is to negotiate with it, to allow it into one's emotions. Those who do this are likely to be people who are comfortable with ambiguity, alive to carnival and the ridiculous. Two-dimensional Superman for instance, either in costume or as clean-cut Clark Kent, would not be a marginalist or corner-folder. Batman, a figure more at ease with the diversity of life, would be. His homoerotic partner Robin indicates an impatience with the societal Book of Love. His on-equal-terms ease with the fatherly butler Alfred signals an absence of oedipal complications or sado-masochistic leanings. His secret doorways to the subconscious-symbolizing batcave make his house a place of acceptance, of anarchic fun. Here is a man likely, in his beautiful library, to wield a pen in the margins and exclaim at the pied beauty of human nature shown on the page, whilst Superman fondles his Kryptonite and checks his hair in the mirror.

In my years of interviewing potential booksellers, I always tried to really discover the nature of candidates, since true booksellers bring themselves to work rather than leave their nature at home. One of my most productive questions was 'Who would win a fight in a pub car park between a vampire and a werewolf?' The question got the interviewee talking about the relative natures of the two, cold and calculating versus wild and instinctive. The werewolf, as Stevenson realized when he had animalian Hyde write 'startling obscenities' on the pages of one of Jekyll's pious books, would be the marginalist.

Personal Politics

With his scribbling habit, however, Hyde would not have lasted long under Henry VIII. In religious books of the Henrician years a 'remarkably widespread obedience', and even Orwellian fear, are in evidence. After Henry's break with Rome, over and again readers defaced references to certain saints, especially that bane of past monarchy, Thomas à Becket, whose great shrine was destroyed in 1538. Prayers to him were scrubbed out; if they were too big, pages were pasted over them. In Ipswich, someone scratched his name out and wrote 'God Save the King'. Purgatory was out too, erased from prayers even when this made them nonsense. The Pope got the worst beating: his crown was scrubbed out, his title changed to 'bishop' and Antichrist comments were frequent. Some of this was aimed to please Thomas Cromwell's thought police, like the book of hours mechanically annotated: 'I utterly repudiate and remove the name of the Pope.'

Richard Topcliffe revelled in his task of torturing what he called in his book-margins, 'lewde Popish Beasts . . . backwod' types. In his copy of a history of the Reformation he drew gallows 'for the Pope', whom he called on other pages 'viper' and 'bastard'. He went off the book near the end – it was by an Italian – and fantasized: 'I wish that I had the author of this book in St John's Wood with my two-handed sword.'

A prayer book in the British Library has a heart-breaking page that takes us into the crucible of the Reformation. Henry VIII himself wrote in it hoping that prayers be said for him, and Catherine of Aragon wrote, 'I think prayers of a friend the most acceptable under God and because I take you for one of mine, assured I pray you remember me in yours. Katherine the Queen.' Then her daughter Princess Mary has written, 'Remember me in your devotions.' After Henry's divorce, both women's signatures were carefully and ruthlessly blotted out.

That the world of spells and fairy lore made it through both the Reformation and the Puritan Republic is remarkable. Spenser's *The Faerie Queene* (1590), Shakespeare's *A Midsummer Night's Dream* (1595) and Purcell's *The Fairy-Queen* (1692) were all highly successful. One 1611 copy of Spenser's poem shows violent enough opposition to indicate how divided the national psyche remained. It was bought for £8 – cheap because it was annotated – in 1953 from David's Bookshop in Cambridge by the now-retired Professor Stephen Orgel. The shop is still there, 300 years old, in a leafy pedestrian passage. The first owner wrote uncompromisingly in the book: 'fairies are devils, and therefore fairyland must be the devils' land.' Jove, mentioned nearby, is called 'what else but a devil', St George 'a popish saint created by Idle Monks', and a mention of the Virgin Mary prompts a little rant about idolatry. At the same time, we increasingly discover, Virgin statues and relics were being privately revered and frequently secreted in walls and attics for better days.

In Portobello Road market, *c.* 1938, my now long-dead father found another political time-travel book, for a few bob, one which graphically illustrates readers making historical parallels in ink over a 300-year period. It lives in my house now. It is Plutarch's *Lives of the Noble Grecians and Romans*, published in 1595 by Shakespeare's publisher and fellow Stratfordian Richard Field. The translator, Richard North, used vivid Elizabethan prose, so good that Shakespeare lifted whole phrases: he used this source a lot for *Julius Caesar* (1599), *Antony and Cleopatra* (1607) and *Coriolanus* (1609). All the lives in my copy of Plutarch concerning those three plays have marginal brackets and underlinings, and several comments in a Tudor hand, so Shakespeare was not the only Tudor to draw contemporary parallels from them. *Coriolanus*, the play, was a safe way for Shakespeare to examine the Essex rebellion against Queen Elizabeth in 1601. Essex, the much-loved favourite who once played cards and relaxed all night with Her Majesty, entered London with a rebel army and was beheaded as a result. In the margin of the life of Coriolanus, the Tudor reader has written 'like ye Earl of Essex his going into ye citie', one of two marginalia about Essex which hint that the Globe Theatre audience would have understood the layered meaning of *Coriolanus*. I cannot be sure the marginalia are by any old Tudor. I did get a shiver down my spine just now when I saw the underlining of the Ides of March passage in the life of Brutus. But surely Shakespeare's own *Plutarch* ending up in Portobello Road is too unlikely.

After the Civil War the book was owned by a John and Elizabeth Doxford, who both lavishly practised their signature on several pages. About a century later, in November 1772, Elinor Day proclaimed her ownership; two years later she hastily recorded, upside down in Alcibiades, a payment 'Received of Robert'. The Victorian owner – whom I date to after 1839 by his mention of a forgotten book by a J. Hollings, wrote over a dozen detailed comments, such as 'Thus too much power leads to audacity' and 'Such factions are the ruins of states.' After this, about 300 years after it was first sold in London, the book faced its most traumatic event, a rebinding which involved cutting down the margins, thus slicing off chunks of all the marginal notes. Finally, in 1965, my sister Ann, a librarian, pencilled in how she worked out from minor printing details, despite the missing title page, that this is the 1595 edition.

The Civil War era changed political marginalia into what the historian Professor Steven Zwicker calls 'a battlefield of correction, denial, and repudiation', complicated by a blizzard of pamphlets. This politicization of reading, Zwicker thinks, 'scripted a new political culture in which debate and engagement were normalised – the culture of coffeehouse and club, the politics of party'. So scribbling in the margins helped us to challenge authority. There is a direct line between the quiet scratching of a quill in a Tudor chamber and the turbulence of debates in Parliament. One did not cause the other, but inky dissent certainly helped to get us used to vigorous disagreement with the status quo. By 1772, anti-slavery campaigner Granville Sharp chooses to rebut the arguments in a slave-owner's book point by point, underlining every justification for slavery and replying in the margin.

Some notable instances in our own times give a flavour of this continuing process. Surprisingly perhaps, one of Edward Said's admired sources for his theory of imperialism was William Blake's fiery marginalia on Joshua Reynolds' *Discourses*. The margins in Mao's and Hitler's personal libraries are littered with self-justifications and apocalyptic predictions.

More recently, Graham Greene was keen to set the record straight when he got a copy of Christopher Andrew's history of British intelligence, *Secret Service* (1985). He corrected several points about Guy Burgess so as to distance himself from that defector. Sexual politics developed in the margins too. When Vita Sackville-West was reading Edward Carpenter's *The Intermediate Sex* she carefully wrote 'Middlesex' by the title, reflecting her conviction that over time gender fluidity would become accepted, and that her whipcord breeches and laced boots would raise no eyebrows. In recent times, history students in an Oxford library don't hold back. Their forensic analyses have included 'wanker!' and 'Oh, the 80s'. The comment, in a history of the Hundred Years War: 'The Scots are such a dull and dour lot', stung – one presumes – a Scot to reply in a way which had brevity if not eloquence: 'Fuck off'.

Creative Conversations

Annotators are critics' ancestors. What they lack in polish they make up for in immediacy and hot engagement. Readers – more than critics, I speculate – do actually throw books at the wall in anger on occasion, a milder version of Topcliffe's St John's Wood fantasy. A toddler and I were once so annoyed by a fairy tale I was reading out that we agreed to throw it out of the open second floor bedroom window. Doing so was cathartic. Come to think of it, my ex-wife must have experienced the same release, post-separation, as she threw one of my favourite books out of our bedroom window (we are friends now). This week I threw a new Oliver Reed biography down the stairs because it said his sword-fighting was so realistic in *The Three Musketeers* that 'stuntmen were seen retching in the corner'. Great story, but stuntmen? I just could not credit multiple stuntmen throwing up. Shabby storytelling, I thought, as the book clattered downstairs to shouts of annoyance from family members below.

This feeling of the book as a live entity sometimes washes uncontrollably over readers, as it did for this recent scribbler on a work by David Shields: 'I'm going to punch this book in the face if it makes this point again.' As viscerally, a reader experiencing the last paragraph of *Madame Bovary*, wrote 'motherfuck!', and then 'utter, utter cynicism'.

In marginal comments you can sense the frustration of Oxford students setting aside their youthful pleasures to plough through works of criticism which have invaded their bedroom and their book-love: on a Pindar analysis, 'moonshine from start to finish'; on an abstruse take on Flaubert, 'Do not use this book. It is all complete bollocks.' The Oxford University Marginalia group, to whom I owe these examples, was born in 2012, when the student April Pierce encountered an annotation, a reminder that books are about life, not the other way around:

> Let us suppose that we have recovered the poetic experience, of which the text is merely a trace as the trace in a cloud-chamber shows where the photon has been.

As marginalia are being widely digitized and celebrated, it is becoming clear that vigorous critical reaction on the page is the secret history of literary criticism. On the quiet, we've made anvils of our books. Jacques Derrida, the French critic who dethroned the authority of the text and was metaphorically the principal violinist of postmodernism, loved marginalia and, in one book he authored, he even had his own annotations printed in his margins, an act of almost onanistic intertextuality.

Blake, who reinvented what a book could be, was free of text-reverence, writing vigorous criticisms, especially in works by his aesthetic enemies, the philosopher Francis Bacon ('Villain!') or the portraitist Joshua Reynolds. A fawning biography of Reynolds was turned into a demolition job by Blake, all digitized now on the British Library website. On the title page he declares: 'This Man was Hired to Depress Art. This is the Opinion of Will Blake my Proofs of this Opinion are given in the following Notes.' His notes in this biography, including comments such as 'all sublimity is founded on minute discrimination', make it a great source for understanding Blake's mind. Scholars agree that, tonally, he was aiming his marginalia at posterity, intending them to be read one day by a wider public, as when he annotated Johann Lavater's *Aphorisms*:

> I hope no one will call what I have written cavilling because he may think my remarks of small consequence, for I write from the warmth of my heart, and cannot resist the impulse I feel to rectify what I think false in a book I love so much.

Coleridge coined the term 'marginalia' and his comments were so polymathic or poetic that Charles Lamb even lent him books to get his annotations, joking that it would triple their value; the poet was also a lecturer of Žižekian popularity in his time. Like Blake, Coleridge sensed that his marginalia would have a wider audience; they now comprise six volumes of his collected works. In the margin of a work by Schelling, the German philosopher, Coleridge gave his marginalia manifesto: 'A book I value, I reason & quarrel with as with myself when reasoning.' Edgar Allan Poe similarly read with pen in hand, for 'thoughts, agreements, and differences of opinion'. This honing of the mind using a book can be seen in Petrarch's annotated *Livy*, Christopher Columbus's *Marco Polo* and Gibbon's *Herodotus*.

Keats's annotated *Paradise Lost* is particularly thrilling, because he is marvelling at how Milton gets effects by odd but magical conjunctions, and then actually working out how to emulate the magic. The two-volume copy, now in London's Keats House collection, has such copious notes that they amount to a book within a book. They have recently been digitized. He praises Milton's 'stationing', a visual arts term of the day for the evocation of a moment: Adam witnessed the eating of the forbidden fruit and was not just horrified, he:

Astonied stood and blank, while horror chill
Ran through his veins, and all his joints relaxed . . .
Speechless he stood and pale

Keats commented: 'he sees beauty on the wing, pounces upon it.' He was deeply impressed too by the way Milton sang of sadness, of what he calls in the margin 'black brightness'. Throughout *Paradise Lost*, Keats's notes show that he is experiencing the poem as a sensory roller-coaster, learning from the evocation of sounds, smells and tactile experiences. He told Leigh Hunt that he thought Milton became, in his blindness, a sensual epicure. Keats notes that even sensory revulsion was 'stationed' in *Paradise Lost*, as when fallen angels tasted food as ashes and 'with spattering noise rejected . . . with hatefullest disrelish writhe their jaws'. As if enchanting his own talent by proximity to Milton's, Keats wrote his poem 'To Sleep' on the flyleaf of volume two.

Another instance of artist-on-artist notation has opened a window on that central dichotomy of nineteenth-century aesthetics, the passionate differences between Coleridge and Wordsworth. Wordsworth margin-noted that some Shakespeare sonnets were 'harsh obscure & worthless'. Coleridge exploded: 'I can by no means subscribe to the above pencil mark of W. Wordsworth; which however is my wish, should never be erased . . . Englishmen have degenerated.' In his desire for the preservation of the comments, he was way ahead of his time. His own marginalia were, right into the twentieth century, ignored or even destroyed, as were some of Milton's. Coleridge used many other books as workshops, annotating, for instance, Blake's *Songs of Innocence and Experience* – though the copy is lost – and William Godwin's play *Abbas*, which bears comments such as 'flat or mean', 'common-place-book language' and 'bad metre'.

The Tudor owner of *George a Greene*, an anonymous play, wrote some marginal speculations about its authorship, including this startling line: 'written by a minister who acted in it himself said W Shakespeare'.

Jane Austen's marked-up Goldsmith poems show her mind at work, and near the end she concludes to herself that Cowper is preferable by far. A little later, the historian Thomas Macaulay used Milner's lengthy *History of the Church* as his workbench, dialoguing with it until near the end: 'Here I give in. I have done my best – but the monotonous absurdity, dishonesty and malevolence of this man are beyond me.'

Rupert Brooke marked up profusely but languidly in pencil, as a chum noted, even on the River Cam: 'He would keep the paddle going with his left hand, and with the other make pencil notes . . . steadying the text against his knee.'

James Frazer had this sort of textual back and forth, but with himself. His first edition of *The Golden Bough*, in 1890, was in two volumes, a leviathan analysis of myth and magic around the globe. Although some Christians were scandalized by this masterwork of comparative religion, the Glaswegian chemist's son had only just started. So that he could add to the first edition, he had a one-off version printed with interleaved blank pages. His additions in ink on these pages eventually added up to the final, 1915 edition of twelve volumes, a founding text of anthropology.

Sometimes, as when Hyde defaces Jekyll's book, annotations show personality in flux. Alexandra Molotkow, when she packed up her first studio apartment to move to a bigger place in Manhattan, cringed at the explosive and arrogant marginalia in her books written when she was '25 and cocky'. In her own defence, like a sort of lightweight Hyde, she mused that she had used the margins for 'identity formation'.

Although T. S. Eliot was less likely to leave cocky juvenilia on the page, he did leave some charmingly personal effusions in Edmund Husserl's *Logische Untersuchungen*: 'What the devil does this mean?' 'damn'd Locke' (Blake would have smiled) and '*es sollte überhaupt Kuchen geben*' '(there should always be cake)'.

Sometimes a mere marginal mark signifies a change in the literary landscape, like a jet of lava from a dormant volcano. In a copy of Thoreau's *Walden*, next to an underlined 'the traveller must be born again on the road' is a small neat tick. The copy, borrowed from a library in 1949 and not returned, was marked by Jack Kerouac.

Love and Death

It is said that there is a secret tunnel between love and death. Both are escapes from the everyday to mysterious lands. Faced with such puzzling glories, we have often resorted to the secrecy of between the pages to open our hearts. When a diary seems too cold and a letter too public, Biblia and Intima will understand.

Coleridge celebrated annotation as a way to cheat death. In a copy of Lamb's *Plays of Beaumont and Fletcher* he wrote, 'I will not be long here, Charles! & gone, you will not mind my having spoiled a book.' Others have used the lasting nature of a book to mark a death. In 1348 Petrarch pathetically noted the death of Laura from the Black Death in his copy of Virgil. The night before his execution, Charles I gave his copy of the collected works of Shakespeare to his servant, Thomas Herbert, who made a note of his master's passing beneath the royal signature. When the great modern expert on marginalia, Heather Jackson, was introduced at a book event as someone who studied the annotations of the famous, she thought, 'Actually, it's the reverse: marginalia are mostly the voice of anonymous people.' In that vein, an unknown late-medieval owner wrote this touching side-note on a devotional calendar page, next to 27 November: 'my moder departyd to god'.

And now to love. One lover-like friendship is lost to history except on a page in a New Testament, now in the British Library. There, Queen Elizabeth I wrote a heartfelt plea which resonates for anyone burdened by their job: 'Among good things I prove and find, the quiet life doth most abound, and sure to the contented mind, there is no riches may be found.' This is signed to her maid Anne Poynts, 'Your loving friend', but, remembering her position, the Queen has crossed out 'friend' and written 'mistress'. Anne wrote after this, in verse of her own invention:

> More swift than swallows flight
> our young days fly away
> then age calls us for his right,
> and death will have no stay
> both by day by night.

There is almost a lover-like warmth here, and Anne pointedly ignored her mistress's decorum in signing herself, 'Your friend Anne Poynts'.

Elsewhere in Tudor London, an anonymous lovelorn male used a dull textbook as lovers use trees to write their feelings on: 'Elizabeth Taylor is the Beauty of Chanell Row' (this narrow street, called Canon Row now, is still there, a stone's throw from Big Ben.)

An American woman had a similar outburst in a 1790s book of sermons, interrupting a list of goods – 'matches two cents, lard eight cents' – with 'my Dear Mister Brown I love you With all my heart and I Hope you do the same.' In the same decade the Irish romantic novelist Regina Roche portrayed the erotic charge which annotation could hold for a lover. In *Children of the Abbey* (1796), lovelorn Amanda finds 'fresh objects to remind her of Lord Mortimer': books with notes 'by his hand, for her particular perusal. Oh! What mementoes were those volumes of happy hours she had passed at the cottage.' Amanda stays up 'weeping the night away'. Her male parallel is Lockwood in *Wuthering Heights*, whose late-night discovery of margin notes by Catherine 'covering every morsel of blank that the printer had left' kept him up. 'An immediate interest kindled within

me' and 'I began forthwith to decipher her faded hieroglyphics.'
Glorvina in *Vanity Fair* tries in vain to use margin-notes as love
charms when she lays siege to Major Dobbin, borrowing his
books and 'scoring with her great pencil-marks such passages of
sentiment or humour as awakened her sympathy'. 'Bah,' Dobbin tells a fellow officer, 'she is only keeping her hand in.'

As the admirer of 'the Beauty of Chanell Row' knew, love-
marginalia console the aching heart. This feeling has survived,
yea unto the very wall of the public lavatory – a folk-magic
voodoo belief that forlorn love can be recorded in earth-
memory, be made real by writing it out. It can even apply to
self-love. The chanteuse of falling in and out of love, Marlene
Dietrich, poured her *Weltschmerz* on to her book margins as
she lived out her last decade in her upstairs flat in Paris. The
street, in a poignant coincidence, was named after another
reclusive annotator: Avenue Montaigne. After her death, aged
ninety, in 1992 the American Library in Paris had just a few
hours' notice of the arrival at their back door of a truckload of
Marlene's books – over two thousand in English, French and
German.

Goethe, whom she 'deified' is enthusiastically marked, and
in more recent books there is much setting-the-record-straight,
in several colours of pen. There is information about Heinrich
Mann's influence on the 1930 movie of his novel *The Blue Angel*,
her breakthrough film, made when she was twenty-nine. A
biography of her by Charles Higham is a veritable palimpsest:
'All lies', 'Untrue', 'why do I always wear grey stockings?' and
'I hated cats all my life.' Although these detailed comments
might bear out her daughter's allegation that the real love of
Marlene's life was Marlene, with one little circle she also
revealed the long shadow of one great unconsummated love:
Ernest Hemingway. Their thirty-year correspondence was

erotically charged and intellectually stimulating for both; Hemingway sent her several story drafts for comments. As he put it, they were simply 'victims of unsynchronized passion'. Her German dictionary has only one word carefully ringed: 'Kraut', his nickname for her.

The Once and Future King by T. H. White has been a satisfying escape for many thousands. Neil Gaiman and J. K. Rowling both acknowledge the influence of its eccentric wizard, and of its mythical characters made warmly human. Sadly, its author never escaped his own psychological torments, which started with his alcoholic father and a brutal boarding school. He once said that school canings made him a flagellant. Even more than Dietrich, he shared his torment with the margins of his book collection. Sexually fluid in an age of straight-imperialism, he reflected in a diary on his 'hideous fate', having 'an infinite capacity for love and joy with no hope of using them'. The nature writer Helen Macdonald thought him 'one of the loneliest men alive'. An elaborate dreamer, White read Freud, Adler and Jung for insight. In the margins of Freud's theory of dream analysis he urges himself: 'Read this repeatedly.' Jung prompts him to extensive analysis and argument. The idea of parts of houses in dreams as symbolizing parts of the mind excites him: 'I feel sure that this is right.' Later on, White hares off into free association:

I tried to die of dysentery. Wine. Dis-entry. De sentry. To die of dis-entry. Failure to enter. Silk. Sick. Six. Beating . . . My mother's name was K for con . . .

The novelist Jim Crace, a T. H. White admirer, was moved to tears when he consulted the White archive, which includes his 400 books, many of which are annotated. Like Coleridge,

White certainly wanted his marginalia to survive and be studied as part of his work. In this he was nailing himself out for public inspection, turning a horrible process into a message, recklessly punk in a way he could never be in the creaky BBC TV interview conducted by an oleaginously supercilious Robert Robinson, who makes White clam up. White's notes are troubling, but they make one realize how much more layered authors can be if they flick on the odd light backstage. Helen Macdonald's excellent *H is for Hawk* certainly drew its naked honesty in part from White, who is the dark engine of her book.

Patina or Damage?

Some customers demand a discount for the slightest mark on a book, but others cheerfully pay full price even when I point out damage they have not noticed and offer money off. I used to think the latter folk were either rich or in a hurry but I came to realize that they genuinely don't care about the odd knock or dent. This split in our psyche goes way back, and it exists within attitudes to marginalia, corner-folding and all sorts of wear.

For some, marks of use are marks of love and messages from history, but for others? Here is Lydia, Sheridan's rich heiress in *The Rivals* (1775), expressing her disgust at a book which has been truly DNA'd by another:

> Heigh-ho! – Yes, I always know when Lady Slattern has been before me. She has a most observing thumb; and, I believe, cherishes her nails for the convenience of making marginal notes.

Her maid agrees, calling the book 'so soiled and dog's-eared . . . it wa'n't fit for a Christian to read'.

Charles Lamb actively wanted such signs of the body on his books. Of used books, he wrote, 'How beautiful to the genuine lover of reading are the sullied leaves, and worn-out appearance, nay, the very odour . . .' Lamb is portraying true reading as a broad engagement with humanity in all its diversity and knockaboutness. For him, old books 'speak of a thousand thumbs'. In a marvellous image, he warms to an imagined 'lone sempstress . . . after her long day's needle-toil', reading 'far into midnight to steep her cares'.

Lamb's cry for secondhand books, 'Who would have them a whit less soiled?' is the voice of the Romantics, close to unmanicured nature, human or otherwise. When Coleridge and Hazlitt found a worn-out copy of James Thomson's *The Seasons* on the window seat of a Devon inn, Coleridge exclaimed, 'that is true fame!' – meaning use and love, rather than a canonical presence in a great library or an antiquarian's bookcase. Thomson's poem from 1730 entered everyday life to such a degree that 250 years later my mother was unconsciously quoting it when she told us eight children to eat only 'an elegant sufficiency'.

George Eliot, writing in the 1850s, signalled a delight in used books. In *The Mill on the Floss*, Maggie's *The Imitation of Christ*, got for sixpence at a bookstall, with its 'corners turned down in many places', has marginalia in 'strong pen and ink . . . long since browned by time'. The patina of this 'little, old, clumsy' book linked it, for Maggie, to the mysticism of the text, an essay in Christ-like humility and unattachment to possessions, its secondhandedness presciently Thunbergian. George Eliot, like Dickens, celebrated patina in an age of growing utilitarianism.

Heather Jackson found that annotations in books were actively prized in sellers' catalogues up until 'about 1820'.

The Industrial Revolution cut off many from the natural world, and a new authoritarian attitude to the bodily biome dictated that we should not leave our mark on books, which themselves became, more often than not, texts sacralized by the cleric and the lawyer, the politician and the teacher.

This hygiene-fever peaked in the high Victorian age, after the marginalia-filled medieval-to-Romantic epoch. A library historian writes of 'the sensory deprivation of the post-1850 public library, where food was banned along with talking'. In a supreme irony, the sound of uncut pages being sliced open in an unread book was even frowned at (a sound beautifully recalled in fiction by Lucia Berlin in *A Manual for Cleaning Ladies* as 'like a sigh').

Martha Dewing was a late-nineteenth-century American version of today's Marie Kondo, the clutter-clearing crusader who has inspired mass clear-outs of any book which does not 'spark joy'. In *Beauty in the Household* (1882), Dewing recommended a small bookcase with doors, so that 'one does not soil one's hands' with 'the corrupting moth and dust' of books left on open shelves. Maybe this was an American Puritan hangover. Dewing's evangelical contemporary in London, Charlotte Yonge, warned readers about servants 'soiling' books. Marie Corelli, an overtly Christian novelist described by James Agate as having 'the mentality of a nursemaid', was even more popular in her day than Conan Doyle. The royal family and the middle classes gave ear to her decent-minded views on life, the stridency of which contrasted with the covertness of her bisexuality. For Corelli, used books were all wrong:

The true lover of books will never want to peruse volumes that are thumbed and soiled by hundreds of other hands. To borrow one's mental fare from Free Libraries is a dirty habit . . . like picking up eatables . . . One book, clean and fresh . . . is worth half a dozen of the soiled . . . volumes . . . which carry disease-germs.

Monique Hulvey of Lyons's municipal library inspected hundreds of old books from several European countries and is able to confirm the nineteenth-century itch to blitz. She writes:

The destruction of manuscript annotations reached its peak in the nineteenth century, when printed leaves were washed and bleached in a concerted effort to 'clean' the margins of the books, and the edges were cropped as much as possible in rebinding, in order to get rid of 'mutilating marks'.

This desire to remove annotations was part of an industrial-age respect for new products. Mass production made new things more widely available, and so secondhand things became a mark of lower status. To be rich and modern was to possess new stuff. In attitudes to books, this had bizarre manifestations. A craze for pristine books became almost provenance-phobia, a sort of War on Terroir.

The Desire for Pristine Books

The fear of pollution from books was literalized in the fear of 'dirty books'; 1857 saw the Obscene Publications Act, intended to outlaw what the Chief Justice called 'a poison more deadly than prussic acid'. All these chemicals: a new awareness of the potential of acids engendered a chemical warfare on books and, as we shall see, in the home.

Library reformer Frederick Greenwood took the idea of books as filth-carriers to its logical end and recommended the use of 'book disinfecting apparatus'. As he contentedly reported in his 1890 *Manual for the Management of Libraries*, Dundee Library used a lidded 'tinplate' cupboard and at Sheffield they heated books 'to the temperature of boiling water'. He thought carbolic acid a good fumigator, although he admitted that the smell lingered for a while. His ultimate gas oven is described with true left-brain attention to metrics:

> The simplest and best arrangement is . . . a metal fumigator made from 16th wire gauge sheet iron, with angle iron door-supports and side-shelf rests. Its weight is 3cwt 1qr and the cost of it is £5 10s.

Gentler readers should skip the next bit:

> Compound sulphurous acid is burned in a small lamp . . . The shelves should be perforated in order to allow of a free circulation of the fumes of the acid.

This muscularly Christian and authoritarian hygienism was a zeitgeist, no mere eccentricity. Parliamentary time was used in 1910 to pass an Act forbidding the kissing of bibles during oath-taking. It's lucky for the blood pressure of that Act's supporters that they never read the obscure account I found of seventeenth-century Indian converts in Virginia getting lusted-for bibles off ships from England and ecstatically stripping off to rub the holy book all over their bodies.

Women and the poor were often infringers of godly cleanliness. In the 1920s Arnold Bennett feverishly conjured a double whammy:

> Go into the average home . . . in the quietude of 'after-tea', and you will see a youthful miss sitting over something by Charlotte Yonge or Charles Kingsley. And that something is repulsively foul, greasy, sticky, black [with] personal dirt.

'Why' does not 'the Municipal Sanitary Inspector' destroy the maid's book? It is significant that the biographer of that scourge of germs Pasteur was vocal on women's dirty habits with books: 'A book, in their eyes, is nothing more than a newspaper: they fold it, crumple it.'

M. R. James had a marvellous antiquarian imagination but it stopped short of books containing marginalia, 'medical receipts and so forth'. Cataloguing books at Cambridge in the early twentieth century, he described such signs of use in hygienist terms, as 'a residue – one is tempted to call it a sediment'.

Coincident with the Bennett quote, householders, unaware then of both the ubiquity and necessity of bacteria, began a scorched-earth policy in the home. Hydrochloric-acid-based Harpic came first in 1921, then a dentist-devised bleach-based Domestos in 1929. The napalm of the lavatory, Brobat, was launched in 1935. The Domestos newspaper ad played upon dirt-guilt with a spruce maid saying, 'Surely you do too?'

The degradation of the body in the First World War – lice, mud, walking over rotting corpses – was an unprecedented episode of European collective shame. We in the West had all been complicit in a previously unimagined vortex of dehumanizing poor hygiene. Partly in reaction, Tolkien created the often foul *Lord of the Rings*, and Kenneth Grahame by contrast retreated into the idyll of *The Wind in the Willows*, where Mole and Badger, not corpses, inhabited underground dugouts. Norbert Elias, a medical orderly on the German side, reacted with his monumental two-volume *The Civilizing Process*. The gravamen of the work was the rise of the 'civilized' individual, but a central part of that process was identified as the development of personal hygiene. Elias, supporting what Bakhtin was to argue and Rabelais had played with fictively, says that we all have a post-medieval prudishness about our bodily functions. His book was only gradually translated, hitting English academia in 1969. His complex but influential identification of hygiene with virtue helped to perpetuate the atmosphere in which marginalia were either ignored or removed.

As late as the 1970s, when Heather Jackson first encountered Coleridge's sea of marginalia, she was advised by a senior academic to 'rub them out and say no more about it'. Anna Midtgaard has argued that librarians remain psychically divided about signs of use. She works in the Rare Books section of Copenhagen's Royal Library and notes that librarians these days have custom-made vacuum cleaners for books, and that many 'find it important as far as possible to remove stains and dust from old volumes, thinking of the new volume as the ideal'. Others around the world, Anna reveals, both clean and iron books. Depending on the librarian, a stain can be either dirt or patina. But the tide is turning. Used books now fascinate social and book historians. As one of them puts it (albeit in an image which makes one not want him to tutor one's children): 'like dolls that cry and wet their pants, past readers come to life through secretion.'

Women philosophers of dirt are counteracting the Arnold Bennett/Norbert Elias mindset. Mary Douglas in 1970 argued that Western cleanliness is 'thoroughly ritualistic', no better than those religious taboos from which mostly women have suffered. Julia Kristeva, whose Eliot Lecture I attended in Canterbury in 1992, characterized ritual cleanliness as a freakish idea of bodily integrity, a fear of being 'swallowed up by the mother – the all-embracing Mother which is also Nature'. Martha Nussbaum argued in 1999 that our Western concern with cleanliness is 'inherently hostile to life': 'disgust expresses a refusal to ingest and thus be contaminated by a potent reminder of one's own mortality and animality'. Another minority-group philosopher, the Polish Jew Zygmunt Bauman, linked dirt-disgust to ethnic cleansing. The Finnish philosopher Olli Lagerspetz takes comfort from the idea that hygiene can be suspect:

> As a sometimes negligent householder . . . I am naturally soothed by the idea that exaggerated cleanliness is not next to godliness but to fascism and xenophobia.

Happily, there are now hundreds of academics working on restoring and digitizing marginalia. Major libraries are taking a patchy interest, although the science of cataloguing has yet to embrace recording annotated books. Thanks to Lisa Jardine and a grant from Pittsburgh's Andrew Mellon Foundation, there is now the Archaeology of Reading project, run by University College London and Princeton, dedicated to digitizing marginalia. Its clean, classy website is – to someone like me who has been lurking in rackety marginalia studies for decades – awe-inspiring.

Auden's official biographer put the cap on the new attitude to book use with his comment on the poet's dictionary, which he found 'all but clawed to pieces': 'This is the way a poet and his dictionary should go out.' Antiquarian booksellers' catalogues have even stopped referring to 'soiled' copies and, with estate-agent-virtuosity, started calling books with signs of use 'honest copies'.

Nothing lasts. Our frail idea of self morphs and shape-shifts, then becomes a line on a death certificate and a few family anecdotes. This is both sobering and liberating. As Forster says of Aziz in *A Passage to India*, 'yes all that was true of him, but his essence was slain'. Our essence might be more contained in a battered, perhaps annotated, comfort book than in our job title, or our position on a family tree.

What if the layers of the societal self were burnt away, could some idea of our individuality live on in a book, if that book was written in, even cut and pasted with thoughts and cuttings?

It's an intuitive idea, and indeed when interviewed about how he thought up *The English Patient*, Michael Ondaatje almost shamefacedly said he did not think it up, it just started with an image which flashed into his mind: a patient, unrecognizably burned in a desert plane crash, who cannot tell of his identity and so is outwardly without one, but who has managed to hold on to a book, *Herodotus*, heavily annotated.

Let us DNA our books. One day they may be all we leave behind.

9. Surviving the Sorbonne: The Book in the Ancien Régime

Several French interns have worked in my Canterbury book-shop over the last thirty years, and this has made two things clear to me: the French take bookselling very seriously as a pro-fession, and French institutions love paperwork. The various universities sending me interns have posted thick contracts in triplicate, requiring several signatures and rubber stamps. For-tunately, I was able to disinter the shop rubber stamp – unused since the eighties and bearing a fax number – to complete these bulky documents. Perhaps it's all about passion, the passion for books displayed by the interns, the passion for control demon-strated by French bureaucrats. Evelyn Waugh's account of an upstairs Parisian restaurant where senators ate 'in absolute silence' exemplifies the French passion and reverence for food, just as the Académie's fervent attempts to control the French language betoken a passion for words, and for policing them.

The history of the book in France before the Revolution is a tale of passion versus control, and much of that struggle took place in one small riverside district of Paris: the Latin Quarter. In today's Latin Quarter, where Robert de Sorbon founded a university and a library in 1257, Sorbonne students still argue ideas in cafés, and there are still good bookshops. In the Middle Ages, the area was the French centre for monastic manuscript production, and, with the dawn of print, the Latin Quarter made Paris second only to Venice as a European centre of book printing in quantity.

The first presses were run by immigrants, mostly from Germany. Johann Heynlin for instance, who ran the very first press in the Sorbonne, from 1470, and at his premises created an early *'cliché'* – the sound a group of often-combined words makes as its metal letters drop into place on the compositor's tray. Early Parisian printing was conservative, using Gothic type to emulate manuscripts, and even leaving blank spaces for illuminations to be added by hand.

Print terrified the Parisian authorities, already struggling with Protestant heresies and with the liberating influence of humanists such as Erasmus. The University of the Sorbonne, in particular, developed what the foremost historian of French print, Lucien Febvre, called 'an outright policy of repression'. Sorbonne theologians became the ultimate judge of a book's legality. When the French aristocrat Louis de Berquin translated Erasmus, he was arrested, under pressure from the Sorbonne, and forced to watch his books being publicly burned. His tongue was pierced and he was sentenced to a public repentance, to be followed by life imprisonment with no books. Refusing to repent, he was burnt at the stake.

Soon afterwards, in 1535, astonishingly, the Parlement de Paris banned printing altogether and burned twenty-three people associated with the book trade after, one historian remarked, 'tortures which, had they not been the invention of Christian priests, we should have thought only fiends could have invented'. The Cnut-like ban on print was short-lived, but was followed by a fusillade of regulation, among which the Edict of Montpellier demanded royal approval of every book, while the Ordinance of Moulins licensed only printers authorized by a new government censor.

The theatricality of the punishments meted out to printers showed how exercised the authorities were over the explosion of books. Étienne Dolet was a tragic victim. A likeable, witty scholar, he particularly loved music and wild swimming. Appointed French Ambassador to Venice, he fell in love with Elena, a local girl, to whom he wrote fine Latin poems. On his return to France, the King personally licensed him as a printer for ten years. Emboldened by his Venice-inspired love of new literature, Dolet printed a variety of dangerous texts, including his own pioneering translations of Plato and the writings of his avant-garde friend Rabelais.

Frequently Dolet was almost carelessly brave, as in his conflict with Gratien du Pont, the seneschal (governor) of Toulouse. Toulouse was the most repressive and fanatically run city in France, the home of the French Inquisition. The Toulouse authorities kept a salaried Inquisitor-General in a palace until 1772. Du Pont wrote an epic poem against women, claiming to paint them in their true colours as agents of the devil and oppressors of the male sex. His wife left him. It is to the honour of France that the poem was widely judged 'the nadir of French poetry'. To one critic it was 'a series of tedious harangues'. Another, Abbé Goujet, roasted it in Volume Eleven of his 1759 history of French literature as a work in 'barbarous style which disgusts the reader, graced with neither wit nor ingenuity'.

Dolet, who once said that his wife, Louise, was his treasure, more than any gold or silver, mercilessly ridiculed du Pont's book in Latin verse, suggesting that its best use was for grocers to wrap food in or, on second thoughts, that it was fit only for lavatory paper. This Rabelaisian poem was very popular; a fellow poet even published a Latin response to it: he had tried out du Pont's pages in the lavatory but the verse was too uncultivated and rough for such use.

Dolet was imprisoned, but befriended his jailer and suggested to him a) that he let him go home because a certain debtor would only repay him there, and b) that, whilst there, they could share a fine bottle of Muscat which he had been keeping for years. When Dolet was taken home by the credulous official, he escaped out of the back door and fled to Italy.

After a few months he returned to France to live with Louise and their son. He continued printing, and opened a bookshop. Outside, he hung a sign showing the golden axe which cuts away ignorance; the axe was also the printer's mark which appeared at the beginning and the end of the books he printed. At this time he championed print-workers' rights against an edict banning their association into any union or society. This latter activity of Dolet's may have done for him, by making master printers, the employers of those print-workers, into his enemies.

The package of radical books delivered to Paris which was addressed to Étienne Dolet and conveniently intercepted by customs was almost certainly a sting organized by master printers. Dolet was arrested, and interrogated over a two-year period. It was remarkably hard to convict him, partly because of the stupidity and vanity of the court President, Pierre Lizet. An Auvergnat peasant, he was 'inordinately addicted to wine and women, with an extraordinary redness of face and nose'. His terrible Latin was said to have inspired the King to ban its use in law courts, and he hated booksellers and printers, even paying a bookseller to spy on his fellows.

Dolet rebutted the evidence of the book package: he had nothing to do with it. The court President challenged him for having satirized corrupt clergy and pompous Sorbonne academics: he defended his right to do so. Hadn't he also eaten meat during Lent? Yes, replied the prisoner, but under doctor's orders and with Church permission. What about walking around during mass? 'Stretching my legs,' replied Étienne.

It took the casuistry of the Sorbonne's theologians to convict Dolet. They found just three words in his Plato translation which seemed to imply heresy. Despite a high-level appeal for clemency led by the book-loving Princess Marguerite, he was taken to Place Maubert, in the heart of the Latin Quarter, and burnt on a pyre of books from his own bookshop.

The square was chosen for its centrality and busy-ness, the site of the ancient Maubert food market which is still wonderfully atmospheric today. It is worth visiting both for the food and to stand and remember funny, brave, forgotten Dolet, whose statue in the Place was melted down for armaments during the German occupation.

Over the following centuries, until the dam-burst of the Revolution in 1789, Parisian printers and booksellers continued to circumvent censorship in various ways. Unlicensed booklets – known as *livres bleus* – could be quickly run off by back-room printers and sold by street pedlars or along the Seine, where unlicensed bookstalls sprang up from the 1500s. *Livres bleus* are largely lost to history, but scholarly detective work has recently clocked over 400 different titles published in Paris in 1589 alone. And book smuggling became a large, almost professionalized, sector. According to one estimate, by 1789 Paris had 300 bookshops and over 100,000 books for sale along the Seine, but 40 per cent of all that stock was illegal.

Neither the Inquisition nor the Sorbonne could stop Parisians' passion for books and ideas. It looks almost as if the sheer extremeness of censorship and control fuelled that passion. An eighteenth-century German visitor was astonished:

Everyone in Paris is reading. Everyone, but women in particular, carries a book around in their pocket. People read while riding in carriages or taking walks; they read at the theatre in the interval, in cafés, even when bathing. Women, children, journeymen and apprentices read in shops. On Sundays people read while seated at the front of their houses: lackeys read on their back seats, and coachmen up on their boxes, and soldiers keeping guard. (quoted by Belinda Jack in *The Woman Reader*)

This despite the way Rabelais and Montaigne could only be legally published outside Paris, Pascal's publisher was put in the Bastille indefinitely, Molière and Racine were heavily censored and Voltaire was frowned upon. His *Candide*, which still sells daily around the world – for pleasure and not only as a set book – was banned from the get-go by the Paris authorities.

Like *livres bleus*, the book smugglers of *ancien régime* France were scrappy, disreputable and are largely lost to history. But we now know that the Enlightenment simply would not have happened without them. Voltaire called pirated editions and *livres bleus* 'basse littérature', or 'low literature', but the mass of people only accessed the new world-changing *philosophes* via smuggled books and abridged versions. It has been said that without piracy and smugglers the Enlightenment 'would have remained in the salons'.

One man has done more than anyone to uncover this disreputable trade, with all the care and attention of an archaeologist to its filigree-like remains. Robert Darnton, a *New York Times* reporter turned Princeton historian, has visited French archives annually over a fifty-year period. In his beloved French provinces, he has practically become part of the families of the archivists he stays with.

Abbé Le Senne is a typical Darnton discovery, an eighteenth-century cleric determined to popularize Enlightenment ideas, even including opposition to clergy corruption. He edited selections of Voltaire and other radicals, wrote broadsides himself, was repeatedly arrested and moved house almost as often as he changed his name. In one raid alone, the police confiscated 2,000 books from him. Like a Graham Greene character, he seems to have combined ideological commitment with dodginess. A fellow bookseller thought him 'a man of no integrity, and sordid morals'. One of his longer-lasting residences was in the Rue St Honoré, near the river, at the house of M. Quinquincourt (such an enjoyable name to say), a retired member of the King's Guard. From there he published using the imprint 'At the Sign of the Golden Sheaf'. He used the house as a major book-smuggling distribution hub, after somehow nobbling the Lieutenant-General of Police, Jean-Pierre Lenoir. Lenoir would allow Le Senne to import all manner of liberal books, but not pornography.

Le Senne wrote florid letters to his Swiss book suppliers, portraying himself as a noble defender of truth. In one, he begged for urgent help, because his bishop had identified him as an anti-clerical polemicist. He wanted only to live in a Swiss mountain hut, 'like a philosopher', but, if possible, could he bring his 'sister-in-law' (mistress) and her (their) son?

When the Swiss could not help, the Abbé fled Paris for a chateau sixteen miles north, in Auxerre, then entered a Chartres monastery under an alias, but was rumbled and became a monk at Provins, then Troyes, from where he again pleaded with Swiss contacts, saying that he was reduced to travelling on foot, 'spattered with mud'. The last we hear of Le Senne he is using a grocer's shop in St Denis (today still a pleasantly raffish area) as a depot for smuggling texts into Paris.

Things were tough for Le Senne partly because he stayed around Paris, with its vigilant censors. The other great centre of bookselling and printing in pre-Revolutionary France was Lyons. Ancient history helps explain Lyons: a Roman settlement with good routes to Germany, Switzerland and Italy, it was always more open to classical learning and radical European ideas than priest-haunted Paris. Throughout the Renaissance it was the intellectual capital of France, and during the eighteenth century it was relatively free from the sinister influence of the Sorbonne, Church and Court. The Lyons Fair was something of a free-trade festival. Twice a year for fifteen days, throughout the early decades of print and into the early eighteenth century, the fair took over the streets. Merchants from anywhere were allowed to set up shop throughout the streets and on bridges, without a licence or any immigration checks. Merchandise brought to the fair was exempt from import duty; and booksellers were at the heart of this great market. Then as now, Lyons was wealthy and liberal, edgy and studenty.

The biggest single reason for Lyons's cultural eminence was its large immigrant population – fifty-nine Florentine dynasties alone – drawn by its silk industry and the fact that it was the clearing house for all commerce between France and Italy. As early as 1485 it had twelve printing presses, and by 1490 it was the third most active centre for print in Europe, after Paris and Venice. Lyons pioneered printing in Greek – the city had both more scholars of ancient Greek and more Greek immigrants than anywhere in France – and in Hebrew – at a time when Paris had banned even the study of Hebrew, to prevent anyone getting uppity ideas about what the Bible really said. Another sixteenth-century Lyons phenomenon has been celebrated by an English historian: 'In no other world city were there so many cultivated women. Here women showed themselves worthy companions and rivals of the other sex in the pursuit of higher things.'

Louise Labé, La Belle Cordière ('The Beautiful Ropemaker') 1524–66, is a fair representative of Lyonnais liberalism. With a

face 'more like an angel than a woman', she was also multilingual, a poet later admired by Rilke and still in print today, a
voracious reader, fine singer and lute player, and superb horse-
woman. Men buzzed around her like bees, and several
contributed to a book of poems about her. Even her persistent
cross-dressing did not faze contemporary Lyonnais. Only later
did grubby-minded male historians try to brand her 'a
whore', and even (unsuccessfully) ascribe her writings to men.

Lyons booksellers used a sophisticated network of book
smuggling over the Alps, dignified in fine French style: smugglers were *'assureurs* (insurers)', smuggling fees were 'insurance'.
Smuggling brokers were commissionaires. There was even a
euphemism for en-route bribery: *'lisser la voie'* – smoothing the
path. Unlicensed wandering booksellers were *colporteurs* (pedlars), and they frequently sold books *sous le manteau* (under the
cloak). Pornographic works were *livres philosophiques*, and not
as base as they might sound. Dominated by tales of lustful
clergy, they fuelled that anticlericalism which was a crucial
strand of revolutionary thought.

The Lyons smugglers' supply chain hub was Switzerland,
principally Geneva. Books were baled up in cloth, disguised as
other goods, and carried on mules or on the backs of schnapps-
fuelled men, over the snowy passes to selected inns, run by
'amis secrets' on the outskirts of Lyons, where they were
repackaged for sale. On at least one occasion the smugglers
fought off customs men with pistols. They were amusingly
protective of their reputation; their indignation at ever being
called smugglers indicates how the Lyonnais regarded book
censorship – all run from the Paris customs house – as an
unreasonable intrusion. This provincial spiritedness is alive in
the English West Country today. I remember locals, digging
an illicit access ditch with a small JCB under the Glastonbury

Festival fences, responding to challenges by saying, in Somerset tones, 'We always get in free, an' we ain't stoppin' now.'

An eighteenth-century travelling publisher's rep found Lyons booksellers of the *ancien régime* exceptionally self-confident and commercially savvy. He remarked of one: 'A double-edged sword, better not tangle with him.' Of another: 'shrewd and tough', and of a third, the Perisse brothers: 'My God, they play their cards close to their chest.' Upon leaving Lyons the rep reflected: 'I have been in this city a long time, but when you try and talk to these gentlemen, they never listen. It's as if they had empires to govern.' They did, of course: their own extensive smuggling network. If the customs men circled too closely, Lyons booksellers bribed the Head of Customs, or fired off a few *lettres ostensibles* – another great euphemism – Mary Whitehouse-style missives decrying revolutionary trends and the decay of French morals, carefully designed to be intercepted and read by the police.

Imports of books into Lyons fed a whole capillary system of revolutionary ideas across France, to centres such as Poitiers, Bordeaux and Marseilles, but also to Spain. Book pedlars carried baskets around their necks (the *colporteurs*) or drove horse-drawn vans which converted into pop-up bookshops, unlicensed and untraceable.

The most extraordinary book city which Lyons did business with, usually by barge straight down the Rhône, was Avignon. Again, ancient history explains Avignon's candle-flame importance in Europe's Enlightenment. In 1305 the Conclave of Cardinals in Rome could not agree on a new Pope. King Philip of France broke the 'no deal' deadlock by forcing them to elect as Pope Raymond de Got, Archbishop of Bordeaux. The new Pope, who took the name 'Clement', decided to live in Avignon rather than Rome.

The 'Avignon Papacy' officially ended in 1376 but relaxed Papal legates supervised the enclave of Avignon thereafter. Until about 1780, French customs had no jurisdiction in Avignon and it was a book pirate's paradise. In 1760 it had 60 printing presses and 22 bookshops, for a population of only 23,000. (Canterbury in 2019 has 43,000 people and 2 bookshops.) Avignon printers were technologically advanced. They used Roman, not Gothic type, and it is now thought that the wonderfully named and mysterious Czech Procopius Waldfogel might have invented printing in Avignon before Gutenberg. As Vincent Giroud put it in his history of the book in France:

> Humanism, as has often been pointed out, came to France as a result of the sojourn of the popes in Avignon, which brought Petrarch and Boccacio to the country.

This deliciously bizarre fallout from a papal squabble ended with the Revolution, when Avignon was fully absorbed into France. Humanism in France eventually triumphed, broadly, over bigotry. But the Enlightenment and the Revolution were not only achieved by the likes of Diderot and Voltaire, Danton and Robespierre, but by a forgotten rag-tag army of pedlars and market traders, smugglers and *livre-bleu* writers, idealistic scholar-printers and heroic booksellers.

Today the French government, no longer manipulated by the Sorbonne or the Church, gives the world a lesson in how to support the physical book. It subsidizes bookshops and legislates against rogue discounting. In 2013 Culture Minister Aurélie Filipetti, despite a huge budget deficit nationally, announced a €5 million fund to give cheap loans to booksellers. She is a novelist. France supports booksellers the way

Britain shores up farmers. One French bookseller mischievously explains this by saying that in Britain the farmer is God, in Germany the musician, in Italy the painter, in France the writer. Whereas Britain in 2019 has about 800 independent bookshops, France has 2,500.

10. Booksellers of the Seine

In the 1950s the young actor and aspiring film director François Truffaut was browsing the bookstalls along the Seine in Paris. His discovery of a battered copy of the forgotten autobiographical novel *Jules et Jim* was to change cinema history: Truffaut's film of the book brought French New Wave cinema to the wider world. Discovering that the elderly author of the novel, Henri-Pierre Roché, was still alive, Truffaut tracked him down; the two became friends, the younger man entranced by Roché's memories of Picasso and Duchamp, of Gertrude Stein and bohemian Paris before the Great War.

These Seine bookstalls are an unchronicled marvel, the biggest open-air secondhand bookshop in the world. Occasionally a writer counted the stalls: by the early 1700s there were 120 booksellers along the river, in 1864, 68 booksellers selling over 70,000 books from 1,020 boxes; 1892 saw 156 booksellers and over 97,000 books on sale. To give a context, Steven Fischer's 2004 *History of Reading* refers to 'about 100,000' books being on sale in conventional Paris bookshops by 1800, 'a figure typical of the book trade in most European cities'. The Seine bookstalls were no mere peripheral street market, therefore.

Picking up unexpected serendipitous discoveries in the open air lends itself to enchantment, to little fizzes of destiny; thus Steven Greenblatt picked up Lucretius' *On the Nature of Things* from a pavement box in New York, attracted – he admits – by the sexy girl on the tacky sixties cover. That discovery led him to reshape ideas of Renaissance origins. The actor Anthony

Hopkins had an even more unlikely chance encounter in 1970s London. Hopkins was offered a part in an adaption of George Feifer's *The Girl from Petrovka*, but couldn't find a copy of the book anywhere until he sat down on a bench while waiting for the tube and found one next to him. Two years later, George Feifer mentioned to him that a friend had sadly lost Feifer's own copy of the book, which had all of his notes in the margins. The book Hopkins had happened to sit down next to was, incredibly, the writer's original.

The Seine booksellers are *bouquinistes*, pronounced 'bookyneest'. Of the several theories about this word's origin the academically preferred one originates it in German, the nationality of many of Paris's earliest printers. It is a frenchified version of 'little book'.

Bouquinistes have been trading for over 500 years. They started on the Pont Neuf and, when banned from that bridge, moved to the riverbanks. There, before the nineteenth-century embankments were built, booksellers could claim their pitches without paying a licence fee. Throughout the Wars of Religion and the Revolution, *bouquinistes* sold a range of secondhand books and manuscripts, and always much banned and underground literature.

As subversive as pirates, they were piratical in other ways too. They were exposed to all weathers. A regular nineteenth-century customer was Paul Lacroix. Inclined to love unofficial Paris – his 'exhaustive' six-volume history of prostitution was perhaps exhausting too – he noticed that 'the *bouquiniste* partakes of the condition of his books – exposed to all the vicissitudes of the weather, shrivelled in the sun, beaten by the wind, smoothed by the rain'. Like sailors, they could read the skies; Parisians commonly asked them for forecasts. Just as pirates expressed their extra-societal identity by wearing earrings and exuberant clothes, Seine booksellers of both sexes dressed with eccentric panache, with a raffish style you can even spot among today's *bouquinistes*.

The psychogeography of rivers – their psychofluidity – affects their denizens' way of being. In 1908 the traveller E. V. Lucas wondered why the Thames never hosted booksellers as the Seine does. Old Father Thames is male, majestic, melancholic and a river of twilight, of night. As the road to empire it has a Conradian poignancy. Tower Bridge, macho and castellated, is unimaginable on the Seine. The Seine is female, named after Sequana, the Celtic goddess, revered by the Romans, who built a temple at its source. It is a river of light and creativity, like the city it runs through. Lovers and book-browsers seem like natural phenomena on the Seine's banks.

Octave Uzanne, mentioned earlier, was a nutty forgotten *fin de siècle* mingler with the *bouquinistes*. Let him take you down to the river. He tells of Gallandre, the ex-railwayman who wore an adapted SNCF livery, of tall, prosperous Rigault, known for his sonorous voice, black deerstalker hat and complete refusal to deal in 'current books'. Of Correonne, the ex-soldier of the Republican Guard who displayed his books in perfect order and in little fortresses. Of Chevalier, who gave up being a waiter when he became too old to clear tables; his daughter was the brains of the stall, in charge of buying, display and any serious negotiations. Nobody seemed to know tall, shaky Vaisset's story, but he was widely liked, 'Sack-of-Bones' his affectionate nickname. In general, Uzanne found that stall-holders looked out for each other; one often minded up to three stalls whilst owners went on errands or, in winter, slipped into one of the many nearby bars for a warming Cointreau.

Old Debas's knowledge was legendary, but mainly of what

he called the 'great century': the eighteenth. Vocal against government, any government, he was irreverent about priests, police and several of his regulars, including Victor Hugo, 'a bit of a windbag'. Debas seemed happy, a small man sitting on his bench with a pot of glue, mending damaged books from his beloved century. The now obscure writer Anatole France – admired by Orwell and Proust – noticed Debas's contentment, calling him 'an artist and a philosopher'. Debas sold books for sixty years until, broken-hearted after the death of his wife, he succumbed to the severe winter of 1893. The weather seemed to benefit Rosez though, who ran his stall until he was eighty-three, having only started selling outdoors to get tobacco money, after his wife told him he could not afford to smoke on the profits from their stationery shop. Similarly, Malorey the Norman worked for sixty-two years until he was eighty-two, kept young by daily conversations such as those with Uzanne ('often on a sunny day I chatted for an hour with this good man') and many others, who enjoyed his gift for mimicry.

One of Malorey's targets was easy to imitate: short, fat, self-important Maynard had aristocratic airs and boasted of friends among right-wing deputies. With his habit of laying a grand Persian carpet in front of his stall, he insisted he was a book-seller, no mere *bouquiniste* stall-holder. His nickname was 'The Baron'. Old Charlier was even odder: he manned his stall daily but glared at customers and barked, 'Don't touch!' if they seemed about to look at a book. His disdain was a luxury afforded by a mysterious income of 6,000 francs a year.

Lécrivain presented a different challenge: 'his breath was enough to make an Auvergnat drunk,' but by mid-afternoon he was usually tipsy enough to sell stock cheaply and cheer-fully. Few approached Isnard or his stock. A one-time barber in the American Wild West:

He dressed in fetid rags. He lived on bread and garlic, abandoned all notions of cleanliness, and became a moving mass of vermin, in which his crapulous soul found a suitable habitation.

But nearby was young, ever-cheerful Raquin, fluent in Ancient Greek, with a fine stall of Renaissance books and incunabula, mentored perhaps by the veteran stallholder Achaintre, a scholarly editor of Horace and other ancient classics, whom Uzanne observed smiling quietly to himself when a customer asked for one of his translations. What a contrast with Lequiller, ex-village shopkeeper, who knew little of books but estimated prices 'by sight and smell'.

Confait occupied the same spot by the Mint taxi-rank for fifteen years. With his bulging eyes behind huge silver spectacles and long stiff hair, he sat with his 'equally striking' wife and a slightly crazed poodle. Boucher, the ex-lawyer whose love of books sent him to the stalls, ran a fine orderly operation with his wife, Mimi. As a newcomer he was assisted by kindly veterans such as old-fashioned, white-haired Rosselin, who wore peasant clogs, large blue spectacles and a loose white ruffled shirt under his coat.

The scepticism of the old guard about a bookseller called Delahaye's novel idea of opening after dark – using a row of paraffin lamps – was justified. In those biodiverse Parisian days, moths and mosquitoes quickly made such trading impossible.

Chanmoru was one of the many socialist *bouquinistes*, on a mission to sell radical literature. In his choice of dress, he also displayed a magnificent and gender-fluid radicalism. He either wore the red cap of liberty or the tall sixteenth-century-style *'toque'* which has only survived as a chef's hat. His long golden hair was tied in a chignon with a blue ribbon; white clogs denoted peasant solidarity and long ruffled shirts completed the outfit. Despite frequent arrests, Chanmoru never failed to shout, '*À bas les voleurs!*' ('Down with thieves!') at passing politicians. His twenty boxes of books were beautifully presented and classified, and a sign banned smoking near his stall, for fear of dropped ash.

Uzanne's love for these booksellers fed into his involvement in the Symbolist movement, that regard for 'liberty, strangeness and personal variegation' which was to morph into Surrealism, Situationism and Punk.

It is a global miracle that the *bouquinistes* have survived the centuries. Bookshop owners regarded them as lower-class citizens, and resented the way they could avoid rent and thus keep more of their profits. The *bouquinistes* were first moved off the Pont Neuf by the city authorities, but only in response to pressure from bookshop owners. *Bouquinistes* were an Amazon-style threat – unfair, and with dubious tax arrangements.

In a city riven by fanatic divisions – the 1572 St Bartholomew's Day Massacre saw at least 2,000 killed on the streets – censorship was severe and enforced with draconian measures (although the protectionist Finance Minister Colbert, 1619–83, was chagrined to discover his coachman using his own carriage to smuggle banned books). Many booksellers and publishers were burned at the stake over the centuries. This made the roguish *bouquinistes* all the more important as an outlet for underground literature. Denis Pallier, a French print historian, worked out in a 1975 study that 2 million illicit books and pamphlets were printed in Paris in 1589–90 alone. The safest place to buy these was down by the river. Just how the *bouquinistes'* impact has been lost to history is evidenced by their total absence from Lucien Febvre's seminal *The Coming of the Book:*

The Impact of Printing, 1450–1800 (Paris, 1958), a work rich in detail about on-street bookshops. But then, looking at photos of Febvre in his bank manager suit and tie, one can deduce that he would have regarded the Seine booksellers as a First Sea Lord might regard Caribbean pirates.

Paris historian Andrew Hussey, a more up-to-date voice, insists that 'the French Revolution was partly down to the *bouquinistes*'. After the Revolution they were still in trouble. An 1822 police chief issued an edict to control them because they 'frequently sell books dangerous or contrary to the law'. An 1829 edict demanded they record all sales in a register, and all names and addresses of those who sold them books. Furthermore – mean-spiritedly – impoverished students, children and servants were banned from selling books alongside the *bouquinistes*. Both edicts were observed fitfully at first, and then not at all.

A bigger upheaval challenged the stalls in the nineteenth century: the building of the now much-loved stone embankments along the Seine. Although we now visualize these as the home of *bouquinistes*, they represented a new era of regulation. This was the age of Baron Haussmann. This career civil servant made it his life's work to demolish much of medieval Paris in favour of long, boring boulevards. The boulevards' subtext was panoptical: they were too wide to be barricaded, and easily policed. Trafalgar Square's fountains have a similar secret purpose of breaking up mass gatherings.

Haussmann's self-confidence was steamrollerish. Interior Minister Persigny gave an almost homoerotic sketch of him:

Large, powerful and energetic, he would have talked for six hours without stopping on his favourite subject: himself. There was a cynical brutality about this vigorous athlete,

broad-shouldered, bull-necked, full of audacity and cunning,
a tall, tigerish animal.

The Baron took a clinical view of raffish parts of the city, having been a sickly asthmatic there as a boy. He rarely visited the
areas whose doom he plotted daily in his office from 6 a.m.
Even when out in his carriage, he never alighted to engage the
locals. One historian put it thus: 'he had little tactile contact
with the city. For him, Paris had limbs and arteries, but no
heart.' He made a huge, 160 square foot map of his ideal Paris
and called it his 'altar'. The map showed more than just boulevards for, incredibly, Haussmann was to actually flatten
over-hilly areas, a feat which involved lifting an entire historic
tower up and lowering it back on to the new level.

There were implications for retailing style: the big boulevards meant big shops and multiple chains. He relished
clearing up the Île de la Cité, 'inhabited by bad characters', he
thought. As for the *bouquinistes*, they disgraced the city and
must be cleared off the embankments. In Uzanne's words:

> Such irregular and curious excrescences vexed his aesthetic
> soul. That long low wall must be cleared of parasites, made
> rectilinear, cleaned with potash, and rubbed with pumice.

'Rectilinear': the preferred Cartesian shape for all left-brain
dominant types like Haussmann.*
   The left brain is the source of language and order, but

---

* For a fascinating analysis of rectlinearity in the neuroscience of history
see *The Master and His Emissary: The Divided Brain and the Making of the
Western World,* by Iain McGilchrist (expanded 2nd edn, Yale University
Press, 2018), pp. 446–9 and 509, n. 129.

the right brain makes stories from that language. The Seine booksellers themselves were fairy-tale characters abusing the utilitarian language of capitalist architecture. This conflict was both commercial and philosophic. Baron Haussmann wanted stories to be straightforwardly housed. He proposed to his close friend the Emperor Napoleon III that the *bouquinistes* all be relocated to a market hall, a sort of bibliographic Arndale Centre. They would be charged higher rents. It is hard to imagine the likes of radical Chanmoru, learned Raquin and crapulous Isnard making the move. A contemporary Paris librarian and collector of fine bindings piled in: 'Things are worse than ever on the quays, where one sees only silly odds and ends of literature . . . [the *bouquinistes*] profane the name of the book.'

Satisfyingly, Paul Lacroix, our prostitution expert, was also in the Emperor's confidence, and approached him directly, persuading him to come and see the Seine booksellers for himself; Lacroix would escort His Imperial Majesty. The booksellers were not all on their best behaviour for the royal visit. Old radical Père Foy was busy ripping pages out of a book to feed his stove. When the Emperor enquired what book was so expendable, Foy quietly handed him the title-page: *Conquests and Victories of the French*. Nevertheless, the visit was sufficient to persuade Napoleon III to resist Haussmann's plan and save the *bouquinistes*. Uzanne said that in old age, about 1880, 'dear old Lacroix, when the evenings came to an end, used to delight in relating the affair, and it was a pleasure to listen to him'. The would-be booksellers' market hall is now a bus station.

Haussmann's hubris had its nemesis: a pamphlet – surely a hot seller by the river – started it by attacking the Baron for saddling Paris with a debt of 400 million francs. The Baron's image cracked like a papier mâché statue as the press exposed his two mistresses – a ballerina and an opera singer – and even alleged that he procured his daughter Fanny for the Emperor's satisfaction. In 1870 Napoleon dismissed the Baron formally, in the course of a two-hour meeting.

By 1888 stallholders could leave their book boxes fixed to the parapet overnight, but at a cost: the boxes had to conform exactly to a certain size and be painted a regulation green, and they carried a rental charge.

In this turn-of-the-century era, Xavier Marmier was one of many long-term customers. He specialized in obscure folklore and Italian literature. He was polite and kind-hearted, and there were many accounts of his generosity to beggars and of his special book-browsing coat, its pockets 'as deep as sacks' for purchases. Marmier's will had a surprise:

> In remembrance of happy hours I have passed among the bookstall-keepers of the quays – moments which I reckon among the pleasantest of my life – I leave an amount to be expended by these good dealers in paying for a jolly dinner and spending an hour in conviviality thinking of me.

Ninety-five booksellers, men and women, attended the dinner, which began with *'champagne frappé'* and closed with coffee and cognac.

The twentieth century presented new challenges. Under German occupation the Nazis closely controlled bookshops. Shakespeare and Company was closed down, and the Gestapo actually staffed the famous W. H. Smith bookshop in the Rue de Rivoli – imagine the customer service – and filled the window with Nazi literature. The *bouquinistes* were seen as less important; there are several photographs of German soldiers browsing the stalls, unaware of the high level of resisters among the Seine stallholders, who braved death by running a system of coded messages left in books.

The 1960s saw another threat as ex-bank manager President Pompidou ordered expressways to be built along the Seine (Princess Diana would die on one of these speedways). His reply to protests 'Paris must adapt to the car' now seems benighted, and indeed those expressways have since been partially dismantled. A later President, ex-Resistance fighter Mitterrand, was a frequent stall-browser.

And now? There are still, despite the increase of souvenir stalls, over 200 *bouquinistes* trading by the Seine. Magical serendipities continue there, such as the American Anne Parrish's discovery of a copy of her own childhood comfort book, *Jack Frost and Other Tales*, a find made astonishing by her childhood inscription in the front. Somehow the book had travelled from Colorado to the Seine.

The goddess Sequana has two reasons to smile: Atlantic salmon returned to her river in 2009 and, as I write, UNESCO has declared the Seine bookstalls a World Heritage Site, of global cultural significance.

11. *Why Venice?*

The patron saint of booksellers is St John of God, a slightly annoying Spanish purveyor of religious tracts, prone to self-flagellation. The little-known Venetian friar Paolo Sarpi would be a more inspiring choice, heroically defending as he did all booksellers in Renaissance Venice, 'the cradle of publishing', against the Inquisition.

Venice was the doyenne of book cities in the Renaissance. Although printing first flourished in Germany, scores of German printers soon migrated to Venice, 'La Serenissima'. As early as 1480, when the printed book was, historically speaking, still in its cradle, forty German typesetters lived in Venice. Twenty years later the clacking of 200 printing presses drifted over the canals, and there were several hundred bookshops in the city.

Even after the decline of the Venetian republic, in 1750 Venice had fifty-one bookshops. Today Venice is known for architecture and atmosphere, but has fewer than twenty bookshops: its hidden history as maker and defender of books is easily forgotten. It was the fairy godmother of the printed book.

Why Venice? As a hub of maritime trade, it was full of wealthy people. In Renaissance style, they spent their money on classically inspired culture. There was an old Greek colony in the city, as well as many caches of Greek and Latin manuscripts awaiting first-printing. It was a polyglot place which needed, for its prosperity, to welcome all races. As a result, the

Renaissance lust to rediscover Greek and Roman classics could be satisfied in Venice, uniquely. Latin was widely known, and Greek typesetters were on hand. Imagine the excitement in the room when Nicholas Jenson, an ex-silversmith of the Paris Mint (type-makers were usually ex-silversmiths) oversaw the first-ever printing of Aristophanes (446–386 BC) – 'the Father of Comedy'.

There was also the tradition of superb Venetian paper-making. Pre-nineteenth-century paper retains a beautiful whiteness to this day because it was made from rags rather than wood. Venice was the European hub for importing such rags. The Doge – perennially a leader of sound commercial nous despite his funny hat – limited the export of Venetian paper to ensure a supply for the city presses. Venetian ink, too, was the best in Italy. Finally, Venice's free trade philosophy extended to ideas. Generally, the city hated censorship.

The prince of Venetian printers was Aldus Manutius, 1449–1515; he was also the most prolific. Highly learned, his academy for like-minded lovers of classics centred on legendary banquets, where diners were fined for not speaking Greek. But Aldus was the opposite of elitist. In his passion to popularize learning via printed books, he was a spiritual ancestor of Allen Lane, originator of the Penguin paperback. Aldus made the Penguin possible, pioneering small, pocket-sized books. He devised a new, crystal clear typeface, and invented italics. To him we owe the appearance of the comma and the use of the semicolon, new tools to make print user-friendly. Sophocles and Plato, Aristotle and Aesop, were all first printed by Aldus. To ensure that people could read these works, he printed some of the first dictionaries of classical languages. Although he died in poverty, he was widely loved: his body lay in state in the oldest church in Venice, surrounded by editions of his books. Models of beauty and clarity, they now command high auction prices.

Renaissance Venice had bookshops worthy of such books. They dominated the Merceria, a maze of streets now the home of fashion shops such as Gucci and Prada. Nobody could open a bookshop unless they had served a five-year apprenticeship and passed an oral examination conducted by a panel of veteran bookmen. The exam covered nature, philosophy and several languages. Bookshops were hothouses of culture and debate, democratic places where customers paid in money but also in whatever they had: wine, flour and oil were common currency.

Venice, then, was a sparkling Renaissance Republic of Books, but many churchmen felt threatened by its freedom to propagate texts to the populace. The Vatican saw the printing press as a potent source of evil. For centuries the Church, especially monasteries, had controlled book production. Significantly it was a monk, Savonarola, who conducted the infamous 1492 'Bonfire of the Vanities', burning musical instruments and printed books in Florence. Savonarola, with his private army of enforcers, went too far even for the Pope, who, in a frenzy of 'pyro-FOMO', burnt Savonarola's own books, then had him both hanged and incinerated. Books were to arouse the burning urge all the way down to Hitler and beyond.

In 1562, Pope Julius III told the Doge that all new books in Venice must be checked by an Inquisitor before going on sale. This did not sit well with Friar Paolo Sarpi, the quietly spoken legal expert at the Venetian court. Sarpi's friends included Galileo and he corresponded with William Harvey and Roger Bacon; as an all-around Renaissance man of learning he was to inspire the historian Edward Gibbon. Sarpi was well-placed to argue with the Vatican, having written authoritative theological texts, and been a monk since he was fifteen. The learned friar kept up a stream of pamphlets arguing against the censorship of books, and even went to Rome to argue with the Pope in person.

Unpersuaded, the Pope ordered the publication of the *Index Librorum Prohibitorum*, or 'List of Banned Books', a publication which continued until the final, 1966 edition, which included the works of Sartre and Simone de Beauvoir. The Venetian Inquisitor and his team began a witch-hunt in the city for those who might possess books on the *Index*. They searched the palazzo of the bookish aristocrat Zuan Sforza. Unable to find banned books, they asked about a locked chest. When refused the key, they broke it open: the books within earned Sforza an excommunication, meaning that he was barred from mass, the sacraments and heaven: he would have to serve at least a lifetime in purgatory. Any other dodgy books from Venice reaching Rome were put in a Vatican basement called 'The Prison and Hell of Heresy'. Nuns tended this bizarre library of sin, presumably having the odd peek.

Sarpi resisted the Inquisitor subtly but decisively. Ordered to burn all books on the *Index* in Venice's cathedral, he organized a small fire of a few, in an obscure parish church. A Papal Bull (edict) threatening booksellers and book-buyers with excommunication was similarly posted in some little-visited church rather than St Mark's.

When the Greek scholar Margounios, resident in Venice, was summoned to Rome for abetting heretical printing operations, Sarpi penned an eloquent rebuttal of such an invasion of Venetian authority. Unsurprisingly, Pope Julius's reply – that Margounios would not be harmed, only interviewed by the Inquisition – did not change Sarpi's stance. The Pope's next move was to instruct the order of friars which took most confessions, to report any inappropriate reading revealed by penitents. On Sarpi's advice, the Doge responded by exiling the entire order.

A contemporary noted Sarpi's 'remarkable tenderness for the book trade': even when the Pope demanded bibles be displayed in every bookshop window on Sundays, the friar protested that Venice would never open shops on the Sabbath – a wily untruth. In 1607 a new Pope, Paul V, the persecutor of Galileo, excommunicated Sarpi and placed Venice under an Interdict, forbidding Christian rites and even Christian burial services. He then paid assassins 8,000 crowns to kill the 59-year-old friar: he survived, badly injured, and the assassins were jailed. The second assassination attempt ordered by Pope Paul involved fifteen dagger thrusts. As Sarpi lay in hospital he joked that it was a typical Papal botched job.

This tale ends happily: Sarpi lived on in a monastery until he was seventy-three, defending Venetian freedom to the last and dreaming of moving to London, where, he heard, you could buy any book. He outlived Paul V by a year, and heard that Gregory, an enlightened reformer, had taken over at the Vatican.

Sarpi had won the battle of the books. A fine statue of him now stands near the site of the second assassination attempt. He is holding a book.

12.   'Organized Funkiness': New York Bookshops

Whatever else anything is, it ought to begin by being personal.

Meg Ryan in *You've Got Mail*

London is satisfied, Paris is resigned, New York is always hopeful.

Dorothy Parker

My own experience of New York was a nomadic visit in 1986, sleeping rough and treating myself to a night in the Chelsea Hotel.

I found it a friendly city, fulfilling Tom Wolfe's adage that, whether you've been there for five minutes or five years, you feel welcome. Even the gang of muggers who woke me up on the subway steps to ask for my wallet seemed friendly as I groggily – I am not a morning person – reached into my jacket for my wallet and they ran off shouting, 'Shit, he's packin' somethin!'

Otherwise I remember the wonderful bookshops. Thomas Hardy said real morris dancers look like they are not enjoying it, it's only the revivalists who grin, and New York booksellers seemed to do their job seriously as if under a wider cosmic compulsion, like harbour pilots.

'Someone's staring at you in Personal Growth.' It's 1989 in New York and Carrie Fisher's line to Meg Ryan in *When Harry Met Sally* starts an intimate encounter. For film-makers, a New

York bookshop is a place where the plot suddenly moves on in unexpected ways, as if the quick wit of the city mixed with the weight of past literature are the sulphur and carbon that make up gunpowder.

1957: *Funny Face.* Fred Astaire walks into the Embryo Concepts bookstore in Greenwich Village. Astaire and his team are seeking a dark setting for a fashion shoot and they inform bookseller Audrey Hepburn that her shop is ideal – 'movingly dismal'. She tells him to get out, and treats him to a vigorous harangue on the exploitative nature of the fashion industry, whilst he perches elf-like on a low bookcase, visibly entranced.

1977: *Annie Hall.* Woody Allen's bookshop exchange with Diane Keaton is that rare thing, a flirtation centred on the fact that misery is more cheerful than death.

1986: *Hannah and her Sisters.* In the Pageant Bookshop Barbara Hershey explores connections with already-married Michael Caine: 'Do you like Caravaggio?' After his tactical reply, 'Oh yes, who doesn't?', he finds the e. e. cummings poem which becomes an emotional causeway between them.

1998: *You've Got Mail.* Tom Hanks enters Meg Ryan's bookshop with his kids. She is disgusted to discover that he is the corporate bookseller Joe Fox: 'You probably rented those children.' But they fall in love: it turns out more connects booksellers than divides them. At heart, Fox is a New York bookman, as this exchange with his father illustrates:

> Nelson Fox: Perfect. Keep those West Side, liberal, nuts, pseudo-intellectuals . . .
> Joe Fox: Readers, Dad, they're called readers.
> Nelson Fox: Don't do that son, don't romanticize them.

1999: *The Ninth Gate*. Johnny Depp's book business in Polanski's satanic tale is truly sulphurous – the gateway to hell.

2004: *Eternal Sunshine of the Spotless Mind*. A bookshop is a natural in this time-slipping tale. Kate Winslet's bookseller is as feisty with a customer as Audrey Hepburn half a century earlier:

> Too many guys think I'm a concept, or I complete them, or I'm gonna make them alive. But I'm just a fucked-up girl who's lookin' for my own peace of mind; don't assign me yours.

Before all these films Christopher Morley's forgotten 1919 novel *The Haunted Bookshop* makes a Brooklyn bookshop the crux of the plot. It is haunted by all the revolutionary ideas in the books, and finally blown apart by a German spy's bomb.

New York's polyglot fluidity means that its bookshops are somehow allowed to be nodal, chakra-points, centres of change. There are theories for the city's creative identity: some cite the 500-million-year-old rocks the city sits on, older than Tibet. The rocks surface like a whale in Central Park and it is on them that Ralph Fiennes' senator sits to compose his speeches in *Maid in Manhattan*. More obviously, New York has been populated by immigration from everywhere, especially Europe.

As early as 1806 the traveller John Lambert noticed that the city's bookshops were 'numerous' and that a lot of people seemed to be reading in coffee shops. Two early characters were Emanuel Conegliano, one of Mozart's librettists, who ran a specialist Italian bookstore so compendious that Columbia University bought up his stock; and the 1830 immigrant Scot William Gowans, parts of whose shop, with its piles of books up to ten feet high, had to be navigated with sperm-oil lamps.

At home, Gowans shared a staircase with Poe, whom he found 'gentlemanly and intelligent'.

From 1880 cheap steamship travel and pogroms in Europe led to a mass influx from Central and Eastern Europe: 2 million immigrants between 1880 and 1930. They forged that unique New York/European wit, quintessentially heard in the voice of Groucho Marx.

The whole culture of New York bookselling, and of New York itself, was profoundly influenced by one of the most remarkable and unlikely bookselling quarters the world has ever seen, centred on Fourth Avenue – 'Book Row'. Famous bookshops, such as Scribner's and Brentano's, were uptown, but Book Row was metaphorically upstream of them, with a wider range of books at lower prices, including tattier books and the sort of ephemeral pamphlets and chapbooks which were on sale almost nowhere else. Two booksellers, for instance, regularly rose at dawn to visit a Salvation Army warehouse and meet the donation trucks to cream off the donated books. These were the twin Wavrovics brothers. They lived on a barge, specialized in house clearances, used a low-rent warehouse for storage and sold books by the truck-load to Book Row. Sometimes they lived on out-of-date food but, as one of them put it, overall 'We hustled, we prospered.' Book Row eschewed the meaningless division between antiquarian and secondhand. Scouts – book-hunters who made a living by buying cheap and selling on to high-rolling bookshops – used to scour Book Row and take their treasures uptown to sell at a profit.

Book Row represented something else too – an immigrant rebelliousness and inclusivity, and a Mitteleuropean mournful love of learning, broad and deep, a special mentality reflected in the shops. Think Flourish and Blotts – the chaotic magical bookshop in *Harry Potter* – with added *Weltschmerz*. The buildings were labyrinthine, stock Alexandrian, and service a roller-coaster ride to rival Coney Island's buttock-clenching Cyclone.

At its height, Book Row had forty-three bookshops in a small six-block zone. By the 1980s they had all petered out or, like the now-iconic Strand Bookstore, moved out. This sounds gloomy but need not be: city bookselling ecosystems are entropic – energy never disappears, it just changes manifestation. Like a big forest, trees fall and make clearings, in which saplings grow. Barnes and Noble was the overshadowing cedar in New York for a few decades, *c.* 1950–2000. Its Fifth Avenue store was bigger than Foyles by 1974, but the chain suffered with age: by 2018 it was losing $17 million a year and in 2019 was bought up by a new owner, who began to rescue it from indirection by deploying someone who started out with one independent bookshop: James Daunt. What remains in the air of New York from Book Row is a unique bookselling fire, and the tales of some extraordinary men and women. Both the fire and the shamanic booksellers will last as long as New York.

Before Fourth Avenue, from the 1850s booksellers congregated two miles south in Ann Street, a narrow rat-infested cut-through in Manhattan. The low rent and heavy footfall – a bookseller's dream – had attracted the great showman P. T. Barnum to open his American Museum of oddities there.

The change of location happened because of a family of German fur traders, the Astors. When John Jacob Astor opened a library on Lafayette Street in 1854, it kickstarted a new cultural zone, which included Fourth Avenue. Not only was the library free – it later moved and morphed into the New York Public Library – its specifically Germanic architecture sent a homely signal to European immigrants. By 1890, as the city exceeded a million people (8 million today), Fourth Avenue was paved and gaslit, a big step up from Ann Street.

Jacob Abrahams, an immigrant from Poland, where he had been more of a scholar than a businessman, opened a bookshop at 80 Fourth Avenue in 1893. The building is still there, now a paint shop for decorators. Jacob was still in business on Fourth Avenue at the time of his death in his eighties in the 1930s. Like many booksellers, he was frustrated at how a lot of the best books were out of print and so, long before the Gutenberg Project, he set up a scholarly reprint service, which long outlasted his death. Abrahams' shop set the Book Row tone of inclusive browsers' paradises. This was to be the only city bookselling quarter where African Americans felt welcome.

One story illustrates Abrahams' relaxed attitude to browsers. During the First World War the FBI discovered that the shop was being used as a dropbox by a German spy. A Congressional committee grilled the staff: 'Didn't you notice the same man lurking at the back of the store repeatedly?' No, replied bookseller Herman Meyers, we let customers browse without interference.

Up the road at number 69, George Smith used $63 to start up his notoriously successful rare book business. 'Notoriously' because he was a legendary shyster, 'assailed as a tyrant and accused of questionable ethics' on both sides of the Atlantic. I cannot find anything questionable in his practices; it seems he was just too flash and successful for the trade. He dressed like a bookie, arrived at auctions in his Rolls-Royce, and cheerfully admitted that he mainly read the racing form. He did not disguise his pleasure at 'the squeal of the English' in 1914 when he bought the Devonshire family collection. The now massive Huntington Library owed so much to Smith's artfulness that its founder said he simply could not do without him. A Gutenberg Bible, Shakespeare First Folios and first editions of Milton and Spenser are some of its treasures. Smith was recognized as the greatest book dealer in America by the time he died of a heart attack in 1920, working as a bookseller at his smart new East 45th Street shop.

Peter Stammer, the 'King of Fourth Avenue', was a bookseller stranger than most characters in the novels he sold. Born in Russia in 1864, he emigrated after he sliced off a general's ear in an altercation about tutoring the soldier's son. In 1900 he opened a bookshop in a Fourth Avenue basement using his own books as the initial stock. By 1919 he had a building of several floors crammed with books, including bargain bins on the pavement. The building was proudly signed 'the House of a Million Books', and he kept the business running until he was eighty in 1945. A visitor recalled:

> The old man was sitting alongside a pot-bellied stove reading [this stove usually had orange slices on it, the olfactory memory of many visitors]. He scrutinized me as if I were a book thief and barked, 'Mister, what can I do for you'.

One scout called him 'eccentric and rough-tongued' – if you haggled he might double the price or rip the book up in front of you – but worth dealing with for the breadth of his knowledge and stock.

Not only were New York's immigrant booksellers long-lived – because of all the good conversation, theorized one – they shunned retirement. Many had epically long working lives, starting in their teens or, in the case of Haskell Gruberger, aged seven. An extreme case is David Kirschenbaum. Born in Poland in 1896, he was selling books with his father off a street cart aged eight in 1904 and still bookselling in his nineties, having never missed a day's work. He ran several shops, but his Book Row building was the biggest, a four-floor Aladdin's Cave with over 100,000 books.

Even it was dwarfed by Schulte's a few doors away, established in 1917 and the biggest secondhand bookstore in the Americas, source of happy finds such as a T. S. Eliot first edition for a few cents, a Scott Fitzgerald letter for $2 and a Hardy letter complaining about expurgation which fell out of a copy of *Tess of the d'Urbervilles*. Wilfred Pesky, who took over after Mr Schulte died in 1950, had a different, adverse reaction to the shop's diverse holdings. They challenged his sense of order and he became submerged in obsessively recording the minutiae of the stock in a way that his staff eventually refused to emulate. Pesky, a gentle scholar who co-founded the American Association of Antiquarian Booksellers, was widely loved by authors and customers. He died at fifty-three in 1966. Schulte's closed in the 1980s but it sold so much weird stuff that its archive is housed at Columbia University.

Dauber and Pine, opened in 1923 by an Austrian and a Russian, worked as two businesses: new books on the ground floor and a network of rooms below ground which extended under adjacent shops, known as 'the catacombs'. These rooms, some unwired and requiring flashlight navigation, housed secondhand books at all-over-the-place prices. One bookseller remarked that it was no fun selling to those who could afford any book, 'the real pleasure is in serving the true students, who are hungry for books'. Dauber himself found the greatest sleeper of the catacombs one evening in 1926 when he knocked over 'a pile of pamphlets which had been gathering dust for years . . . from heaven knows what sources' and unearthed a rare first printing of the first ever detective story, Poe's *Murders in the Rue Morgue*. An attorney bought it for $25,000 after a nervous consultation with his wife, and in old age gave it to the

New York Public Library. Only when beret-wearing Nathan Pine died aged ninety did the shop close, in 1982.

Lou Cohen was another childhood entrepreneur, a baker's son who earned nickels from the age of eight by offering umbrella cover to commuters as they emerged from the subway on rainy days. In 1926 he opened Argosy Books in Fourth Avenue, where customers included several presidents and staff included Patti Smith. The shop is still open, run by Cohen's three daughters, who get about three calls a week from developers offering to buy the building.

As a bookseller I first encountered the name Samuel Weiser and its ankh symbol as the foremost publisher of occult books, but Weiser was responsible for one of Fourth Avenue's many specialisms, a store which opened in 1926 and became a shrine to magic. Harry Houdini was said to have visited the shop before he died; his books are some of the treasures sold there.

The specialisms of these shops account for the archival legacy of Book Row. Separate shops also specialized in areas as diverse as aeronautics, theology and theatre history. Most shops accepted ephemera in their labyrinthine premises, and this benefited the new breed of book historians, who now search out pamphlets and chapbooks eagerly as 'ground-level' evidence of reading habits. The big libraries often ignored such ephemera and sometimes even threw them away. One historian, Maggie Duprest, got lucky when she casually mentioned her interest in 'unofficial publishing' to Sid Solomon of the Pageant Bookshop. 'Oh,' he said, 'I've got tons of that stuff in the attic.' When she went up there with him she was astonished to find he was not using a figure of speech: there were literally tons of ephemera, in boxes piled up to the ceiling. Another hoarder of ephemera, Frank Thoms of Thoms and Eron, donated his entire ephemera stock to the Brooklyn Library just before he retired.

Walter Goldwater specialized in African American history for fifty years, so that by the time his shop closed he had probably 'the largest collection of black studies . . . in the world'. New York University bought his stock for $47,000. His wife, Eleanor Lowenstein ran a nearby cookbook shop and was such a world expert that she wrote a global bibliography of the genre. In the course of her career she visited ninety cities worldwide, and over 300 bookshops, hunting down books on food and cooking. After she died a friend went to the shop basement, and a typical Book Row one it was:

> The floor was covered with several inches of water. The lighting was terrible. And there we found box after box of books, wonderful, extraordinary books.

The University of California purchased the collection. Bookseller Haskell Gruberger, who at just seven years old persuaded his father to buy 5,000 books for $75 from a bookshop which was closing down, built up such a sociology collection that when his shop folded McGill University bought 52,000 books from him. A much-loved specialist was the Russian Leon Kramer (1890–1962). He arrived in 1912 on a small steamer – too poor to travel steerage on the *Titanic* – and worked at odd jobs, playing chess in Central Park until he got into bookselling. He developed such a depth of knowledge of socialism and radical history that he was frequently cited in academic histories. From his bookshop he founded the world's first Yiddish newspaper. Seymour Hacker started making bucks as a kid in the twenties by reselling printed matter thrown in the bin by his Bronx neighbours. In Hacker's adulthood, his Hacker's Art Books became the city mecca for regulars such as Jackson Pollock and Willem de Kooning.

All this hoarding of orphaned books is against the grain of clutter-clearing self-help books, but a form of psychic self-protection was at work among these booksellers. Descendants of a rag-tag army of recent refugees, they gave rag-tag refugee books a home when nobody else would. I saw a similar behaviour with my father: orphaned and abandoned when young, adopted by a book-hating harridan, he compensated by keeping thousands of books, so many that the front wall of our house cracked. In one room there was only one narrow chasm you could walk through. His protective instinct towards all books included ephemera and, as with Book Row, his legacy included many valuable treasures, hoovered up by him on Portobello Road buying trips.

Book Row booksellers, Jewish immigrants mostly, ran chaotic emporia where alphabetization was not the norm, and unclassifiable ephemera were welcomed. A *Village Voice* reporter evoked the vibe at Goldwater's premises: 'Despite what appears to be chaos,' he wrote, there is an 'organized funkiness' which is 'the heart and soul' of the shop.

Dewey and Shurtleff, the two progenitors of the most powerful book classification systems, were both prominent and active anti-Semites who vigorously opposed immigration.

In bad times, classifiers of books can become classifiers of people. A bit of chaos in the garden makes for a healthy ecosystem. Immigrants, victims of history, keenly preserve history in all its diversity, so that, ironically, Book Row immigrants did more for American cultural heritage than Dewey. 'Organized funkiness' mirrors the way we think and browse better than a decimal system. I see the human craving for serendipitous opportunities daily in my shop, when customers peer at stock trolleys, 'return-to-publisher' piles, even other customers' orders, seeking a shamanic union of time and chance. Less wordily, we all love a surprise karmic bargain. In New York, an old Judaeo-Catholic labyrinthine spirit breathed in bookshops, whilst the more doctrinaire Puritan heritage lived in Dewey's system and in the panoptical Library of Congress.

The tale of one Jewish refugee from Tsarist Russia illustrates the potential of New York booksellers' eclectic funkiness. Ze'ev Chomsky arrived in 1913 speaking no English, but his son Noam ended up a New Yorker and one of the most eloquent challengers of the political status quo. One historian of the city has insisted that, rather than academe, 'Chomsky relied on Fourth Avenue shops to supply him with the scholarly and radical literature that nourished his career.'

The mystery of Book Row's wayward attitude to customer service remains. It combined rudeness and kindness in a grainy authenticity, but the rudeness has been more reportable. As well as the ordeals recounted above, customers recall Abe Geffen ('an unpleasant little man') and Sid Solomon ('gruff and aggressive'), Jenny Rubinowitz ('tough as tenpenny nails . . . if you asked for a discount . . . madder 'n hell'). A particularly bizarre customer service story is told of Jenny's husband, George. Bill Weinstein had asked over the years for anything by George Kunz (I hadn't heard of him either). One day in 1950 Mr Rubinowitz sent him downstairs with a clerk, to a series of basement rooms. Some were lit by bare bulbs, some unlit, but all were full of books, including a whole dusty box of Kunz books. The conversation upstairs as Weinstein paid for the whole box tells us much about the Book Row milieu, and was recorded word for word in a later interview with Weinstein:

BW: 'Mr Rubinowitz, I like you, you seem a nice man. I'm curious, how long have you had these books that you knew I've been trying to find for a long time?'

GR: 'Oh, maybe ten years.'
BW: 'So why have you never told me you had these?'
GR: 'There was no one here to take you down. I don't go downstairs anymore.'
BW: 'Why didn't you just let me go downstairs?'
GR: 'Oh, I knew you'd come back.'

Another customer recalled Eleanor Lowenstein's selectivity about which customers she would serve. It is reminiscent of Bogart's admission nod in *Casablanca*'s Rick's Café:

You would go in there and see her at her desk through the locked door. She let you in if you passed inspection; if not, she ignored you and carried on working.

Why all the angularity? These booksellers seem to have turned retail on its head, but this was because they regarded themselves, like the Cree Indian elders who kept tribal stories in their heads, as shamanic scholars. The idea crops up in Michael Ende's *Neverending Story*, where the bookseller's role is to unite certain books with certain people in the cause of magical reality.

As admitted by Chip Chafetz, co-founder of Pageant Books: 'Book Row sellers derived satisfaction from sharing in America's scholarship and weren't focused on buying and selling.' This sounds uncommercial, but was married to a market-trader flexibility which less long-lasting book chains have lacked. One shop occasionally put out an 'Any Book 25 cents!' sign, another regularly slashed all prices by 50 per cent to move stock through. Book Row discount signage never had that annoying chain-store asterisk-and-small-print 'Selected Items Only', nor did they mess about with the equally annoying 'Up to 50% off' line. One shop slashed prices if the book had not sold after just one week – imagine the freshness of his stock. They all had bins and tables for cheaper books on the pavements, even after 1941, when the police said they could not. And they opened late long before chains thought of doing so. The two great late-night-walking book-lovers who especially liked this aspect of Book Row were Tom Wolfe and Leon Trotsky. As you might expect, Book Row sellers attracted a constellation of writers: Kerouac and Ginsberg, Lowell and Frost, Thornton Wilder and Edna St Vincent Millay, to name some of the most regular browsers.

One veteran bookseller of Fourth Avenue, asked how the hell they survived the Depression and two world wars, said simply, 'our wives worked', and most shops were family businesses, with the sort of family commitment night and day which drove shopkeeper's son Kafka near-crazy. Families could be made too: Jenny Rabinowitz got hired and then married the owner after being spotted kissing a copy of *A Midsummer Night's Dream*.

One shop which relocated from Book Row is now New York's most famous. Broadway's Strand bookstore, still run by Nancy Bass, a descendant of its Lithuanian Jewish founder Benjamin Bass, is one of America's best-loved bookstores, with about 200 staff. Now as much a tourist destination as Shakespeare and Company in Paris, a comment by Benjamin's son Fred Bass in 1998 indicates that it remains a proper Book Row portal of serendipity: 'Every time I make the place too neat, business goes down.'

There are so many other landmark bookshops in the city, such as cool and confident McNally Jackson, intimately cheering Three Lives and the apparently timeless Corner Bookstore, established 1976. Alabaster Books, est. 1996, is doing well, back on Fourth Avenue where it all started in 1893. You can imagine some cities without their bookshops, but not New York.

13.   Bookshops

Latham's Uncertainty Principle:
Serendipity in the bookshop

We've all been there. The social occasion where the conversation clunks on to well-worn rails, usually a news item, TV or
the kids. The opinions are forgettable and recycled. The Merlot
beckons. In desperation at a suburban dinner party, my sister
once shrieked, looking at a top shelf, 'What's in that box?' John
Gielgud's solution to conversational lowlands was to ask, 'Has
anyone had an obscene phone call recently?' The lowlands
were famously avoided by 'Conversation' Sharp, a humble hat-
ter, who, by good storytelling and the avoidance of malice,
became renowned company, sought out by Boswell and Burke.

'All progress depends on the unreasonable person,' said Shaw.
So at various times in history it was unreasonable to condemn
slavery, support universal suffrage or decry caning. All progress
away from those views was achieved by unreasonableness, by
uncovering the irrationality of prevailing mindsets. We all, it
seems logical to conclude, currently subscribe to some views
which future generations will think laughably outmoded. How
can we leave the trodden paths of thought? Not entirely by thinking great thoughts in a university department or think tank.
It seems, indeed, such institutionalized thinking is less likely to
be mould-breaking; whereas a bookshop, used open-mindedly
enough, uniquely challenges the normative thinking which
dulls our reason and clouds our souls.

'Where is your Cosmology section?' asked one of my book-shop customers in 2016. After my initial annoyance – what the hell is cosmology? – I realized it is rather wonderful that some-one just goes into a shop to learn about the cosmos.

There is another, even more cosmic way of discovery via books – aimlessness. Heisenberg's Uncertainty Principle states that you cannot know both the position and velocity of an object because everything is both particle and wave. I now pro-pose Latham's Uncertainty Principle, which states that, upon entering a bookshop, you cannot know both who you are and who you might become, because you are both memory and instinct.

Something strange happens when you wander aimlessly among books: you lose yourself, you begin to shed your iden-tity. The Greeks called it *kenōsis*, an emptying of self in preparation for being invaded by the divine will. If we are all a series of impersonations, and all the world's a stage, book-browsing is a way of going backstage in our minds. Chance finds free the mind, unmoor the soul, still the windmill brain. Suddenly the engineer looks at a poetry book, or the poet reads physics, the academic remembers the *Beano* annual, the account-ant stumbles upon Vonnegut.

In 1990 I thought I had created a pretty full-on new book-shop in Waterstones Canterbury, having ordered 35,000 books after a month of poring over publishers' catalogues on my kit-chen table. Until Tim Waterstone visited: 'Hmm, not quite . . . it just doesn't have that Aladdin's Cave feeling.' The metaphor is interesting, with its implication that among books one might find a magic lamp, something unexpected. As the crime writer Laurie King said about the first time she entered, as a student in 1966, the Santa Cruz Bookshop in California:

with its creaky wooden floors and scattering of well-used arm-
chairs, always occupied . . . I suspected there were magicians
in the basement, alchemists maybe.

Ah, bookshop basements. My Canterbury Waterstones basement was insulated from all noise and somehow timeless. A
Roman bath-house floor was visible behind glass next to History. An old African American man from Alabama asked me to
show him the basement. We looked at books in History. The
Persian Empire sat with Marathon and Caesar, the Hittites
were nearby, and a book on Cleopatra. As I rambled on, a funny
feeling came over me. I was getting an actual sense of Roman
times, of when Roman soldiers walked. I checked in with my
interlocutor. Was he getting this actual timeslip feeling? 'I'm
getting it, boy, just carry on talkin' – I only came in for a god-
damned thesaurus, by the way.'

Dave Eggers thinks about the building itself too. His favourite bookshop in California, Green Apple, has thousands of
handwritten recommendation cards but 'even without these,
something in the building casts a light of wonder on everything they carry'. It might be the 'psychic wounds' of its history,
which includes two earthquakes, or just that 'If a bookshop is as
unorthodox and strange as books are, as writers are, as language
is, it will feel right and good and you will buy things there.'

The right book has a neverendingness, and so does the right
bookshop, with shelves that disappear into the gloom, ideally
somewhere, as Terry Pratchett wrote, which looks as if it was
'designed by M. C. Escher'. Such a shop can seem inevitable,
henge-like, a site-specific nexus of magic and mystery – and
this is no invented romanticism: I am merely reporting what I
see in customers' eyes and hear in their sighs. The first hit they

get is often an olfactory one. Many, many times I have seen
someone enter the shop, stop, deliberately breathe out through
their mouth, then in through their nose, close their eyes and say
something like – to directly quote a recent customer – 'There
it is, that smell.' We in bookish countries with decades of peace
can easily take our bookshops for granted. Yesterday a young
woman with blonde hair and a bulky coat piled up *Sherlock Holmes*
and various classics. She looked English, a local student I
thought, but oddly not buying the expected mix of set books
and cult fiction. She put them on the counter in an unusual
way, the way priests put the chalice down on the altar just after
transubstantiation. As she paid, she suddenly gestured around
the shop with her arm and said, shy about her broken English,
'Your shop – I am from Georgia. Do you know where that is?
Do you know what it is? I think you cannot understand . . . a
shop like this.' The thought flowered more in the air between
us for her not putting it in exact words.

Virginia Woolf loved to lose herself in a late afternoon winter walk in London: 'We shed the self our friends know us
by . . . the shell-covering which our soul has excreted to protect itself is broken.' For Woolf, reversion to a fluid, eel-like
self was the best way to begin trawling for new books:

> Here, none too soon, are the secondhand bookshops. Here
> we balance ourselves after the splendour and misery of the
> streets, among wild books, homeless books . . . in this random
> miscellaneous company we may rub against some complete
> stranger who will, with luck, turn into the best friend we have
> in the world. There is always a hope, as we reach down some
> greyish-white book from an upper shelf, directed by its air of
> shabbiness and desertion, of meeting here with a new friend.
> ('Street Haunting')

In that open-minded state, life-changing and mind-opening books can be found, for don't we all sense that we have other, unexplored selves? Although Greta Garbo is known for saying she wanted to be alone, her truer weariness, as she confided late in life, was that she was 'tired of being Garbo'. It fits my theory of bookshops as looseners of the swaddling of identity to discover from Antonio Ximenez, bookseller at Rizzoli's in New York, that Garbo 'would spend hours exploring' that shop, 'nobody but us knew she was there'.

Serendipity Books in Berkeley, California, ran on the aimlessness principle for forty years. On several floors, over a million books were arranged at random. The notoriously brusque owner, Peter Howard, once said to a customer, 'If you're focused, go to a library.' When the shop closed in 2012, Bonhams held six auctions to sell the books. I chortled when I read that they found, among other literary curiosities, a spear owned by Jack London – but then I remembered that in my bookshop only I know where there is an 1870s Zulu shield made of kudu hide.

Other randomized bookshops remain, and they will always exist, because of the human need for them, a need demonstrated by the customers of my bookshop who love to rummage under tables or in clearance boxes, in search of strangers, and of other selves. The Dutch writer Cees Nooteboom felt this need on his 1991 ramble around Spain:

> Tucked away in each provincial capital I found at least one obscure little bookshop, a treasure trove of curious editions which seldom travel beyond the town or province, local publications mostly, by authors unknown to me, crammed with fascinating information, regional histories, poems by poets I have never heard of, and recondite cookery books [he found

recipes for baked lizard, and dried cod with honey 'as cooked by the monks']. Tiny, cluttered shops where I knock over a pile of books in reaching for a title, where the bookseller's eagle eye follows this odd-looking, clearly foreign visitor searching among the very volumes most people ignore. (*Roads to Santiago*, 1997)

Such chance finds can become consoling objects. Many readers have a comfort book issued by a long-defunct publisher, printed at a long-closed printing works and inscribed by a long-since skeletonized hand. It has no cloud of contemporary associations, nor shouty reviews by living worthies. I particularly cherish an ochre cloth hardback, *Cues and Curtain-Calls* (1927), by Chance Newton, a Dickensian theatre critic who extolled the long-forgotten stars of his day with colloquial intimacy. You can almost smell the greasepaint in this production of a back-street London publisher. Books like this are cosy reminders that reputation is mostly bubble. In a world of hype, it feels good sometimes to be the only person in the world reading a certain oddity.

A bookshop in Toronto, The Monkey's Paw, has mechanized the serendipitous discovery of such gems with a 'Biblio-Mat' machine, a Wallace-and-Gromit-type dispenser made from skateboard bearings and upcycled machine parts. For $2, you get a random book. 'This! Is! Brilliant!' commented Margaret Atwood. Neil Gaiman said simply: 'I think I'm in love.' Pre-Biblio-Mat, back in 1992, I installed a big section near the front door of Canterbury Waterstones called 'Serendipity'. No algorithm informed what went in there. It was a home for the misfits and mutants of the stock. Some of the books looked odd, some simply dull, but all had special powers for the right finder. Here, finally, we sold the taxidermy book *Much Ado*

About Stuffing and *Chinese Snuff Boxes*. In the same spirit I discovered that, although I could not sell the *Klingon Dictionary* from Science Fiction or the *Star Trek* section, it sold consistently from 'Dictionaries' between Japanese and Korean.

Browsing is non-linear, and yet productive, as behavioural economist Malcolm Gladwell insists:

> although I have to screw around online . . . I walk the bookshelves regularly, because of the way ideas cluster on shelves: more thematically and more randomly.

Ideas come not only from linear thought, but also like lightning from the synaptic soup, a soup full of randomly gathered information. To access it, Sherlock Holmes sat with his pipe for as long as it took. I thought I had invented the faux-Yiddish dismissive 'Google-Schmoogle', but I discover it is a thing: people who unthinkingly use Google for answers, as if it was the cardboard god Vaal in the 1967 *Star Trek* episode. Do you use a computer's suggestions to break what Blake called 'the mind-forg'd manacles'? No. Its suggestions are based on algorithms which assume your brain has the potential of an old IBM PC. Even the most updated algorithms are both reductive, inhibiting and past-based.

I once went around a sailing ship at Chatham Dockyard and that night dreamed my shop was the ship, commercial but undeniably romantic. The guide said that the 1878 ship had steam engines but that the wind could drive her faster. Serendipity is the wind that drives bookshops faster and more beautifully than search algorithms. In bookshops we are psychonauts.

The Bookseller's Tale, London to Canterbury

'The beginning of everything was in a railway train upon the line from Mhow to Ajmir.' This opener from a Kipling story shows an awareness that the significant moments in life happen *en passant*. While we think we are going from A to B we are crossing bridges unnoticed, or slipping through invisible portals. I will tell how it all started for me in 1986. I was cycling from a flat in Battersea to various part-time history lecturer jobs. I was only paid for 'contact time', actual teaching; there was no pay for preparing the lecture or marking essays. I was married then to a hard-working speech therapist and I needed a full-time job. Cycling down the King's Road in Chelsea I saw a new bookshop, Slaney and McKay, advertising for staff.

Sally Slaney was an ex-publicist at Collins Publishers, and Lesley McKay already ran Sydney's best bookshop. After a short interview, they took me on: I had stumbled into a vocation. As manager they had hired Ruth Hadden, a young foul-mouthed Liverpudlian with a *Flashdance* hairstyle which framed her head like a sort of Aztec headdress. Many mornings she had sore feet from her almost dervish level of dancing in London clubs. I had never met someone who so flung themselves into living, and yet she would suddenly enthuse to me about, say, Froissart's medieval chronicles – how she loved them and was 'dead chuffed' that a customer had come in asking for Froissart even though they called it 'Croissant's Chronicles'. She laughed often, a rich, filthy laugh that made me think she took life seriously enough to not take it seriously. Low-paid bookshop manager she might be, but she seemed to be queen of her life, and happily married to Ivor, a darkly handsome cockney.

She came from another remarkable bookshop run by two

women, the now-forgotten Collets in Charing Cross Road. There Ruth's independent spirit had soaked up the habit of rebellion, and the vision of a bookshop as a launch pad for change. Eva Collet (1890–1976) and Olive Parsons (?–1993), life-long Communist sympathizers, had set up a large bookshop near Foyles stocking Communist and progressive literature, periodicals from the Eastern bloc and, pioneeringly, world music. It was said that you could get books and periodicals about any liberation movement in the world there. Collets was more than anything a free-thought bookshop, although MI5 took a dimmer view of it, bugging Eva's phone and reading her mail.

Eva Collet's passion was fuelled by what she saw of conditions in her wartime factory work, informed by her time in the Labour Research Department, and deepened by her decision, at thirty-one, to do a Philosophy degree at UCL (she got a First). Collets spawned a Chinese bookshop near the British Museum and branches in Manchester and New York.

To illustrate the opinionated atmosphere of Collets it is worth recording that Ray Smith, who ran the music department (which later became Ray's Jazz Store inside Foyles) took pleasure in shattering 78 rpm 'Melodiya' records with his air gun, demonstrating his contempt for the state music label of the USSR.

Ruth Hadden, schooled in Liverpool's sense of community and Collet's radicalism, was an inspired choice to run Slaney and McKay. Despite the posh location, Chelsea then was hot with change. Vivienne Westwood's shop was up the road, Lucian Freud and Francis Bacon were at peak penetration artistically, and punks from all over the world hung out outside the Chelsea Drugstore, which the Stones had made famous in 'You Can't Always Get What You Want'.

Ruth abandoned all ideas of traditional bookshop classification and turned much of the ground floor into a fluid but connected mixture of new thought, art, fashion and music. The imported gay fiction of Phil Andros sold especially well, alongside books from Women's Press, then making its name with Alice Walker. Hadden got an eight-by-five-foot black sign fixed across the back windows to give this new section a name, in the same typeface as the Sex Pistols' most celebrated album cover: 'Style and Gender'. Sally Slaney and Lesley McKay began to wonder what they had unleashed.

Chelsea didn't. Francis Bacon was a regular, buying art and Andros, and filling the shop with that faultless adenoidal enunciation, bookie-posh, which Derek Jacobi nearly captures in the biopic *Love is the Devil*, a voice so eerily plangent that I could hear him from the ground floor till when he was in the basement. One summer morning Bacon met another regular, Anthony Hopkins, and the two conversed at length, the future Hannibal Lecter and the creator of *The Screaming Pope*, two artists who, to borrow Bacon's great phrase, 'unlocked the valves of feeling'. My conversations with Hopkins were about what might now be called New Age stuff. He was still boozing in those days, staving off the feeling of acting being a frippery field populated by shallow bores.

Sally Slaney always knew what fiction people should buy – I phoned her recently and found her still voraciously up to date – and she became Joan Plowright's personal shopper, keeping the ailing Laurence Olivier in comfort reads. Thanks to her enthusiasm for fiction, the shop hosted a Julian Barnes launch party, and, thanks to her passion for art books, Mick Jagger was a regular, stocking up with John Singer Sargent and the Pre-Raphaelites.

The veteran actor Michael Hordern came in just after Eve,

his wife of forty years, died, to learn how to cook. Sally had suggested he buy *One is Fun* by Delia Smith. As I put it in a bag he said with a crack in his voice, 'One is not, though.'

Alan Jay Lerner's sadness was that, despite me repeatedly checking the microfiche (5 x 4 inch celluloid sheets listing books in print which we viewed like holiday slides on a device which most customers called 'the computer', although it was just a monitor-shaped box with a light bulb inside), there was not a single book on musicals. Surely, he said, shows such as *Gigi* and *My Fair Lady*, which he wrote, had a place in cultural history?

The tide-rip between the wealth of Chelsea and its creative radicalism never quite went away. We were the local bookshop for a lean young Bob Geldof. He and Paula Yates enjoyed the books while daughter Fifi and friends ran amok in the children's section. As Live Aid towered into reality, driven by Geldof's iconoclastic fire, he walked in one morning after I had put a £120 book on Tamara de Lempicka in the window and asked, quite reasonably I thought, 'do you know how many fucking sacks of rice I could buy for that much money?' After Live Aid, he sought advice on good modern autobiographies as he wrote his own, *Is That It?*

Ruth was pleased that the punks who paraded King's Road like high society on Rotten Row in the 1850s flocked into the shop. One extremely pinned and mohawked crew alarmed Sally Slaney particularly, until they paid from rolls of £50 notes, as Ruth whispered that they were The Shits, or some such distinguished punk combo. I too was not au fait with The Shits' oeuvre. I only occasionally attended punk concerts, feeling out of place in my cords and worn Harris tweed jacket, with only a CND badge to confirm that I was not a trainee gamekeeper amid the leather trousers and flying spittle.

The shop proved a lesson I have to keep relearning, one simply expressed in Groove Armada's 'If Everybody Looked The Same (We'd Get Tired Of Looking At Each Other)': you need diversity in a team, despite the conflicts it can cause, despite one's desire to be with like-minded colleagues.

Each bookseller in the small team clicked for different regulars. Our part-timer Ursula Mackenzie was a confident resource for almost anyone who just wanted a good read. Her later career evidenced her skill as book pharmacist: as CEO of Little, Brown she would publish Donna Tartt and J. K. Rowling's crime books, and be one of the first women to get the Pandora Award for Women in Publishing. A sympathetic figure, she now presides over a charity which helps low-paid initiates of the book industry get starter homes. Olivia Stanton, a painter herself, looked after the handsome American R. B. Kitaj, an ex-GI turned painter who, with his friend Hockney, regenerated English figurative art. It seems so odd that my memory of him was of especially relaxed charm, but that on looking him up now I see that at seventy-four he suffocated himself on purpose with a plastic bag.

Olivia also attentively cared for an old crook-backed man who came in a lot, wearing a long tweed greatcoat in all weathers, always with his wife, who sported big hats and flowing scarves. Olivia supplied them with mystical texts and books on the English visionaries. They were Cecil and Elisabeth Collins, painters I had never heard of but a couple as significant in art as 'The Shits' were to punk. I wish – as we all do of old folk – I had spoken more with them. Cecil had a major retrospective at the Tate later on and had exhibited in the legendary 1936 Surrealists Exhibition, whilst Elisabeth had known Gertrude Stein in Paris. Nowadays, because of unthinkingly missing out on people like the Collinses, I actively try and pump old customers for their stories.

Another customer memory from Slaney and McKay reinforces that feeling: I liked the cheerful and faun-like Welsh surrealist photographer Angus McBean, but had never heard of him. He had some nice pics of Vivien Leigh and we agreed to launch a little book of his photos in the shop. We all drank a lot and a very old, still beautiful screen actress told me I 'reminded her of Marlon', whom she had known. Only now do I discover that McBean is a cult figure who had a) served four years in prison for homosexuality, b) designed sets for Gielgud in 1933, and c) did the photograph for the Beatles' first album cover.

Ruth's fluid classification system in the shop attracted the Scottish pop art pioneer Eduardo Paolozzi (he did the big Newton statue outside the British Library), who became a loved regular with his gravelly voice, smiling creased face and fat cigars. It also suited Brian Eno's eclectic avant-gardism. Eno would have liked the anecdote Nabokov told in a 1942 interview to support his own wariness around classification: in London, a scientist walking to his publisher's offices with the final text of a definitive guide to British beetles noticed, crossing the pavement in front of him, an unknown beetle: he crushed it underfoot. On one visit Eno wistfully asked if there was a book about all music, covering all styles and instruments. On the microfiche, fag in hand, I found *The Grove Dictionary of Music and Musicians* (1980). Eno ordered it, all twenty volumes. He collected them on foot in several trips. I really only knew him as a fascinating softly spoken man of my age, also prematurely balding and also a fan of weird music. At home I was listening to Talking Heads and David Bowie albums, unaware that Eno had produced them. The internet did not exist outside the military so there was nothing to look him up on.

The Hollywood star Dirk Bogarde was so used to being stopped and hassled that he was a furtive and silent shopper in Chelsea, until he encountered the irrepressible flamboyance of Pascal, our high-camp (but straight) bookseller, who had changed his name to honour the French philosopher and to forget being called Graham. In 'Pasc', Bogarde found someone with a deep and unaffected knowledge of his two great loves, French cooking and French films. Pasc was so unaffectedly egotistical that he had no interest in feeding off Bogarde's aura.

The diverse team thing is best if not wholly human: at the moment three spiders over the front door in Canterbury console me and another arachnophile bookseller as we lock up; they are reassuring ambassadors of a besieged ecosystem. To stop the window cleaner killing them I have told him they are being studied by the University of Kent Urban Ecology Unit. In Slaney and McKay a cat was on the team: Brando, a tabby who adopted the punk zeitgeist by posing charmingly on the till but taking a right hook if stroked, a move he deployed indiscriminately, even on the pedigree Scottie belonging to the shoe designer Manolo Blahnik. (The dog's face was badly gashed, but Manolo, one of our all-time nicest regulars, took it philosophically and refused our offer to pay the vet's bill.) We had rescued Brando from a tarring by urchins so he was entitled to be touchy.

Often, bookshop conversations lack the customary limitations because, to repeat Virginia Woolf's idea, in bookshops we can lose the carapace we excreted for self-protection. I have seen this so much over the last thirty years: bookshop conversations go off-road. These exchanges can be brief but resonant. Charlie Watts, the Stones' drummer, ordered a lot of military history – his unlikely passion – and we shared that unfashionable interest (my PhD included some forgotten battles in India). One bad morning, when I was post-divorce, he asked what was amiss: when I adduced the whole thing, life, he said simply, 'Ah, life' with such a 'yes-it's-a-bitch-but-never-for-long-trust-me-as-someone-who's-been-around-the block' warmth, that it still consoles me recalling it.

Ruth Hadden did more, though, to get me through my youthful shyness and sadness and learn to live a little, telling me once as I brooded and smoked that if I would just put myself into it I could be a fantastic bookseller. I was a bit surprised, lacking much self-esteem (or wallowing in that excess of it which stops some people competing) and furthermore still thinking that bookselling was a fill-in job.

In 1989 Ruth was invited to a party where the dancing would go on late, on a riverboat called *The Marchioness*. When I heard that it had sunk and she had drowned in the Thames, that someone who seemed to me to be life was dead, it took about thirty seconds to register and then a pressure wave of grief hit me as if from an explosion. Such a ruffianly taking. Shakespeare put it well: 'Now boast thee Death, in thy possession lies a lass unparallel'd.'

Slaney and McKay closed after a rent hike, and Sally, who had not cried when her mother died, wept for the first time since childhood. Elisabeth Collins wrote a letter in a spidery hand saying the shop had been a luminous place, a haven. A few years later, Pasc and Bogarde died; they probably discuss the perfect sauce in heaven.

I went to sleep after writing the above sentence, and dreamed vividly of the shop closing but, in the dream, when we took the bookcases out there were inscriptions on the walls by various writers. They had, dream-logic said, accumulated there quite naturally because of the stories in front of them. I awoke happy that this always happens, thinking it a real phenomenon. The message seemed to be that, if you make a bookshop, stories leach out of it, new stories, timeless lines.

Bookshops, happily, are victors over death, full of ideas from the dead but peopled by the living (although I wonder about a couple of our regulars). Since Ruth, Sally and Lesley taught me a bookshop's potential, I have had thirty years of working in shops which are safe harbours for the stories of authors and of customers.

After a spell in the secondhand sector – at Any Amount of Books on Charing Cross Road – I worked a few years in Waterstones' Kensington and Cheltenham branches. The Kensington shop felt good because my father bought women's corsets there when the building was Pettits, an old-fashioned womenswear shop. He took the whalebone strips out of the corsets because, as a practised dowser, he found them excellent for making divining rods. There being no whalebone in the earth, they give a pure signal when used to search for anything. When I blurted this out to Tim Waterstone he looked understandably nonplussed.

Bookshops always subtly partake of their psychogeography, far more than, say, a hardware store. The Cheltenham Waterstones, perhaps in reaction to the town's staid reputation, was staffed by a crew of baroque eccentricity, who stocked it with an almost Alexandrian completeness. Biography held all eleven volumes of Byron's letters, History held the complete works of Churchill and two editions of Gibbon. Travel, I remember, had three books on the island of St Helena.

I was Assistant Manager to the elegantly drawling and roll-up-smoking Harrovian Andrew Stilwell, who later became the first manager of the London Review Bookshop. He collected rare hard-boiled American crime and art books, and held the place together with an unsurprisable amused gravitas. Frequently, a rhythmic quaking of his shoulders announced the beginning of his creaky laugh at some new absurdity. Stilwell's tolerance impressed me especially when Ian, a burly Scottish bookseller, took to practising kendo – Japanese stick fighting – in the spacious manager's office, with its three Venetian windows overlooking the Promenade. Ian cavorted and screeched athletically around the office, leaping desks and piles of unsold books as Andrew sat in a cloud of smoke studying the Thames & Hudson catalogue.

Ian the Scot ran Graphic Novels and turned it into an empire, with visitors from afar. He championed rare comic books and, if challenged on his spending, fired off a defensive fusillade of sales figures for superheroes who even now have not reached the screen; he got me to read some tales of 3D Man and Bulletwoman, and even Arm-Fall-Off Boy, who seemed a real one-trick pony.

The elegant Mary van der Plank, now a mother of two in wildest Devon, liked to cat nap on her breaks. To maximize the time and find darkness she curled up inside a cupboard behind the ground-floor till. Getting a new till-roll out without waking her was a delicate operation, and so was managing customer incredulity when, break over, she unfolded out of the cupboard with a tousled mane of black hair and a sleepy, 'Who's next?'

John, the fiction buyer, was forever nipping over the road to swap ideas in the cosy basement bookshop run by Alan Hancox; William Golding was there with Alan once. The now gigantic Cheltenham Festival of Literature was saved from extinction by Hancox who, after an emergency meeting with the Town Clerk in the sixties, decided to lure big names to the town. He succeeded. W. H. Auden, Ted Hughes and Seamus Heaney all gave talks. Although in Heaney's 1988 talk – now a cassette in the Faber archives – the poet calls Hancox a Yeatsian figure, a 'hearkener', the current slick Festival site has no mention of Alan. If I have just exiled myself from ever speaking at the Festival, I am nevertheless glad to have named a much-loved and unduly neglected bookseller.

The bizarre cultural microclimate of Cheltenham's still hollow in limestone hills is symbolized in my memory by one day in particular. As bookshop events, Stilwell double-booked an ale-tasting with a wood-carving demonstration. The carver was thin, bearded and intense. Flying chips of wood repeatedly winged the waistcoat-wearing real ale fans, so that their appreciative sighs and lip-smacking were punctuated with yelps of pain.

On another day, we held an event for Melvyn Bragg's biography of Richard Burton and afterwards Bragg pointed out that a shop, if it thought both global and local, could reflect the spirit of the age, even contribute to it in a small way. The conversation lingered in my mind during my next job.

In 1990 I opened Canterbury Waterstones. Tim Waterstone had interviewed me and asked why he should give me such a sought-after opportunity. I said – I was young and callow – 'Because I'll set Canterbury on fire.' A. S. Byatt opened the shop, and left her glove somewhere, a loss which turned into a bit of a saga. As her minder said, everything becomes a fairy tale for her, a fact which I thought made her the ideal bookshop-opener. Fables suit bookshops. The subconscious, like the childhood imagination, knows this: after Philip Pullman gave a talk in the café about the second *Northern Lights* book I dreamed I went to the basement (subconscious-representing) of the shop and found an armoured polar bear prowling among the customers, with neither animal nor people being surprised.

Two children taught me how bookshops don't just sell books, they are so charged up by people opening up their imagination hatch that stories quietly explode there time after time. We have two rocking-horses in the Canterbury shop, which I ordered in 1990 from the Queen's rocking-horse maker, Stevenson Brothers. (Naturally I asked Tony Stevenson the same question which, delivering a big horse to Windsor, he had asked a footman; 'Does she go on it?' – she does, or did.) The horses were one of my more eye-watering petty cash slips, although nothing compared to the one for the archaeological dig under the shop which uncovered the Roman bath-house remains. That one is still the biggest extraction from the takings in Waterstones history. Girls love the horses the most and they usually start singing on them or engage in quite complex dialogue with their silent steed. The girl I overheard told more and more baroque fantasies to her slightly younger sister on the other horse until the sister got suspicious and said, 'Now you're just telling me stories.'

'Well,' said the unfazed storyteller, 'we are in a bookshop.'

J. K. Rowling felt comfortable making up stories too, and before her talk on the second *Harry Potter* book she used the shop phone – these were pre-mobile days – to read out a made-up bedtime story to her six-year-old daughter Jessica.

Storybook characters, and the dead, feel more alive in a bookshop. Recently, the Canterbury Cathedral Dean came in to find a reading for his sister's funeral. As we wandered the floor he said, almost to himself and as if his sister was still alive, 'She'll want a bit of Maggie.' My fleeting fear that he was considering an ex-Prime Minister was dispelled as he headed for George Eliot and inspected the feel of the paper in two editions of *The Mill on the Floss* (he meant Maggie Tulliver). He preferred the cream paper OUP edition. The bright white paper seemed a bit stark. As he paid, he said that the Cathedral and the bookshop were both spaces where people can wander for solace without being hassled, and maybe find it, or maybe just mooch about and commune.

I have hoarded an untold story from this winter, waiting to tell it here in the privacy of the page. It is a story of no one famous: I don't even know her name. It was an indifferent morning last month. You know those days when you can conceive why Keats was 'half in love with easeful death'. *Moby Dick* starts with such a morning, when Ishmael amusingly finds himself 'stopping before coffin warehouses, and bringing up the rear of every funeral procession I meet'. In this chapter I seem to be talking about death a lot, but only as love's sibling. Bookshops suit both. City Lights in San Francisco had a letter from a customer confessing that she had, as directed by her father, distributed his ashes around the store, behind some of his favourite books. I used Lesley McKay's father's ashes – a nice heavy box – to prop up art books in Slaney and McKay's window. She was startled when she saw this, but admitted she had been stumped to do something significant with them. I have seen plenty of heart attacks in my bookshops over the years. A woman customer, resuscitated in Classics after a coronary, held my hand as paramedics trolleyed her out to the ambulance and said, 'I do love it here . . . it would've been a great place to go.' As for love, bookshops are fruitful meeting places, and at the Strand Bookstore in New York they get asked so often to be a wedding venue that they have an established routine for ceremonies.

Back to my melancholy morning. It made me think of Charlie Watts' 'Ah, Life'. Instead of Watts I got a tall woman with a good strong face, weather-beaten complexion and a real workwear anorak, browsing Poetry. I was to learn that she was an engineer in her fifties, a person of few words, with things going on; she wore a heavy-duty ID lanyard, not some flimsy academic one, with a fob for site access to some launch pad or Hadron collider-type place.

She wanted help finding a certain sea poem, one of the poems which her late father used to read to her. One line about 'the old grey Widow-maker' – the sea – kept coming back to her. We looked in various anthologies and I suggested 'Butting through the Channel in the mad March days' from John Masefields 'Cargoes', but she said, 'No, hang on, I'm just going through "Sea Fever" at the moment.' She was actually hearing Masefield's 'Sea Fever' in her head, the whole poem, going through it for the Widow-maker line; her Dad had put a sort of audio recording in her head of these poems. Meanwhile I found the poem she wanted, 'Harp Song of the Dane Women', by Kipling. It's about Viking women waiting at home while their menfolk go off, leaving just 'the sound of your oar-blades, falling hollow'. The refrain is:

What is a woman that you forsake her,
And the hearth-fire and the home-acre,
To go with the old grey Widow-maker?

Having found it, I read it to her – it's not long – and although her voice was unchanged as she thanked me, when I looked up from the book, tears were streaming down her face.

Booksellers and Customers

Booksellers are a free-floating breed, neither professional nor proletarian: they shape-shift daily from literati to cashiers to, quite often, care-workers. Interviewing for the initial team of booksellers in Canterbury I looked for this adaptability, for learning lightly worn and open-mindedness about human nature. It takes a certain resilience and discernment to appreciate the gamut of customers, from the geek to the literary snob, the builder after site regulations to the refugee after citizenship guidance, the romance reader to the Barbour-clad memsahib who strides in and asks, 'Are you the help?'

When I opened the Canterbury branch I hired a young graduate to run fiction. He quickly engaged in long conversations with most customers. In his curiosity he reminded me of the story about Kipling who, waiting for a train once, used the time to find out all about the life of the porters, the ticket-office clerk, the stationmaster, the level-crossing operator and the signal-box man. Tim Waterstone wrote a handwritten report on this fiction buyer – David Mitchell – as he used to on all booksellers he met, but it failed to predict that, with books such as *Cloud Atlas*, he would have a permanent place on Waterstones' shelves. Mitchell's unclassifiable books, which Ruth would have put in 'Style and Gender' have spawned debates with his editor, centring on whether he was becoming 'a sci-fi author'. The same problem afflicts H. G. Wells. Is *The Time Machine* Sci-Fi or classic fiction? Is Lovecraft 'Horror' or just classic fiction? Should Neil Gaiman be left in Sci-Fi but *The Handmaid's Tale* enshrined in literary fiction? Beware the entomologist's boot.

My conversations with Mitchell, which unspooled once onto a long night walk on Whitstable beach, his Doc Martens crunching the pebbles, seemed all part of that nineties' optimism which made history hot and relevant, that decade in the wake of the fall of the Berlin Wall, when apartheid collapsed. I got hate mail for hosting a talk by Ronnie Kasrils, a burly ANC fighter whom the Home Office nearly banned from entering the UK. Later he would be free South Africa's first Deputy Defence Minister but a USSR-trained freedom fighter talking about a book called *Armed and Dangerous* was not a typical Home Counties book talk. During the talk, in pre-mobile 1994, I went to get rid of someone who had somehow got the number of the only unmuted phone in the shop, an old payphone in our café. I stopped the talk for Kasrils to take it: it was Joe Slovo calling from Johannesberg to say that the ANC had won the election (a more justifiable interruption than the only other call taken during a talk, the mobile answered mid-flow by Antonia Fraser: 'Hello Harold, yes I'm in a talk. No, I'm giving it, darling.')

Like Mitchell, Umberto Eco recognized the unique cultural vantage point which a bookseller can have. I asked his UK publisher if he would come and 'event' at my Canterbury shop, but they said he never did such things. I phoned his publisher in Milan, who courteously said they would ask him. He replied that what he really wanted to do was work for a day in a bookshop. He did, and even sold one of his books to a customer, without revealing his identity. Somewhere out there is that customer and somewhere too are the several customers who Spike Milligan answered the shop phone to. After his event he insisted on helping us answer the phone. I remember his answers: 'Hello, Waterstones Canterbury, how can I help . . . I'm not sure . . . that depends . . . Who am I? Spike Milligan.' At that point the caller hung up. For a while and for a day, respectively, Milligan and Eco were in the fertile tradition of authors who have worked in bookshops: George Orwell, Nancy Mitford and Alice Munro, most notably.

Robots will replace most jobs, and much of retail, but not the most enjoyable parts: connecting with customers and connecting them with books and with writers. I love nature guides and it really works commercially to go beyond basic bird guides and stock guides to moths and dragonflies, fossils and lichens. I have sold several copies of a £45 moth guide, and sixty-eight copies in two years of a £20 bird guide from an unusual publisher which I always recommend for its having good illustrations of seasonal plumage. Why, I've even sold three copies, in six weeks, of the £39 *Atlas of Britain and Ireland's Larger Moths*. Who on earth was passing by the Nature section and thought yes, something up-to-date about Hawk moths and their allies is just what I need. £39? No problem. It's the same with Hannah Arendt's *The Human Condition*, £20. I ordered this because of a customer recommendation and now it repeatedly sells despite the author not being on telly or social media. I am continually humbled by the breadth of intellect out there. Retailers and publishers often underestimate the curiosity and intelligence of the public, instead jumping on a new craze a bit too late and then flogging it to death and coffee-table-booking every celebrity death or sporting event in a very un-Greta-friendly way. A Gauguin exhibition can spawn a shelf of books on him, squashing space for those he admired. The Olympics kill the Falconry and Darts sections. Poetry sections only sell if they are far more comprehensive than they usually are. The Persian poet Rumi is regularly being rediscovered as the ecstatic mysticism of his paradoxes gives us ways to survive the strangest days. Instagram poets bring hordes of young people to poetry, one of many ways in which the digital life piques the appetite for the physical book.

The bookshop is a place of TV-led fads but also of authentic private enthusiasms. This week I was given warm saved-up coins by a child who was literally jumping for joy at her purchase. A Norwegian Rutger Hauer lookalike, buying *Moby Dick* in the middle of his round-the-world trip, said, 'Now I have the time . . .' A greybeard told me at the till: 'I buy Buchan now to enjoy the language – I know the stories backwards'; and a brisk woman bought three copies of Vera Brittain's *Testament of Youth*, because she always gives it to women she knows as they enter their twenties.

Questions are gloriously unpredictable: 'Where are your technical books on goldsmithing?', 'Where can I get sit-down fish and chips?' 'I want a book which proves the existence of God' was a challenge, but we alighted on Thomas à Kempis's *Imitation of Christ* as, if not proof, damned fine marketing. It was in Tunbridge Wells Waterstones that a well-dressed customer asked for books on the devil. After a civilized chat about what the store had in stock, the customer confessed that he thought them all a bit ill-informed.

'Ill-informed?' said Mike, the shop manager.

'Yes, you see, I am the Devil.' (I never found out if Mike checked his feet, traditionally the one part a morphing Devil cannot change.)

In my Canterbury shop I had a similar surprise when a customer, finding our 'Mind, Body, Spirit' section, held a hand to the shelves and said 'Yes, it's here.'

Self: 'Oh good, glad you've found what you're looking for.'

Customer: 'Yes, this is the portal to the other dimension, here on the wall, I was told it was here.'

Customers enlighten me every day on a less cosmic but more useful level. Earlier today (I'm writing this in bed at 1 a.m.), I learned from three of them in particular. One young woman in running clothes with an Afro recommended the Apocrypha. Although she was no Christian, she told me about Maccabees with all the enthusiasm of someone going on about a Booker winner: 'Revelations did my head in but Maccabees! It's somethin' else.'

Soon after this, a short, busy-looking man with quietly co-ordinated clothes and blue-framed specs was so surprised that I was unaware of the autobiographical *Life Among the Savages* by *Haunting of Hill House* author Shirley Jackson that I resolved to read it: 'You really should, you know; it kicked off this whole genre of domestic chaos stories.'

I nodded, pretending I knew that was even a thing.

I fear I implied that the third customer, a wonderfully dressed woman, was gaga to suggest that Ursula Le Guin, revered cult author of the *Earthsea* books, had written something called *The Carrier Bag Theory of Fiction*. She has. ('Are you sure you mean Ursula Le Guin?') It seemed as unlikely as if Philip K. Dick had written *Pingu*.

Urbanely tolerating my ignorant doubting, the customer sauntered off, saying with magnificent *esprit de l'escalier*, 'Ignota publish it, you must know them.'

What! Who? I thought. What fresh mind game is this, from this woman who seems to be running the secret rebel army of freethinkers, dressed like Artful Dodgers? So they really exist, thank God, living in the outlands. When I looked up Ignota I felt I had fallen through a wall into one of their meetings:

> Founded in the last days of 2017 in the Peruvian mountains, Ignota publishes at the intersection of technology, myth-making and magic. Deriving our name from Hildegard of Bingen's *Lingua Ignota*, we seek to develop a language that makes possible the re-imagining and re-enchantment of the world around us.

Ignota's edition of the Le Guin is introduced by an 'eminent cyberfeminist', so I got a good new word out of all this too. I felt I had wasted those last days of 2017, footling about when I could have been in the Peruvian mountains with Ignota.

Over the years, much of my awareness of subtle societal change has dawned on me thanks to customers (before and after the internet happened); I think you sense it early in a bookshop. In 2003 my art buyer Paul Hayton, a painter in acrylics, started selling an obscure postcard-sized book from his table, next to Blake and Turner. He said it would be big. I queried this oddity but now I wish I had bought that rare first edition Banksy book. I texted Paul just now to ask how he knew about Banksy back then, in Canterbury; Facebook started in 2004, Instagram in 2010. He wasn't sure: 'Just cultural osmosis,' he thought. Manga came, similarly, out of nowhere to challenge our over-classifying minds. It confused the international book data inventory, which scrambled the titles across art, graphic novels, children's and foreign languages. Early fans were Japanese students and European geeks under twenty-five. We responded early and started with a whole two shelves of it; two decades later we have twenty shelves and the genre has its own exhibition at the British Museum.

In Slaney and McKay I found out what punks wanted; in Canterbury I was to discover that steampunks warm to Bram Stoker and Arakawa's *Fullmetal Alchemist*. The sci-fi questers who polished off *Game of Thrones* in the nineties have moved on to Jin Yong, 'the Chinese Tolkien', whose death in 2018 was mourned by millions, and to Proust-in-space, Cixin Liu, whose *Remembrance of Earth's Past* trilogy is much in demand. At the literary end, a customer in 2018 surprised me by being surprised that I did not stock the new translation of the four-volume novel by Uwe Johnson, 'the Sage of Sheppey', published by the *New York Review of Books*. Despite having been asked to write a book on Kent writers I knew nothing of this recluse whom Günter Grass called 'the most significant of all East German writers'. Johnson astonished his admirers by moving to Sheerness, a small town on the generally poverty-stricken Isle of Sheppey in the Thames Estuary, aged forty, in 1974. He was deliberately removing himself from academia and the company of literati; the result was the completion of his epic *Anniversaries*.

Booksellers enjoy such encounters because they tend to have butterfly minds, ill-fitting in a one-note career. They can find unclassifiable books such as Huxley's *Doors of Perception*, know what a rhyming dictionary is, where genealogy books are, and that there is a book on the birds of Trinidad.

Sometimes, a military level of fortitude is required. The frontline of bookselling is justly romanticized but always portrayed in somewhere well-heeled like Southwold or Notting Hill. Bookselling happens too in places most self-respecting retirees with a pension pot and time on their hands would never consider. Bookselling in grittier towns, bravely opening daily to offer Dickens and Lee Child on a tough street, is heroic, bookselling *sans frontières*. A bookseller in Ireland was locking up in the staff areas when an intruder approached her with an axe. In one notoriously tough town, there is a superb bookshop on a ravaged high street. The security radio freaked out a new bookseller there when it crackled out: 'Man coming down the street waving a samurai sword.'

'Oh, don't worry,' said the old manager, 'he's one of our regulars'.

She went for a tea break with relief, only to see old bullet scars in the staff-room window.

Mostly, booksellers walk, cycle or take public transport to and from work (delivering the odd customer order). Their contact with the public gives them, in my experience, a positive outlook on life, revelling in eccentricity. They are often leisurely scholars, or sci-fi lovers who like living in several universes.

They are confirmed readers: a colleague recalls going into the staff room of a big bookshop on her first day and finding it absolutely silent; everyone was reading and she thought, 'This is my tribe.' Being surrounded by such diverse books can make booksellers Renaissance in their mentality. There was multilingual Nick Bray, who when I said I wanted to read Goethe, looked a bit doubtful.

'You're not a fan?' I asked.

'No, no, he's fantastic, I just think you have to read him in German.'

Paul Grigsby used every one of his lunch hours to learn Ancient Greek, and one morning told me he had 'spent a great evening with Aristophanes'. Another bookseller was adept in Latin and Anglo-Saxon, and could recite Chaucer as heard by contemporaries. Children's booksellers have a very particular enthusiasm and tend to be as eccentric as some of the characters in the books they sell. They provide an unsung service in creating havens for children and getting reluctant readers reading. In my shop all ten staff agree on one thing: we want to be more like the children's bookseller, a one-woman literature pharmacist. One child put on her Christmas list, 'Anything recommended by the lady in the children's section', and another grateful mother asked, not entirely in jest, if she could take her home. Only my old colleague Robert Topping, who now runs his own exceptional bookshops, has inspired me more to see the potential of bookselling to change lives in small ways, day to day.

Booksellers have great power to champion or trash books, a power now enhanced by social media. Word travels like wildfire among the world's booksellers. Publishers can bring a new author to market, but the bejumpered bookseller on the ground is the one who decides to keep it there or not. After the initial hype a new book gets, booksellers make or break many an author. I think of Mitchell's successor, Vicky, in my shop, singlehandedly championing W. G. Sebald. 'Why so much of this?' I asked her one day. 'Well,' she replied, 'he's marvellous, and I have sold eighty-two copies by recommending it.'

Bookshop staff combine being shop assistants and literary experts. The job feels more expansive than the word 'career' – that linear, post-medieval word derived from 'racecourse'. It's a philosophic path. At their best, booksellers are shamanic. Pretentious, *moi*? Maybe, but, as Jarvis Cocker added after those words: 'where would we be without pretension? *Absolument* nowhere.' Put booksellers together with serendipitously minded customers in a roomful of books and you are in Ignota territory, where re-enchantment happens.

Graham Greene dreamt so vividly and repeatedly of a bookshop between Charlotte Street and Euston Road that he twice went on walks searching for it. It was not there, and nor was his other recurring-dream bookshop near the Gare du Nord, deep with high shelves, where he used a ladder to find Apollinaire's translation of *Fanny Hill*. We humans continue to dream up vibrant new bookshops, from Brooklyn to Baghdad. In Bloomsbury, Treadwell's occult bookshop currently has a mummy case in the window and the scrying workshop is sold out. In New York there are still tickets for the 'Domesticating *Ulysses*' talk at McNally Jackson. The 'Fellini at 100' talk at City Lights in San Francisco is free. If you don't fancy the Drag Brunch at Toronto's Glad Day Bookshop they host comedians on Gay Friday. In Sydney, Sappho Books' long-running monthly poetry open mic is open to all comers. Globe Books in Prague have a tempting Anti-Valentine's Reading Group. In Paris there are still a few places for Shakespeare and Company's Agnès Varda-inspired Still Life Drawing Workshop. As I write this, in the café of the London Review Bookshop near the British Museum, I can hear a couple deconstructing Kundera.

One day I want to visit the Montague Bookmill Bookshop in Massachusetts. It is in an old wooden flour mill; I hear it has idiosyncratic shelving rules, creaky wooden floors and a café spread throughout the building. The owner says, 'We're not particularly convenient, we're not particularly efficient, but we're beautiful.' You can get a hot chocolate and sit anywhere, and read, or just listen to the river running under the ice outside.

Acknowledgements

Be not forgetful to entertain strangers: For thereby some have entertained angels unawares

Hebrews 13: 2

All of you first; customers and book-lovers: you prove every day that there is more to life than war and laundry. If my dreams of being a full-time writer or academic had come true, my life would have been impoverished without your surprises, your storytelling and your warmth.

I grew up in a house noisy with seven siblings and six tenants; my mother's conversation over the drying-up was a university. My father: every Saturday he took us down 'Portabella' as he called Portobello Road Market in London's Notting Hill. He knew most of the book dealers there, and elsewhere in London we often waited ages while he browsed bookshops, amassing a houseful. My extraordinary brother John read eclectically and deeply; his shade is in this text.

I benefited from inspiring tutors at London University, especially my PhD supervisor Peter Marshall. He taught me intellectual rigour, and has retained his fast-talking charm into his eighties. He seems to value the prize vegetable certificates in his garden shed as highly as the many honours he has received. Even a political opposite such as Eric Hobsbawm has enthused to me about what an exemplary human he is.

Acknowledgements

I found Victor Kiernan an avatar of what humanist learning can do. There's a Buddhist enlightenment-fable of a frog in a well whose head explodes when it sees the whole expanse of the world above. Although I did not shatter the peace of Kiernan's upstairs eyrie in Edinburgh with such a detonation, he did impart to me that sense of global awareness. As Hobsbawm obituarized, 'He was a man of staggeringly wide learning.' At Cambridge Guy Burgess had recruited Kiernan into Communism; he later left the party, but worked tirelessly for marginalized peoples worldwide.

I became a bookseller by the grace of Sally Slaney and Lesley McKay, two fine, funny divorcees who, *Thelma and Louise*-like, let rip and set up shop in the heart of chain-store London. If their adventure was a movie its catchphrases might be Sally's '*complete* nightmare luvvie', '*so* up himself' and the irrefutable 'utter *wanker*, quite frankly'. Lesley was the *éminence grise*, unflappably seeing humour, it seemed, in any situation.

Tim Waterstone gave me a job after the Church Commissioners' rent-hike ended Slaney and McKay. He has done more for culture than a barrowload of Arts Council members, and he invigorated his staff with continual inspiration. Forget 'thinking outside the box': he was innocent of the whole box concept. After Tim, six managing directors were followed by the most intelligent yet: James Daunt, Bach to Tim's Beethoven. I thank him for his tolerance, his Edward Gibbon-like use of language and for saving Waterstones. Many colleagues have made Waterstones thrive again: Kate Skipper, with her Sekhmet powers; Luke Taylor, Daunt's Marshal Ney; Neil Crockett, Pierre from *War and Peace*; Juliet Bailey, whose sense of history enables her to both deal with and see the absurdity of anything; my co-workers for decades Ruth (a loyal friend),

Pete (learning lightly worn), Rachel (the best of us) and all the Canterbury team. Newer booksellers such as Zoe, James and Alfie show me there is no end to reinventing the bookshop. Artful Tucker: thank you.

Jenny Uglow and Katherine Wyndham long ago had more respect for my writing than I did. I took an idea for this book to Jamie Byng at Canongate a decade ago and I thank him for gently telling me – on overlapping Kirghiz rugs in his book-lined Notting Hill back room – that I did not need to hide behind facts. I love him for being the Necessary Outlaw of publishing. Out of an argument with Peter Ackroyd about Virginia Woolf's suicide came similarly sobering advice, to find my own view of things.

Canterbury Cathedral Archivist Cressida Williams read sections of this book with her customary rigour, the iron fist inside her maternal good nature. Anthony Lyons has inspired the young as a teacher, and me as a friend, more than he will ever know. Josh Houston, the Yale University Press rep, supplied key books and quiet conversation through dark days.

Kate Gunning, a de Sévigné figure, is the godmother of this book, and her friendship has been a tree house I can always go to. I did not want to finish the book because Simon Winder's editorship has been so companionable and percipient, and Eva Hodgkin such a wise owl. Jane Birdsell patiently copy-edited. My agent Sophie Lambert guided me away from successive cliff-edges and embodies so much that is good about the book industry. Emma Finn is her kindly consul.

Children underpin this book. Ailsa is more like her hero Margaret Cavendish than she knows, Oliver is the soul-seer from the forest, India's the compassionate firebird, Caspar the Chestertonian Nietzschean and William the wise counsellor.

Acknowledgements

Francesca is Anne from *Persuasion*, Jack's a Karataev figure and Sam embodies goodness.

My wife Claire is wise, funny and reads crazy forgotten books. Our marriage, like the Kon-Tiki expedition she so loves, has been a triumph of hope over probability.

A Note on Sources

Note: 'Princeton', 'Cambridge', etc. are shorthand for their Univer-sity Presses

A night-time comfort read as I wrote this book was the three-volume biography, *Kafka* (Princeton, 2005–17) by Reiner Stach, a portly leather-jacket-wearing freelance writer and Berliner who is about my age, mid-sixties. Even in translation it has several words I did not know; epigonal, for instance. Its steady scholarship is lit up by novelistic insights about humanity. Apart from that, my bedside table has books which are my lightning conductors: *Sherlock Holmes*, Evelyn Waugh and new writers such as Lesley Jamison and Olivia Laing.

Comfort Books and Reading in Adversity

A book by two Frenchmen kicked off the study of people read-ing and caught my undergraduate imagination in the seventies. In the 1930s Lucien Febvre and Marc Bloch founded the Annales school of history. In a radical historiographical shift, it looked systematically at everyday life as well as at more obvious histor-ical changes, and it took an interdisciplinary approach to studying the past. Why the interest in 'everyday folk'? The two men – themselves well-heeled bourgeois – ascribed it to their years of mixing with all classes in the trenches of the First World War. Bloch, who fought through the battle of the Somme, even described the war as a 'gigantic social experience, of unbelievable richness'. A Resistance fighter in the Second World War, he was executed by a German firing squad in Lyons. Post-war, Febvre pursued the Annales mission with renewed vigour. As he put it, he spurned 'those puerile subdivisions based on the artificial distinctions of dates; the kind of thing that is fed to schoolchildren to keep them happy'. His seminal 1958 *The Coming of the Book: The Impact of Printing, 1450–1800* (Verso edition, 1976) spectacularly exceeded his modest aim of producing 'something not too unpleasant to read' about a field which 'no-one has generalized or assessed'.

My wife Claire found Henry Miller's out-of-print *The Books in My Life* in the musty basement of a Brighton bookshop. It is a wonderfully rambling but authentic tour of book love, from the perverse Author's Note at the front telling you that the book bombed and had 'bad reviews' to the chapter on lavatory reading.

Miller should be reprinted, but not the annoying 600-page *Anatomy of Bibliomania* (Soncino Press, 1930). Its author, Holbrook Jackson, tried unsuccessfully to emulate Burton's *Anatomy of Melancholy*. In among all the 'perchances' and 'wilts' I did find much useful information, but I vented my irritation by ripping out the useful pages and defenestrating the book.

If I hated Jackson I think I fell in reader love with Professor Abigail Williams of Oxford University, though I never met her. *The Social Life of Books* (Yale, 2017) is innovative, witty and warm; it was no surprise that her acknowledgements mention her 'kitchen table, the crumbs and chaos of family life'. Less warm but still *the* book on the subject is Belinda Jack, *The Woman Reader* (Yale, 2012).

Jonathan Rose admits that no recent book, but 'a shopworn copy', found in Pennsylvania, of the 1957 *English Common Reader* by fellow American Richard Altick, inspired *The Intellectual Life of the British Working Classes* (Yale, 2001). Rose's book has a following which has included Phillip Pullman and Christopher Hitchens. Like Hitchens, I found it 'lastingly moving'.

Margaret Spufford was home-schooled, and illness stopped her getting a university degree. A lifelong empathy with ordinary people informs her seminal *Small Books and Pleasant Histories: Popular Fiction and its Readership in Seventeenth-Century England* (University of Georgia Press, 1981).

The American Leah Price's *How to Do Things with Books in Victorian Britain* (Princeton University Press, 2012) is a groundbreaker about human interaction with books in Dickens's time, as witty as her YouTube talk which explores how reading a physical book lowers stress even more than listening to music. Deirdre Lynch's *Loving Literature: A Cultural History* (University of Chicago Press, 2015) is a useful survey. Few have followed David Allan into the undiscovered territory of *Commonplace Books and Reading in Georgian England* (Cambridge, 2010).

Like many before me, I drew much from John Brewer's *Pleasures of the Imagination: English Culture in the Eighteenth Century* (HarperCollins, 1997) and from *The Book: A Global History* (Oxford, 2013) edited by Michael Suarez and Henry Woudhuysen. Stephen Greenblatt's *The Swerve: How the Renaissance Began* (Bodley Head, 2011) is a breakthrough in the anthropology of reading. The neuroscience of language and story creation is expounded in Iain McGilchrist, *The Master and his Emissary: The Divided Brain and the Making of the Western World* (Yale, 2009). On reading spaces, Gaston Bachelard's unclassifiable *The Poetics of Space* (Penguin, 2014) was first published obscurely in Paris in 1958. As with McGilchrist, I defy anyone to read it and not be changed by it.

Christine de Pizan's *Book of the City of Ladies* is available in Penguin Classics.

The Strange Emotional Power of Cheap Books

Chapbooks are still largely lost to history, although their digitization is proceeding apace all over the world. The compendious 1882 *Chapbooks* by John Ashton can be bought in a 1994 edition reprinted by the excellent Skoob Bookshop, which still trades in Bloomsbury. The British Library, National Library of Scotland and Cambridge University Library websites all have much information about their chapbook holdings. The East Ender and conscientious objector Leslie Shepard had an extraordinary collection of chapbooks. His *History of Street Literature* (Singing Tree Press, 1973) surveyed the subject decades before academia took it seriously.

Markets, Pedlars and Bookshop History

The position of markets and fairs in our imagination is presented in Katerina Clark and Michael Holquist's *Mikhail Bakhtin* (Harvard, 1984), and in the Walter Benjamin talks printed in *Radio Benjamin* (Verso, 2014). Simon Johnson, a barrister and a regular customer, shared his unpublished dissertation on market law. I found *Fairs, Markets and the Itinerant Book Trade* (Oak Knoll Press, 2007), edited by Robin Myers, romantic and riveting. Myers also edited *The London Book Trade* (Oak Knoll Press, 2003). Henry Mayhew's *London Labour and the London Poor* (George Woodfall, 1851) is a time machine to Dickens's London: oral history on a scale not since equalled.

Jeroen Salman's *Pedlars and the Popular Press: Itinerant Distribution Networks in England and the Netherlands 1600–1850* (Brill,

2013) is pioneering for its region, as the writings of Clive Griffin are for Iberia.

The role of pedlars and bookshops in the Reformation is unequivocally outlined by Diarmaid MacCulloch in *The Reformation* (Viking, 2004) and by Carlos Eire in *Reformations: The Early Modern World* (Yale, 2016). Kevin Sharpe was a typically eclectic Hugh Trevor-Roper pupil. His *Reading Revolutions: The Politics of Reading in Early Modern England* (Yale, 2000) is so good it underlines the sadness of Sharpe's death at sixty-two. As the *Guardian* lamented, he was 'a natural egalitarian', a good tendency for any historian of the book. That tendency is shared by Professor James Raven of Essex University, who works with charities to widen access to learning. His humanism informs his unsurpassed *The Business of Books: Booksellers and the English Book Trade, 1450–1850* (Yale, 2007).

Andrew Pettegree of St Andrew's University is the uncrowned king of book history, not just because of his many works – I love *The Book in the Renaissance* (Yale, 2010) – but because he runs a project to put all early book titles online. And he writes with all the authority and good humour of someone led by the data rather than paradigms.

Concerning modern times, booksellers spill the beans about their calling in Bob Eckstein's *Footnotes from the World's Greatest Bookstores* (Potter, 2016), and authors write about their favourite bookshops in Ronald Rice's *My Bookstore* (Black Dog, 2017).

Libraries

Edith Hall's lectures are noted for their humour and lucidity, qualities encountered in her writing too. Her *Inventing the Barbarian* (Oxford, 1993) ranks with Edward Said's *Orientalism* as a warning to beware of unconscious bias when writing about 'civilization'. Hall's essay on ancient libraries in *The Meaning of the Library* (Princeton, 2015), edited by Alice Crawford, is exhilarating. *Ancient Libraries* (Cambridge, 2013), edited by Jason Konig, is an up-to-date survey of Near Eastern ancient libraries.

The more visceral meanings of libraries are explored by Melissa Adler in *Cruising the Library: Perversities in the Organization of Knowledge* (Fordham, 2017). A brave and funny investigator, she recently wrote an article called 'Let's Not Homosexualize the Library Stacks'. Considering her subject, she might smile to know that if you Google her you get her article 'Wikipedia and the Myth of Universality' in the *Nordic Journal of Information Science*.

Panizzi's victories at the British Museum are recounted in Louis Fagan's *The Life and Correspondence of Sir Anthony Panizzi* (3 vols, Houghton Mifflin, 1881). The online *Oxford Dictionary of National Biography* covers the other Museum notables in the great Reading Room dispute.

Anthony Hobson's 1970 *Great Libraries* (Weidenfeld & Nicolson) is vintage publishing: great paper, atmospheric monochrome photographs which are somehow more evocative than colour, deep research and Hobson himself. Multilingual, cultivated, impeccably dressed with a dash of dandyism, a fun father of three, decorated for bravery as a wartime tank commander, he was Sotheby's book expert but retreated to academia when the company became too corporate for him. I discovered his book, ironically, in a Sussex library sell-off.

Martin Gayford's *Michelangelo: His Epic Life* (Fig Tree, 2013) covers the latest research on the Laurentian Library and its creator.

Collectors

Thomas Dibdin's rambling *Bibliomania or Book-Madness* (1809; revised edn Chatto & Windus, 1876) helped to stoke up the very phenomenon which it chronicled. The bumptious London dealer Walter Spencer's *Forty Years in My Bookshop* (Constable, 1923) details a lost world. Victor Gray's excellent *Bookmen London: 250 Years of Sotheran Bookselling* (Sotheran's, 2011) can (only) be had from the legendary bookshop, off Piccadilly. American book collecting is evoked by Edward Newton in *The Amenities of Book Collecting* (Atlantic, 1918) and by Rebecca Barry in *Rare Books Uncovered* (Quarto, 2015). On French *fin de siècle* collectors, *The New Bibliopolis: French Book Collectors and the Culture of Print* (Toronto, 2007) by Willa Silverman is peerless.

The best introduction to the world's real book pioneers is Tsuen-Hsuin Tsien's *Written on Bamboo and Silk: The Beginnings of Chinese Books* (Chicago, 2004). The British Library-curated International Dunhuang Project is an ongoing online emporium of articles and research from scholars all over the world who have studied the Mogao cave library, where the Diamond Sutra was found. The Sutra itself can be viewed in its entirety on the BL site, and is usually on display in the library's free gallery. I also used *Aurel Stein* (John Murray, 1995) by Annabel Walker.

On Pellechet I used A. Ingold's *Notice sur la Vie et les Ouvrages de Marie Pellechet* (Alphonse Picard Fils, 1902). Ursula Bauermeister, now retired from the Bibliothèque Nationale de France, kindly sent me her article on that forgotten heroine of book collecting.

Marginalia

Marginalia have emerged from sequestered archives with the coming of the internet, but two books still bestride the field like colossi: Michael Camille's *Image on the Edge: The Margins of Medieval Art* (Reaktion, 1992) and Heather Jackson's *Marginalia* (Yale, 2001). Daniel Wakelin's *Scribal Correction, 1375–1510* (Cambridge, 2014) does what it says on the inkwell. *Marking the Hours* (Yale, 2006) by Eamon Duffy deals lucidly with the politics of marginalia in early printed devotional books. Also useful are William Sherman's *Used Books: Marking Readers in Renaissance England* (Pennsylvania, 2008) and Heidi Hackel's *Reading Material in Early Modern England* (Cambridge, 2009). The link between cutting off or scrubbing out marginalia and fear of transgression is covered in Olli Lagerspetz's *The Philosophy of Dirt* (Reaktion, 2018). I found it as I was aimlessly meandering the bookcases in Waterstones Canterbury, a prime example of a discovery no algorithm could have offered me.

Surviving the Sorbonne

Robert Darnton is lord of French regional book trade studies. Of his many books, I found *A Literary Tour de France: The World of Books on the Eve of the French Revolution* (Oxford, 2018) particularly enjoyable. Octave Uzanne's *The Book-Hunter in Paris: Studies among the Bookstalls and the Quays*, translated by Augustine Birrell (A. C. Mc Clurg, 1893), with its street sketches, is reverie-inducing.

Venice

Reading *Shipbuilders of the Venetian Arsenal: Workers and Workplace in the Preindustrial City* (Johns Hopkins, 1991), I felt I could smell the lagoon and hear the city's hubbub. Happily, I also discovered Horatio Forbes Brown (1854–1926) 'a breezy out-of-doors person with a crisp Highland accent'. Reduced family circumstances led him to live most of his life in a canalside house in Venice. A bonus was homosexual freedom: he found love with a gondolier called Antonio. Studying neglected Venetian archives, he wrote the compendious *The Venetian Printing Press: An Historical Study Based Upon Documents for the Most Part Hitherto Unpublished* (Putnam, 1891). Only 500 copies were printed. This book breathes love of Venice and, as a contemporary remarked, 'has a freshness and vigour' not found in 'blasé academic historians'. David Wootton's *Paolo Sarpi: Between Renaissance and Enlightenment* (Cambridge, 1983) remains the best book on the friar.

New York

In Brighton I discovered a copy of *Book Row* (Carroll & Graf, 2004), signed by Marvin Mondlin and Roy Meador at the Strand Bookstore on Broadway. The writers, veteran city bookseller and journalist respectively, interviewed most of New York's leading twentieth-century booksellers and lovingly harvested shop archives. The black-and-white photos are atmospheric, the bibliography extensive. Mondlin, born in 1927 to Russian Jewish immigrants to Brooklyn, was a living link to perhaps the greatest tribe of booksellers to take root in America. He began work as a 'stock boy' in 1951 and died in March 2020.